Leading International Teams

SUE CANNEY DAVISON
KAREN WARD

McGraw-Hill Publishing Company

London . Burr Ridge, IL . New York . St Louis . San Francisco . Auckland . Bogotá
Caracas . Lisbon . Madrid . Mexico . Milan . Montreal . New Delhi . Panama
Paris . San Juan . São Paulo . Singapore . Sydney . Tokyo . Toronto

Published by
McGraw-Hill Publishing Company
Shoppenhangers Road, Maidenhead, Berkshire SL6 2QL, UK
Telephone +44 (0) 1628 502500
Facsimile +44 (0) 1628 770224
Web site: http://www.mcgraw-hill.co.uk

British Libraray Cataloguing in Publication Data
A catalogue record for this book is available from the British Library

Publisher: Alfred Waller
Developmental Editor: Elizabeth Robinson

Created for McGraw-Hill by the independent production company
Steven Gardiner Ltd TEL +44 (0) 1223 364868 FAX +44 (0) 1223 364875

ISBN 0 07 709269 4

McGraw-Hill
A Division of The McGraw·Hill Companies

Copyright © 1999 Sue Canney Davison, Karen Ward. All rights reserved. No part of this publication may be reproduced, stored in a retrieval system, or transmitted, in any form or by any means, electronic, mechanical, photocopying, recording, or otherwise, without the prior permission of Sue Canney Davison, Karen Ward

1 2 3 4 5 CUP 3 2 1 0 9

Printed and bound in Great Britain at the University Press, Cambridge

Contents

How to Use this Book		vii
Preface		ix
Introduction		1

Section I Successful Participation in International Teams 9

Chapter 1	International Teams in the Current Scheme of Things	11
Chapter 2	Know Your Team	33
Chapter 3	The Impact of Inequalities	65
Chapter 4	Implementing Best Practices	88
Chapter 5	Facilitating International Teams and Key Interventions	111
Chapter 6	Leading in the Information Space: Teams and Technology	139
Chapter 7	The Role of International Team Leaders	166

Section II What the Organisation Needs to Do to Support These Teams 181

Introduction for Section Two		183
Chapter 8	Creating the Right Organisational Context	187
Chapter 9	The Role of Human Resources (HR)	213
Chapter 10	Organisational Best Practices for International Teams	232
Chapter 11	International Teams in the Future Scheme of Things	261

Appendix One 275

Appendix Two	278
Annotated Bibliography	283
Endnotes	295
Index	303

How to Use this Book

This book is designed as a resource book for those involved in creating, supporting and participating in international teams. It is in-depth and specific to these teams and it is based on two research projects, an MSc thesis and over 15 years of joint experience of consulting, facilitating and working in international teams. While the model used to illustrate best practices in Chapter Four describes teams that have beginnings, middles and ends, the findings and advice are equally applicable to on-going teams and looser international networks.

The book is divided into two sections. Section I is written for international team leaders and members who need to know what to expect and what to do when participating in international teams in order to be successful. Chapter One is an introductory chapter that looks at the special problems these teams face, where they are in organisations and what they are trying to achieve. Chapter Two is a detailed and comprehensive description of how cultural differences can influence the interaction in a team. Chapter Three uses real life examples and research results to demonstrate how different types of inequality skew the interaction. Chapters Two and Three are there as diagnostic resources for anticipating and understanding what can go wrong. Busy leaders and members with little time to read can head straight for Chapters Four and Five for practical advice of what to do at each stage of a team's journey, how to use a facilitator and the types of tools the facilitator can usefully offer. They can return to Chapters Two and Three when the need arises. Chapter Four describes effective best practices at each stage of a team's life cycle. Chapter Five helps a team leader recognise how and when a facilitator can help and what tools they may use at each stage. Chapter Six explores how teams can best use the technology rapidly emerging to support the rhythm of working together and apart. Chapter Seven ends this section with a summary of an international team leader's role and responsibilities.

Section II of the book is written for senior managers and directors, human resource personnel, sponsors and champions of these teams, as well as trainers, facilitators and those involved in organisational development. It outlines the actions and responsibilities that these players need to take in order to create and sustain effective international teams within their organisations. Chapter Eight looks at the responsibilities of senior management to support these teams through role-modelling, creating workable structures and conducive environments as well as investing in sufficient resources. Chapter Nine suggests ways in which the human resource department will have to re-organise itself and its policies and practices in order to support such teams. Chapter Ten explores how to identify, select, develop, evaluate and reward international team leaders and members. Chapter Eleven summarises the book as a whole and explores important aspects of the future. We expect that those who may start at Section II will come to recognise that they too are international team leaders themselves and will return to Section I to see how they can become more effective in this role. We hope that team leaders and members can use Section II to hustle for the support that they need.

Preface

We the authors were fortunate and, in different ways, have participated in the growing numbers of international teams throughout the nineties. In 1987, having spent six years in the Himalayas, Sue was asked to co-facilitate the Shell Intercultural Communication Workshop with a remarkable man called Peter Aylett. From Peter, she gained a deep appreciation that the best way of approaching cultural differences was to create supportive situations where people can understand and feel their impact for themselves. She also inherited some of the main tools which she has shared in this book.

Thanks to an auspicious meeting with Karl Weick in 1989, Sue decided to focus her Ph.D. video research at the London Business School, on international teams. Aside from support within the school for her thesis, she was also lucky enough to meet David Findley, then Human Resources Director of Wellcome, (now Glaxo Wellcome – a major international pharmaceutical company). David facilitated her joining up with Chuck Snow and others funded by ICEDR* to study transnational teams, which among other things allowed her to video teams in Hong Kong and Singapore. He also introduced her to Karen, who was to play a major part in setting up the support systems for the newly created international project teams in Wellcome. The partnership of an internal and external consultant which has resulted in this book, was born.

Karen had arrived at her role in the T&D function in Wellcome curious about working in a multifunctional and multicultural environment. This curiosity could be traced to the late eighties and a postgraduate work assignment in Ibadan, Nigeria organised by AIESEC (Association Internationale Etudiant Scientifiques et Commerciales – a global academic and business network). Having completed four years of study in international business at European universities, Karen arrived in Ibadan realising that she had been given lots of answers – but to all the wrong questions. A subsequent role with PA Consulting Group based in Germany at the time of the fall of the Berlin Wall, only strengthened Karen's interest in the impact of cultural differences on organisational effectiveness.

*An international consortium of thirty multinationals and twenty international business schools.

A Masters Degree in Organisational Behaviour at Birkbeck College, London, provided Karen with the opportunity to undertake some research to complement her practical organisational experience. When Wellcome decided to internationalise its R&D function, it provided Karen with the perfect research population for the study. Building on the research undertaken by ICEDR, Karen worked with the international project teams and their sponsors, Rick Kent, Trevor Gibbs and Judy Kramer to explore how to apply the existing research findings on international team effectiveness to the dynamic environment of an organisational setting.

Since the work with Wellcome in the early 1990s, both of us have worked with many different companies, facilitating and consulting on international teams. Despite the passing years and the range of new experiences in many industrial sectors, Wellcome's approach has always stuck out as a shining example. An example that many others still only aspire to. Thus, although changes of continent, motherhood and consulting work have delayed this book, we believe the experiments begun in Wellcome are still relevant to many companies today and we want to share the valuable lessons and insights that so many people have given us over the years.

Beyond those mentioned above, there are many people to thank and acknowledge in our journeys along this road. Thanks go to all our clients and colleagues for the support over the years without which the research and consulting work that has resulted in this book would not have been possible. Thanks also to the support of those at the London Business School, especially Nigel Nicholson and Lynda Gratton who saw Sue through her studies. A particular debt of gratitude is owed to Susan Schneider, Peter Frost and more recently, Martha Maznevski for critiquing, supporting and collaborating with Sue's research. Thanks to Farid and Kiran, patient husband and son for putting up with many non weekends in recent years.

Karen's thanks go particularly to her colleagues at Wellcome and Ashridge who have unfailingly supported her work on her Masters dissertation and this book. A special mention must go to John Howarth, partner in crime at Wellcome, from whom she learned so much about her own cultural biases and whose energy continues to astound. To husband Martin, who has patiently tolerated middle of the night phone calls from international team members who have got their time zones confused. Special thanks and acknowledgements go to Claudia Heimer of Ashridge Consulting Limited for her considerable initial input into this book and to Martha Maznevski and Ronny Vansteenkiste for their in-depth feedback and guidance as the book neared completion. Thanks to Joseph Kariuki, a talented Kenyan cartoonist, for turning rough sketches and ideas into our cartoons. Finally we send our whole hearted thanks to Alfred Waller and Elizabeth Robinson of McGraw-Hill for their sympathetic support and endurance far beyond easy limits.

Reviews

'An important and thorough study of an area that will be more and more critical as more organizations globalize.'
Edgar Schein, Sloan Fellows Professor of Management Emeritus, MIT Sloane School, USA

'A deeply insightful, comprehensive examination of a highly relevant topic in an increasingly interconnected world. I am very impressed with the richness of description which brings life into this valuable book. Sue Canney Davison and Karen Ward provide a must-read for international team leaders as well as for senior directors of international operations.
Robert Feller, Vice President Corporate Management Development, ABB Zurich, Switzerland

'Grounded in years of working with real teams, here is a clearly written guide to help us make the most of diversity in international teams. Worth buying for Chapters 4 and 5 alone – detailed, practical and straightforward help for team members and facilitators at all stages of a project.'
Dr Peter Moore, Head of Staffing, BP Amoco, UK

'*Leading International Teams* provides a practical guide to success in all aspects of international teamwork for team leaders as well as for those in top management and Human Resources charged with creating the culture and supporting systems to nurture international teamwork. It is full of case examples and good practice and is essential reading for all international executives and leaders.'
David Findley, Director, Global Human Resources, Glaxo Wellcome, UK

'*Leading International Teams* provides an intriguing and generative approach with strong practical application in this crucial capability for global success. Useful even for those of us who think we know it all.'
Personal commendation by Ed Sketch, Director Education, Training and Development, Global Automotive Company, USA

'Canney Davison and Ward's book in an original combination of numerous practical hints and in-depth research. Reading their work, you wish you had this book before when you were faced with setting up and leading international teams. A seminal book for all managers, facilitators and consultants who want to improve their performance in this area in the future.'
Ronny Vansteenkiste, Vice President, Management and Organization Development, Philips, The Netherlands

'*Leading International Teams* is written with the clarity, conciseness, and currency that today's busy global managers and HR professionals need. The authors give us bold, powerful, and practical solutions to:

- power struggles within teams
- internal competition in corporations
- diversity insensitivity of dominant cultures

The chapter on Facilitating International Teams and Key Interventions is the most in-depth treatment out there. I strongly recommend that one should not employ another team consultant or facilitator before reading this book.'
Diane Woods, (former) Global Vice President of Organization Development, Levi Strauss and Company, USA

'I recomment this enormously valuable resource to team leaders, senior line managers, and organizational consultants. Davison and Ward give us insightful and highly practical guidance, with real life examples.'
Joan E. Roberts, Head of Organization Effectiveness, Glaxo Wellcome Research and Development, USA

Introduction

The world is becoming increasingly interconnected: technology has allowed us to travel and talk to each other across distances; there are more of us with higher expectations; and industrialised nations have saturated their own markets. Along with the commercial activity, an appreciation of the interconnectedness of our environment has been forced upon us by pollution, disease and natural and industrial disasters. The result is that increasingly we have to work with people from other nations to solve complex international problems and to take advantage of opportunities often far away from home. As Michael Schrage reminds us:

> *'Individual genius may spot fertile ground, but it takes a collaborative community to cultivate and harvest it.'*

International teams are increasingly the mechanism used to harness the necessary international collaboration. The goals of such teams are usually broad and intended to have a much greater impact than teams of one nationality based in one place. Often whole companies depend on the quality of their output. The stakes are high. Yet experience tells us that working with people different from ourselves does not come naturally to most. The potential for difficult communication and misunderstandings and worse, open displays of prejudice and ignorance, is very high. Effective collaboration in these teams needs to be actively worked for. This book shares the knowledge, tools and techniques that we have found helpful in establishing that collaboration.

Main Themes

International teams are different from 'other' teams because their participants hold passports from different nationalities. To greater and lesser degrees, this means that cultural differences will add another layer of complexity to the team's interaction. We have a particular view of cultural and individual differences. Writers on international teams have talked about transcending, resolving, fusing and integrating individual cultures to create a new or 'third' team culture and a unified result. In our view, rising above or fusing differences is not only uninteresting, but can lead to instability and rigidity. If we are to maintain a dynamic kind of equilibrium that is adaptable to change, we need to passionately love our differences. To do so, we need to understand them in some depth.

A piece of brown clothe can be made from brown threads all dyed in the same brown dye. Alternatively, a piece of brown clothe can look the same shade of brown from four feet away, but on close inspection is made up of bright blue, red, yellow, green, purple, orange, black and white threads. Unlike the first, this second clothe can be unravelled when it has served its purpose and woven into any colour then needed. People need to remain bright in their own colours while weaving a common purpose and agreed way of interacting. That way they can best manage the creative tensions between global perspectives and local needs. People can also maintain their sense of self worth and create the need for others to learn and broaden their outlook. In other words, we need a way of interacting that adapts not too much and not too little, but creatively, 'just enough'.

Another theme that runs throughout this book is our conviction that cultural differences rarely, if ever, play out on a level field. Certainly the present reality in private business or international intergovernmental bodies is that one or two cultures will often have an upper hand, either because of numbers, power over resources, choices of language or preconceptions and stereotypes about others. We are convinced that whether these inequalities arise from the organisational context of the team, or from the individuals within the teams, they often have a far greater (negative) impact than cultural differences per se. A large part of the work we do with organisations and teams is to lessen the negative impact of power differences through paying attention to a team's processes. Over many years of working, we have become convinced that structuring a teams' processes leads to greater participation, protection of minority views and a huge saving in time. For this reason we have developed a model* that looks at what needs to be attended to at each stage of the teams' life cycle and what interventions are appropriate for speeding things up and raising subliminal issues at each stage. The aim of the model is to make process management within international teams a concrete issue that has a large impact on performance outcome.

Finally, our approach is one of developing an organisational capability to use international teams to respond effectively across cultures and distances. The most practical approach we have found is to work with a whole team as a facilitator, passing on the skills that enable that team to manage its own processes. Team members can then become facilitators of future teams. We have called this a 'systemic' approach. The word systemic reflects the fact that a flow

---

*See Chapter Four.

of learning is created that fans out from core catalytic points and embeds best practices into the very fibre of the organisation. We have also found that senior management, sponsors, and human resource specialists need just as much feedback and coaching on how their current systems, actions or inaction help or hinder teams as well as the flow of learning. No international team stands alone. A team is embedded in the organisational culture(s) and context(s) that it is created to serve. As such, most of the organisation will need to transform its mindset, practices and support mechanisms. In fact, unless organisations recognise the need for this systemic approach to working globally, they can invest significant time, money and energy in their international teams, without developing a sustainable global capability. As a consequence of this approach, this book is primarily focused on the needs of international team leaders and members who are usually the conduit between what is happening in the team and the rest of the organisation.

Information Sources

The information in this book is based on research and consulting experience. In the main piece of research, almost thirty international teams were videoed and surveyed in organisational settings in both Western Europe and South East Asia. The analysis focused on the amount each individual contributed within each team, and the predominant communication patterns that emerged with different team compositions and cultural contexts. It was a study that went fishing for an in-depth view of what was going on in these teams and that revealed the biases in favour of those who belonged to the same nationality as the main leadership group of the company. It also yielded rich stories that are shared in Chapter Three.

Some of the contextual material in Chapter One and Chapter Two draws on the interviews and unused survey data of over thirty transnational teams at the beginning of the nineties, while Chapter Ten draws on Seagram's internal review of its international re-engineering teams and other experiences of working with a range of international organisations. Much of the rest of the book is based on our joint experience of working to support the newly set up project teams in Wellcome from their beginnings and watching the transitions that took place after the merger into GlaxoWellcome. Extensive work with other companies has added more perspectives, short vignettes and different examples. As such, this book is not an in-depth, 'one coat fits all' recipe on the exact steps that each team must take. Rather, we aim to create some insights, to generate discussion and to provide frameworks and guidelines on what team leaders and other key parts of the organisation can usefully do to ensure that they are effective. We do share some of our favourite interventions in Chapter Five.

Rather than become exhaustive, the book builds on a basic understanding of what teams are and of cross-cultural communication, both of which have been well covered elsewhere*. This book looks at the impact of what happens when these two features combine and illustrates both what a team needs to do and the organisational context needed to make such teams effective. As such, parts of it needed to be in-depth and comprehensive. While some readers may find the wealth of information in Chapter Two too much to take in at one go, the bulleted summaries and interim learning points are designed to allow someone to start by taking in the main points and to return to the detail at a later date. One point needs clarification. Almost all this book will be very relevant for international teams working in the same place, but the main focus is on what we are calling 'dispersed' teams. These are teams that meet face to face on a regular basis every three or six months, but then work apart for most of the time. We touch briefly on what we call international 'virtual' teams in Chapter Six. These are, in our parlance, teams that *never* meet face to face. While again these teams need to understand much of what is said in this book and use similar best practices, they are bound by the limitations of communication technology, and have an additional and extensive set of difficulties to overcome that can only be dealt with briefly in this book. We have noticed that many articles and books in America published on virtual teams include teams that meet face to face. This is a looser definition than the one we apply here. So particularly many Americans will find that this book is focused on what they call virtual rather than dispersed teams.

The Structure of the Book

Section One: Successful Participation in International Teams

Chapter One: International Teams in the Current Scheme of Things

This chapter takes a broad look at where international teams are in the current scheme of things. It defines an international team, looks at why international teams are now prevalent in organisations and what differentiates them from teams and globalisation in general. It then briefly explores the added complexities in these teams and shows why they create the need for much greater attention to the process. After giving a sample of what it is like to be in such teams, we focus on the needs of the team leaders.

Chapter Two: Know Your Team

This chapter is a resource chapter on cultural differences. International team leaders need to understand the many ways in which cultural differences can affect the interaction in their teams. Only then can they analyse, anticipate and establish best practices that ensure that these differences will work for the team,

---

* See annotated bibliography for list of relevant books.

not against it. The chapter looks at five cultural and three organisational factors that can have a significant impact. In particular, the role of stereotypes, norms, language and communication patterns are discussed in full.

Chapter Three: The Impact of Inequalities

Using the results and stories from in-depth video research, this chapter illustrates the difficulties caused by three types of inequality. Structural inequality occurs when one nationality outnumbers others. Linguistic inequality arises when team members have different levels of fluency in the working language and communication norms of that language. The third, and perhaps the most insidious, type of inequality is when some nationalities perceive themselves and are perceived as having more status, power, resources and influence regardless of the truth. The chapter ends with examples of when things go right.

Chapter Four: Implementing Best Practices

The message from Chapter Three is that structuring a team's interaction can overcome many of the problems created by different communication styles, behavioural expectations and Chapter Four turns this into a simple four-phase model of a team's life cycle. It illustrates the useful actions that team leaders, sponsors, members can take before a team meets, when the team first meets, during the middle phase and when completing the work. Much emphasis is placed on adequate preparation before a team meets. This will be much more extensive than for other teams. The benefits of applying the model are cumulative. If the right actions are taken before a team meets, then the first meetings will be more fruitful and effective. If appropriate actions are taken in this initial phase, then many of the problems of working together and apart will be averted. If team leaders want a quick, 'what can I do immediately to make my team more effective' fix, then this is the chapter to read first.

Chapter Five: Facilitating International Teams and Key Interventions

As the chapters so far have emphasised, the interaction in international teams needs to be consciously managed to be effective. If the team leader is involved in the content, then using a facilitator can be very helpful in passing on the skills that will enable the team members to manage their own interaction. This chapters outlines what a facilitator can do and when you may need one. It then gives the team leader a set of criteria that can distinguish what skills are essential and complementary to their own. It ends by sharing some of the interventions that facilitators can use at the different stages of the life cycle.

Chapter Six: Leading in the Information Space: Teams and Technology

The revolution in information technology has enabled teams to do much of their work from different locations. It is developing at a rapid pace. However, no amount of technology can create collaboration, if the underlying will and processes are not in place. This chapter starts by outlining how to make the best use of current technology and points the reader to information on future technology. It discusses how cultural differences may play out in the usage of technology, but emphasises the difficulties created by the lack of emotional and sensory data. These restrictions imply that at the moment, there are certain things that teams should use expensive 'face-to-face' time to achieve, and other things that can easily be achieved using existing information sharing technologies. This will create a rhythm and discipline for working together and apart. The chapter ends with a brief look at the special challenges faced by teams that never meet, teams we refer to as virtual rather than dispersed teams.

Chapter Seven: The Role of International Team Leaders

Having illustrated what effects cultural differences and inequalities can have in these teams and how team leaders and facilitators can best make them work for them, this section ends with a summary of the role of the team leader. Given all of the above, it is complex and demanding and is often beset with unrealistic expectations. The team leader needs to decide how to balance the need for both technical and leadership skills and then match the style of leadership to the strategic and operational needs of each stage of the team's development. After looking at the three main facets of the role: managing the boundaries; the interaction; and the task, the chapter ends with a reminder to keep the overall leadership style in tune with the cultural mix and context of the team.

Section Two: What the Organisation Needs to Do to Support These Teams

Chapter Eight: Creating the Right Organisational Context

This chapter urges senior management to take responsibility for creating an organisational context in which these teams can excel. To do this they need to involve key players from the start and, above all, communicate to each international team how its purpose fits into the company's overall strategy. Key managers then have to be proactive in removing out-dated or unintentional structural hurdles while being realistic about the speed at which these teams can reach optimal performance. The best way to achieve such aims is for top teams to learn by role-modelling and demonstrating that going global does not need to result in ignoring one's family and undermining one's health. Organisations also need to be committed to investing in the necessary resources to support these teams and above all realise that they are in for a marathon with steep learning curves, not a sprint. We gratefully acknowledge Claudia Heimer's initial inputs into this chapter.

Chapter Nine: The Role of Human Resources (HR)

This chapter explores the specific role that the Human Resources (HR) function has in supporting an organisational context in which international teams can be successful. This function needs to be a strategic partner in the creation of these teams, rather than being asked to sort out the operational difficulties created by a grand vision. HR need to develop a comprehensive strategy to support team leaders and members. Again, this usually entails walking the talk and reorganising to become high performing international teams themselves. The chapter ends with the various stages that one HR department went through in its steep learning curve to stay one ahead of the teams it was given to support.

Chapter Ten: Organisational Best Practices for International Teams

The chapter begins by considering the organisational practices that focus on identifying, selecting and developing international team leaders. It finishes by looking at the difficulties and key factors in evaluating and rewarding the whole team. The section on evaluation argues a strong case for separating the evaluation of team performance from the effectiveness of the outcome. Both are important. Having watched many companies struggle with international team rewards, we highlight why this is such a tricky issue and why companies are currently best advised to remove obvious inequities. Team leaders and members need to be involved in deciding both evaluation and reward processes, but we suggest that they do not pay for months of expensive internal or external consultant's efforts to make a team's rewards and pay schemes exactly equal.

Chapter Eleven: International Teams in the Future Scheme of Things

This final chapter summarises the key messages for international team leaders, members and senior managers. It then muses on the future. Rapid developments in technology will bring increasing freedom to participate from different places at different times. However, many of the underlying pitfalls and dynamics of working across cultures will remain unchanged. We are therefore of the opinion that even a small shift towards a revolution in human interaction and the way we view each other in the present and the future, will have a much more profound effect on human development. We hope that some of the best practices outlined in this book are small steps towards such a change.

Section One

Successful Participation in International Teams

Chapter One

International Teams in the Current Scheme of Things

Teams are in vogue. So much so that many managers are already tired of the word and people are talking about collaborative workplaces rather than teams. What is clear is that the complexities of local issues, let alone international markets are becoming too much for one brain to grasp, identify and respond to intelligently. Increasingly, just to survive, we need to work together on problems and opportunities that cover much larger geographic areas. This usually means working with people from different nationalities. This first chapter sets the broad scene. It looks at how international teams are different from national ones and why they justify a book all to themselves. It outlines the layers of complexities that exist within such teams and the layers added by the organisational context. All these layers of complexity invariably lead to greater communication difficulties:

> *'none of us have worked internationally before — it is like the blind leading the blind'**

The only way to work through the internal difficulties this creates is to pay as much attention to creating good interaction as to the task. Experience has told us that working with individual teams is the best way to embed international teams skills into the fibre of the organisation. Experience has also shown us that many other parts of the organisation also need to develop and change if these teams are to sustain high performance.

International Teams

An international team can be defined as a group of people who come from different nationalities and work interdependently towards a common goal.

International teams are usually working on a complex task that will have an impact in more than one country. They are usually expected to achieve an

---

* The quotes throughout the book come from the managers and team members of international teams in Wellcome, now Glaxo-Wellcome a UK-based pharmaceutical company with a strong American presence, and Seagram, the international US-headquartered drinks and music company.

outcome that will either serve a very widespread set of customers, solve problems in many areas simultaneously and/or have a very significant impact on increasing or sustaining profitability as the following two examples demonstrate.

> ### The Digital Race
> The R&D function of a multinational photographic company had its best scientists working on the latest digital technology for cameras and film. The company believed it was significantly ahead of its competition in the digital race, until a smaller national player launched its digital products (with a different standard) onto the market a full 12 months early. The race had become one of survival. If the competing technology became standard, years of effort and expenditure in product development could be wasted.
> *The organisation's response*: to create an international multifunctional team with the best and the brightest from R&D, Marketing and other relevant parts of the organisation.
> *Their goal*: to develop and launch their competing technology in all key global markets within six months. A full year ahead of schedule.
>
> ### Simultaneous Registration
> As globalisation extends its reach to all corners of the globe, some regulatory authorities are taking advantage of the advance in technological communications and attempting to harmonise some of the rules and regulations they create. The pharmaceutical industry was quick to encourage its regulatory authorities to take this path, as it promised more rapid simultaneous registration of their products globally.
> One organisation decided to test the system. It was due to register a new product and knew there were potential markets in over 15 countries. The Director of R&D set a challenge to the International Project Team and the regulatory department: simultaneous registration in all countries in three days. The organisation was aghast. The previous best that they knew of was three months and the norm was six to eight months. Yet at the same time the international team knew the cost in lost sales each day a product was not on the market was phenomenal. They accepted the challenge.
> *The result*: simultaneous international registration in three weeks. The organisation was delighted. A new standard had been set.

In fact international teams *have* to achieve such impressive results as they are very expensive to set up and maintain. The increase in the levels of complexity

International Teams in the Current Scheme of Things 13

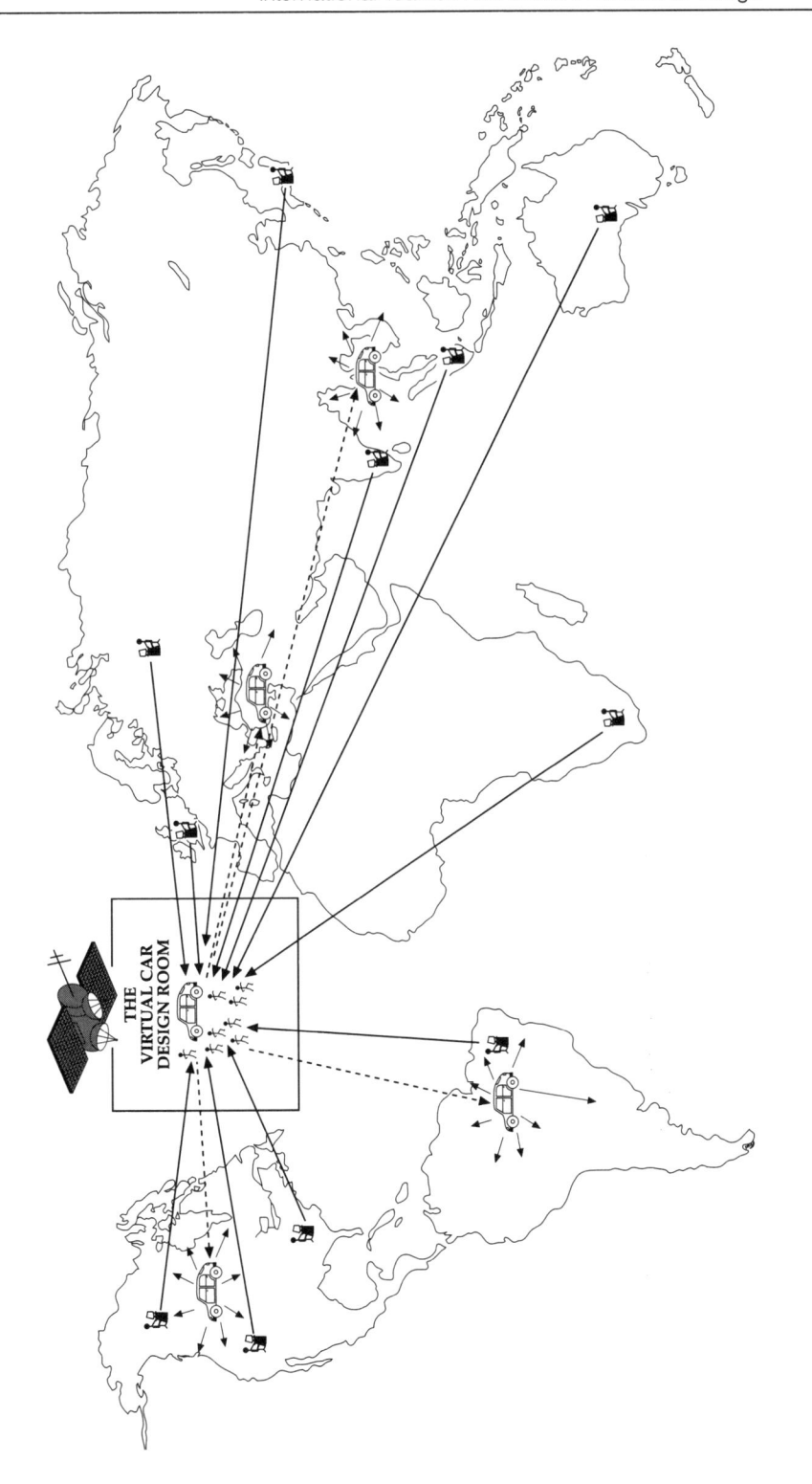

Figure 1.1: The three trends – globalisation, teaming and information technology – creating and distributing the design for the global car to regional production sites

of both the task and the team's interaction demands much higher support and different training than teams of one nationality based in one place. Adding a day of cross-cultural training onto the end of a standard training package for teams is not enough.

Three Trends are Creating the Need for More International Teams

Unlike most national teams, international teams often work apart across cultures and time zones for extended periods of time; they are dispersed. Three major trends mean that these teams are here to stay, that there will be many more of them and that they need to be effective.

Globalisation

The first trend is the perceived need for many companies to go 'global' in order to grow and survive. This has both created and is brought about by 'globalisation' which we define simply as increased commercial and economic interdependence between countries. This growing interdependence is currently relentless and is supported by many joint ventures, strategic alliances and mergers and acquisitions.

Teaming

The second trend is that the increasing complexities of scientific, medical and environmental issues as well as commercial life demand individuals from different backgrounds and different nations to collaborate in order to identify and resolve the problems and to take advantage of the opportunities. Many workforces have been driven to work as accountable, often 'self-managed' teams rather than functional units that do not co-ordinate well. Leadership roles are increasingly focused on creating collaboration; not just across all levels of the organisation, but between suppliers, customers and other like businesses and institutions. Increasingly, the whole organisation at all levels has to be able to perform what were previously management processes; to talk (or at least 'e-talk') to each other, share information, solve problems and make decisions. This has led to such a frenetic amount of 'teaming up', the question now being asked is, 'is it always appropriate, and if so, when'?

Information Technology

Third, and perhaps most importantly for international teams, we are in the middle of a dramatic information revolution. The first major impact of this revolution is that wireless technology is increasingly allowing people to participate in meaningful discussion and interaction wherever they are, at any time they choose. These teams can now work apart as much as together and access and share information as never before. Business will increasingly be done in an 'information' space where, so long as there is adequate communications infrastructure, physical location is much less of a consideration than time zones.

The creation of dispersed international teams is an obvious response to these trends and will continue to be so for some time to come. The trends themselves have set some parameters for these teams. Information, rather than physical products, is becoming a major commodity in its own right. This has created many more 'knowledge workers' in both technologically developed and developing economies. These are people who create, exchange, digest and broadcast information as knowledge.

Recent figures suggest that 82 per cent of the American workforce can now be called 'knowledge workers' as opposed to those doing predominantly physical work, and 20 per cent of the workforce consists of technical and professional workers[1]. International teams are usually made up of such technical and professional 'knowledge' workers.

Shifting physical products by courier, air or sea is still very expensive and awkward, so most production lines are the last places in a company to feel the impact of a greater international spread. However, exchanging information through the internet and e-mail is almost free and relatively easy, even from otherwise under-developed countries. At first glance, it is relatively easy and cheap for professionals in different countries to 'team up'. The costs come in setting up compatible technology and software, facilitating still necessary travel and good co-ordination. Almost every company that has had or is developing international teams, faces the need to make significant organisational changes to reap the full benefit from, as well as fully support and facilitate these teams. Different companies are responding in different ways. Highly dispersed organisations such as the Anglo-Dutch oil giant, Shell, and the large international power company ABB (Asea Brown and Boveri), are focusing on increasing the variety of nationalities within the ranks of management, standardising some management processes and technology and creating international regional teams to serve increasingly regionally spread customers. As the quotes below testify, other organisations, such as Glaxo-Wellcome are seeking advantages from these teams by reducing duplication in different countries:

> 'Creating these teams optimises use of resources — they will cut out a lot of duplication of effort that the previous system had.'
> 'It helps that we are not competing with our overseas colleagues for the same pot of money anymore — it means that the studies that go ahead will be better funded.'
> 'I finally got access to a piece of kit that we only had on the other side of the pond — I'm hoping it will save several months on timelines.'

Yet other companies, such as Ford, Fuji and Xerox have created international teams to develop products that they hope will serve many markets simultaneously. Each of these different approaches demand a formidable response from the organisation to do away with the old systems and attitudes that block these teams and to invest in and create the support mechanisms and infrastructure that help them be effective.

It is, however, one thing to recognise the advantages of international teams and quite another to put strategies in action to overcome the potential downsides and ensure that these teams are operationally effective. Table 1.1 illustrates some of the advantages and disadvantages organisational and team leaders need to take into account if they want to introduce and lead effective international teams.

Table 1.1: Advantages and Disadvantages of International Teams

Advantages of international teams	Disadvantages of international teams
Enables global strategies to be created that are sensitive to local requirements	Individuals can feel torn between loyalty to the team and to their local manager
Enables the organisation to benefit from a diversity of perspectives that more closely match the preferences of their client base.	It can be difficult to reach consensus on a way forward.
Increases organisational learning about the global market.	Language and communication difficulties mean that it can take longer to reach an optimum level of effectiveness.
More efficient use of resources – avoids duplication of effort.	Remote working can feel very isolated and de-motivating and harm family life. It is also easy to get distracted on local issues.
High level of intrinsic rewards, learning a lot from different people, different parts of the company, and learning different methodologies in tackling problems.	Potential for increased conflict due to different opinions.
Extends international development opportunities beyond 'traditional' expatriate manager.	Certain cultural habits, such as talking about oneself, pointing, types of food can be offensive to people from other cultures.
Being 'special' can increase morale.	These teams need high initial investment in people, training and technology to avoid very expensive mistakes.
Team leaders and members usually increase their skills with communication technology.	Difficult to create equitable reward and evaluation.
Enables broader targets to be set that will have an impact in many different countries simultaneously.	

This book is to ensure that companies that are investing in such teams will reap the advantages while not becoming swamped by the disadvantages and possible pitfalls. Many of the advantages accrue at the organisational level, while many of the disadvantages need to be handled within the team and between people. It is imperative that the key players create a facilitative organisational environment which gives the teams the top down, parallel and bottom up support they need to overcome the downsides and become effective. Senior managers who say 'we want the results, it is up to them how to achieve them, but they will hear about it if they mess up' will end up paying a heavy price. As such, international teams are a form of management that incorporate what has been written about teams and globalisation in general, yet go beyond both of them. Since they incorporate what is true for teams in general, it is important to remind ourselves what that is and to see what added layers of complexity they need to deal with.

Teams and Workgroups

A team can be loosely defined as a group of people working interdependently towards a common goal.

Different authors then add in different aspects, such as mutual accountability, complementary skills, additions which apply to effective teams. Some prefer talking about the verb 'to team', to do teamwork, or to work collaboratively, rather than trying to talk about teams per se. This is usually in response to a smart manager saying 'I call my company a team and that is three thousand people'. There is also now talk of workgroups rather than teams and the question arises; 'How do they differ and does this book also apply to larger, more loosely formed international groups?'

The first step in answering this last question is to get past those preaching that teams are better than workgroups. This approach makes statements like; teams work on the big picture and workgroups on the small; teams do whatever it takes to achieve the task; teams are participative and workgroups are autocratic and so on[2].

Much confusion is created by calling an effective team, a team and an ineffective team, a workgroup.

The reality is that certain types of tasks require people to usefully collaborate and co-ordinate to greater or lesser degrees. Workgroups may well have a higher ratio of individual work than teams, but the real difference is in the extent to which people need to co-ordinate to fulfil a common outcome. If you cannot move forward without very frequent interaction with your colleagues, if other group/team members are expected to make up the difference if one person fails, then it is probably important to make the extra effort to become a good team. In many cases, companies create a core team to drive a project forward. This core team will then use a much larger 'work' group of technical experts as and when they need them.

International workgroups with high amounts of individual work will find this book useful. Small groups of people from different nationalities who are working interdependently towards a common, usually significant goal, what we are calling an international team, will find it even more so.

Regular Team Processes

Much is written about effective team processes and most of it applies to international teams. In order not to reinvent the wheel, at this point we presume a basic understanding of what works and what does not work in teamwork in general (see Annotated Bibliography at the back of the book for relevant texts). To summarise, it is now well established that any team will have a greater chance of success if the team as a whole has:

- a clear motivational goal;
- a strong sense of commitment and urgency;
- interdependent work;
- competent team members with complementary skills;
- well set ground rules and standards for good interaction;
- good interpersonal communication and relationships;
- appropriate inspiring leadership;
- appropriately rewarded interim and final goals;
- control over its own resources;
- good boundary management;
- external support and recognition.

Each team member has to believe in what they are aiming to achieve and to clearly understand the benefits of the outcome and the need for it to happen in a timely way. They need to understand what each person can contribute and how their different contributions allow them to meet the overall goal. The different skills need to be integrated by agreeing a structured working process that allows each person to contribute fully without being dominated by others. A good leader will create a role model for good interaction, as well as keep the overall purpose and direction clear while others become focused on the day-to-day details. However well a team works internally, external issues, such as control of resources, external support and recognition, as well as a sense of operational autonomy while being recognised and well rewarded for contributing to overall organisational goals, will all enhance the team members' commitment and motivation.

While these 'team basics' may have very different interpretations in different cultures, they are as important to international teams as they are to national teams. Companies that have already invested in creating good teamwork locally, find it much easier to create effective international teams.

Similarly, working on complex international team processes creates useful lessons for all teams. Zeneca (pharmaceuticals) in the UK, produced a model of best practices written for all teams, in which the base model was for international teams, and national teams were considered as a subset. International teams are not different in kind to national teams. The differences lies in the complexity of the interaction and the scope of the work. International teams need to learn all and more than national teams need to learn because they have added complexities that come both from within and without the team.

The Added Complexities that Come from Within the Team

The most obvious difference between international and national teams is that international teams have people from different nationalities. This means that team members will have:

- different mother tongue languages and communication styles;
- different ways of looking at the world, taking in and processing information and different underlying assumptions about the way reality works;
- different expectations about each other's behavioural norms, especially involving emotional display, decision making, conflict resolution and leadership;
- different stereotypes about each other and perhaps, status within the company;
- varying access to resources within the geographical spread.

One can argue that apart from different mother tongue languages, individuals in national teams will also differ on all the other factors. It is true that our personal identity is made up of many factors or 'different identities'; professional skill and expertise, life experiences, gender, race, ethnicity, marital status, parenthood, age, length of tenure, rank etc. There will be differences between people in many of these factors in any team, which will lead to differences in the above cognitive and communication processes. Some parts of individual identity will be more relevant to each particular task than others. Others will become noticeable perhaps because of the structure of the team, for instance being the only woman, being the only non production person etc. So each aspect of identity will have a different relevance, weighting and history in any team which can lead to potentially complex interaction between the different aspects both within each individual, eg 'Should I stress my expertise or rank at this moment?' as well as between the team members; eg 'They seem to think I am less experienced just because I come from Russia'.

What we are talking about with international teams is degree. While a Californian millionaire may well differ markedly on the above five factors from an Appalachian small holder, sadly it is unlikely that they will be on the same business team. Peers of similar 'social standing' from different countries are likely to differ even more widely across these factors which creates complex interaction that then has to be actively wrought into something that works. Most of the studies on heterogeneous teams have compared them with homogeneous teams. Sometimes they are more effective and sometimes not, however almost always, they have greater communication difficulties, at least in the beginning. Take communication styles for instance:

> *'Communication is so much harder because of the cultural differences – some people respond to your e-mails, some don't – you find you have offended one and pleased another with the very same note – it's mind-boggling sometimes.'*
>
> *'From what I have seen, these teams are very inefficient, they are taking ages to make decisions.'*
>
> *'Sometimes you can't get a word in, there is always one or two dominating the discussion and no-one seems to stop them.'*

As the instances above show, team members will differ in the way they use even supposedly the same language, as well as putting important information in different places in a sentence and by preferring different communication styles, eg formal or informal, making jokes or being serious and are more or less comfortable with different technologies. The seriousness of misunderstandings can range from different interpretations of specific actions and timing to different understanding of whole strategies or leadership roles. Some teams seriously underestimate the time it takes to agree on what is the task at hand. Even simple things can hijack the start such as failing to introduce each other properly, not responding to different communication styles, or failing to unearth hidden agendas or strong cultural biases within the team.

Jaws have dropped when American team leaders have asked their British colleagues for their home numbers during a videoconference:

> *'You mean you are going to give them to our department heads and we have to remain sober after work ... and anyway what constitutes an emergency, you people are always in a panic?'*

When asked to take the lead on an action, some team members think that it is still proper to wait to be told what to do *'Yes we agreed that I would do it, but you did not tell me how'*. Questions such as 'can you do that in your own time?' are interpreted as 'take as long as you like' not as a British way of saying 'please do it out of office hours to speed things up'.

> The most common 'back home after the meeting' phrase that we have heard is *'what are these guys up to, I thought we had agreed ...'* as people wished they had taken detailed minutes or paid more attention when they saw their colleagues nodding in seeming agreement.

This lack of agreement after a meeting is usually the result of rushing into the task while wrongly assuming everyone is thinking the same way, eg that 'things work the same over there'. There are then the 'simpler' factors that disturb initial international team meetings. These range from not accounting for jet lag, airport delays, travelling logistics, food and beverage preferences and the fact that support staff may not understand other currencies, telephone greetings in other languages and switch the fax off when they go home. Out of hours security staff seldom speak other languages to give alternative fax numbers or to take urgent messages.

Aside from the differences created by different nationalities, these teams often need to accomplish more complex tasks that involve crossing not only cultural, temporal and geographic distances, but also functional and professional boundaries. Team members need to be clear about the regulatory, legislative and financial structures in the countries they are working in as well as how to work with their different languages, communication styles and expectations. Working across time zones, it is harder and harder to keep work restricted to office hours. Working across large geographical distances means team leaders, if not members, will often need to travel. Individuals will have different levels of ease with and access to different communication technologies and the teams must learn the most effective uses of technology and expensive face to face time. Different functions speak different technical languages and different professions have very different priorities. These added complexities within the teams mean that international teams need to pay as much attention to *how* they are approaching the task and their interaction as to *what* the task itself involves. Creatively structuring and managing the interaction becomes an absolute necessity if everyone is going to participate meaningfully. As such, these teams are discovering many best practices that are useful for any team, international or national.

In other words, these teams would have to proactively manage inherent communication and procedural complexities even if the cultural playing field was level. However, these teams exist in organisational contexts where the cultural field is seldom unbiased.

The Complexities Added by the Organisational Context

One obvious dramatic difference between donor funded inter-governmental organisations such as the World Bank and United Nations (UN) and most private companies, is the mix of nationalities in the professional layers. Having a long exotic double-barrelled name can sometimes seem to be a recruitment requirement as you scan the nameplates in UN corridors. In the private sector, however, the cultural 'structure' of power often exacerbates relatively innocuous cultural differences. This is because:

- Organisations usually have different international representation and international mobility at different levels of the organisation.
- The range of nationalities is often restricted.

This can lead to a strong bias where one or two nationalities predominate either in numbers and/or in power and influence.

In one study[3], despite 27 different nationalities being represented in the sample, the average number of nationalities per team was four, the same as another study[4], with a minimum of two and a maximum of six. Many had large dominant subgroups of one nationality, usually the same nationality as most of the leadership of the company.

If a company claims to be international, it is often worth taking a closer look. In most international companies, the very top team is often internationally mobile, but seldom culturally heterogeneous. Besides a few worthy exceptions, most of the biggest corporations in the world are still dominated by the culture of the home country. This may not matter if all the management were internationally minded, culturally adept and gifted linguists. However many managers are not.

Whatever happens below, the implicit message that is usually conveyed by having one or two nationalities predominate at the top is that, based more on nationality than skill, some people are more important and have more relevant business experience, knowledge, power (and sometimes even intelligence) than others.

Key posts lower down and in regional sites can also often be held by parent company nationals. Any kind of cultural dominance has a large impact on the international teams within that organisation. It also means that companies and teams can lose good people who leave companies because they feel trapped under a subtle or unsubtle national glass ceiling as highlighted in Figure 1.2.

Well-intentioned attempts to level the cultural playing field can be consistently hijacked by the over-riding national norms. They are so ingrained, that even after discussing them, people cannot see their impact or think of anything different. This leads to dysfunctional attitudes and behaviour within teams that can end up excluding and upsetting one or two team members. The minorities usually stay quiet until they relax in the bar.

In Europe and America, it is common to find teams made up mostly of Americans, mixtures of a few different European nationalities and one or two

Figure 1.2: Equality on international teams

people from Asia Pacific. One usually needs to go either to the UN, World Bank or other institutions based on national representation and quotas to find a team comprised of say a Thai, a Canadian, a Ghanaian, a Kazak, an Icelander, a Guatemalan, and a Dutchman. In these organisations, being an employee tends to be a far stronger identity than one's nationality. As highlighting cultural differences is also loaded with political significance and sensitivities, they are seldom publicly acknowledged or addressed.

> One response to a short training needs analysis questionnaire that asked about cross-cultural communication in the UN was 'why cross-cultural? Surely communication is communication?'.

In the private sector, the dysfunctional impact of cultural inequity is often most easily visible in joint ventures, strategic alliances or mergers and take-overs, where most of the dynamics in teams follow patterns of majority/minority, acquired/acquiree influences rather than a more neutral play of cultural differences and equal power. In Eurocopter, many of the Deutsche Aerospace managers initially felt that their contributions were taken less seriously because Air France was the major partner in the joint venture. In New Holland, American Ford New Holland managers at the executive Committee level initially felt less involved than their Italian Fiat counterparts however much the acquisition by Fiat of Ford New Holland was passed off as a merger and not a take-over. There is one advantage of having a restricted number of main nationalities. Siemens, a large German based electronics company, focused much of their experiential cross-cultural team learning on their US/German project teams, only recently adding in Japanese culture as it became relevant. The general cross-cultural lessons of being open minded, listening, humour, adaptation and awareness of the areas where cultures tend to differ most, are learnt. However, unlike many cross-cultural training programmes, the participants are also able to gain an in-depth knowledge of the other relevant cultures. Experts say that once you have learnt one second language, it is easier to learn others. The same, we suspect, is true of cultural adaptation. Once the seemingly inherent rightness of your own way of seeing the world has been shattered, you cannot restore it.

Different Perceptions of Economic Strength

Now add on to the predominance of one or two nationalities, the fact that an international workforce also usually reflects differences in regional and national economic strength. The picture becomes more complex. Multinational companies emerge from and follow the major regional markets and until very recently, that meant North America, Europe and Japan. Most still feel that operating somewhere in two sections of the 'triad' qualifies as 'international' and three qualifies them as being 'global'.

In ABB, multinational teams are set up to address specific issues of efficiency, transfer of technology and integration. One ABB manager explained how there were 'two Americans, a British man, a French man, a (white) South African, an Australian, and a Canadian' on his 'very international' technology transfer team. Although six nationalities were represented on a team looking at a global issue, the team members were either Anglo-Saxon* or European. Similarly the 'Continental European' management team of a major US investment house based in Luxembourg was comprised of three Americans, a New Zealander and one German.

Aside from causing difficult numerical imbalances in international teams, this lack of representation due to the lack of presence or strength in the global capitalist markets, tends to support existing stereotypes about perceived power and all that goes with it.

> A Ugandan reporter covering the visit of Bill Clinton in Kampala was annoyed by the rough and ready tactics of American security men – ordering people here, directing them there, restricting, hassling, searching. He finally rebelled 'you can't do this! I am a Ugandan citizen and this is Ugandan sovereign territory'. The response: 'Sorry buddy, wherever Air Force One (Bill Clinton's private jet) lands, that's American Sovereign territory.'[5]

* A collective name for cultures now dominated by English language and customs.

As we shall illustrate in Chapter Three, these implicit or explicit messages that some nationalities have more power than others create significant problems in international teams. Moreover, the organisation as a whole will probably not reap the wisdom of even the range of nationalities that they have when they need it. This can mean that they have to learn their 'cultural' lessons the expensive way and not always only on the edge of the industrialised world. Disney is estimated to have lost billions of dollars when it sent 400 mid and upper level American managers to 'jump-start' EuroDisney in Paris[6]. They tried to impose American office rules on dress, labour law, drinking and speaking English (even though less than three per cent of the Americans could speak adequate French).

Despite the often enormous costs of getting it wrong, some senior managers have 'done' cultural integration by mandating expensive one- or two-day cross-cultural workshops that do not touch any of these perceived or real iniquities. They then wonder why they still have problems. We have seen that the few top teams who have themselves gone through the disciplines of learning to be effective multicultural dispersed teams, have a very different view. They appreciate the ongoing expense of creating an international workforce and integrating all levels. As one said 'we have to take a drip drip approach and it is going to take a very long time'. Even if a company has made proactive efforts to level the cultural playing field, still another set of challenges that international teams need to respond to arises from where they are in companies and what they are trying to achieve.

Where Are These Teams?

Many international teams can be found in the middle layers of professional management and expertise, led and supported by less diverse teams.

ABB has 300–500 international managers at the 'next to top' level. They 'could be plugged in wherever we want; they think internationally; identifying and assigning them is a smooth process'. They are mostly used to start up business before local people take over. Otherwise, although engineers do project assignments in other countries, there are very few international jobs as such in ABB's decentralised workforce of 220,000 employees.

In Alcatel, the French based Telecoms company, a Belgian headed up the non-production corporate purchasing team which was based in Paris, but had team members dispersed all over Europe and North America. On the Eastman Kodak CD Launch, an entrepreneurial German was followed by a more integrative Belgian to lead a team spread over fourteen European countries. This level of management tends to be well mixed.

Table 1.2: Nationalities represented in different types of teams

Type of team	No of teams represented	Average number of nationalities
International joint venture	3	2.3
Top management teams	4	3.5
Functional teams, such as R&D, Manufacturing, quality assurance	5	4.2
Business launch, product development team	6	4.5
Regional headquarters teams	6	4.5
Special taskforce and international co-ordination teams and business units	4	5.0
Total numbers for teams*	28	3.84

*Pearsons correlation between type of team and number of nationalities $= 0.5166$, $P = 0.004$

One typology that emerged from the survey of transnational teams (TTS)[7] covered both location:

- corporate headquarters;
- regional headquarters;
- joint ventures;

and tasks:

- business development teams;
- research and development teams;
- special taskforces.

The numbers of nationalities varied in each as shown in Table 1.2.

As the table shows, the *number* of nationalities represented on the team was predictably related to the type of team and task. The table shows that special taskforces and product development teams comprised mainly of technical and professional staff had predictably higher numbers of nationalities than administrative managerial teams in corporate and national subsidiaries. Exxon Chemical's world-wide viscosity modifier team comprised of Argentinean, British, American, Romanian and Singaporean members. A special project team in quality assurance in Wellcome was comprised of British, Canadian, Australian, Nigerian, American, Indian, French, Spanish and Italian.

The number of nationalities represented in corporate headquarters and the national subsidiary top teams indicate the worrying reality that teams at the very top tend to have a narrow international range. At the other end of the scale, despite being managerial and administrative in purpose, regional headquarters teams usually have members of the different nationalities within that region. British Airway's Latin Caribbean office comprised British, American, Venezuelan, Jamaican and Barbadian personnel. Common sense predicted the finding that in teams staffed by technical professionals in joint ventures, only two or sometimes three nationalities are usually involved; a German/French team designing missile launching systems, a British/Italian team to explore Russian Gas, and so on.

The findings re-emphasise the fact that most international teams are found in the professional and technical 'knowledge' levels. The emphasis is on leveraging the advantages in the design, development marketing, selling of products in many countries simultaneously, all of which can be done by sharing and shifting information with relative ease. From the point of view of the task, these teams are faced with much greater co-ordination and workflow challenges than ever before. But that is not all. In this research, special taskforces and product development teams with greater numbers of nationalities were those set up to:

- 'increase the efficiency of the company's international operations';
- 'help the company develop and spread international innovations'.

However, they were also the teams that came closest to

- 'not meeting the expectations and needs of those who rely on the team's output'.

In another study[8], the larger the number of nationalities, the more team members clearly stated that they did not want to work on the team again and the lower they rated their team spirit.

Furthermore, the transnational teams research showed that regional headquarters teams and special taskforces met face to face less regularly than the other types of teams. These two types of teams would spend increased amounts of time working at a distance and/or have greater cultural complexities. Perhaps these two factors explain why, as the number of nationalities increased, there was a significant move away from 'decisions being made by seeking consensus' and 'members caring about each other as people' and a trend towards the decisions being made mostly by the team leader. It seems, despite communication technology, dispersed teams with specific tasks to achieve tend to 'revert' to 'strong' leadership; a point taken up in Chapter Seven.

So greater numbers of nationalities can lead to lower team spirit, greater difficulty in fulfilling expectations and more directive leadership. However, these challenges were faced by *the very project and special taskforce teams* whose success was most critical to the company's' future profitability and strategic goals.

In each case, if these teams were not effective, the companies faced enormous consequences. These are the teams that need to be well led, well trained and well supported. However, while their managers and sponsors can often be less experienced internationally, often so too are their support systems.

At the lower management levels, people tend to be of the same nationality as the site they are working in and not to be very mobile. Information technology is allowing the creation of interest groups and workgroups who mostly work apart. So while as a pool spread across a globally dispersed company they are mixed, they often have little face-to-face experience with other cultures. Some companies such as Henkel, a German chemicals company have made two years' experience in another culture a prerequisite of moving into the upper management layers. What happens at the non-management level depends on the ethnic mix of each country and the type of work. Hence the shop floor workforce in Australia can be very diverse with surprising mixes of different nationalities. A Japanese, American, or Finnish shop floor workforce will seem much more coherent because either people of different nationalities arrived a few generations ago (and are now attuned to the American melting pot for instance), or in comparison to other countries, immigrant numbers have been small.

On the other hand, oil rigs, shipping crews and construction sites for instance, have always attracted migrant workers and been nationally diverse. 'We have had international teams for decades' may be the response of an international oil company. However, it is likely that international diversity at this level has little representational significance within the organisation as a whole. So while middle management and professionals can be internationally competent, lack of representative international diversity may still persist through the top levels of management and the support teams, creating difficulties. And, as if unequal experience in different organisational layers was not hazardous enough, Table 1.2 also hints at another tricky organisational reality.

In most companies, certain key departments start to work across national and temporal borders before others. Yet others may never become very internationally active.

In Wellcome and Ford, the first departments to 'internationalise' were research and development, in Unilever, marketing, in Ikea, distribution. Wellcome integrated parallel UK/US medical development teams, cutting internal competition and freeing up access to resources so that the international teams could be better funded. In Unilever, the company relies more on good presentation, creating brand names, marketing and advertising than on research and development. Each reflects an area crucial to the global success of the company. However, functions do not operate in isolation. For instance, local national accounting offices may be most effective restricting their activities to local offices, but they would then need to collaborate effectively with other local offices in order to support an international team needing regional financial information. The fact that few companies have spent enough time building bridges between localised support systems and international functional teams has led to frustration and inefficiencies.

When one function changes the way it operates, it needs support from other functions. The process usually turns into 'learning by experimenting' and can cause much frustration and de-motivation for new project leaders. Their new role as 'international project leaders' can sound exciting, challenging and rewarding. However, they often soon find out that the lack of any formal job description is strongly linked to a vagueness elsewhere about what their power and influence should be. Other less enthralled departments stick to what they know until told otherwise. Resources have to be argued for and haggled over. The job can quickly turn into an 18 hour a day nightmare.

In summary, aside from the added complexities within the team, the organisational context can create more problems for international teams by:

- having very few nationalities represented at the top, sending a message that however well mixed the 'professional' levels are, certain nationalities are more important and powerful in that organisation than others;
- supporting stereotypes based on economic strength;
- failing to address additional problems created by increased numbers of nationalities;
- having inexperienced support systems;
- having some departments/levels go international before others.

Greater Communication and Functional Difficulties

We have begun to highlight the internal communication and procedural differences that can slow these teams down. To this we can add the fuel of unhelpful preconceptions arising from the organisational context about usually outnumbered team members. Dominant nationalities are likely to create patterns of interaction that suit them and base their listening ability and responses on their underlying attitudes towards others. So, even face to face, the potential for misunderstanding, for missing opportunities, for offence to be taken, for intentionally or unintentionally excluding or underestimating some team members is enormous and happens frequently.

To this we can add the possible lack of understanding of these and other problems from senior management who usually work with people of their own culture and the lack of support systems at certain levels of the organisation and in certain departments to get things done effectively. Clearly these teams have a lot to contend with, but that is not all. Much of the communication within the team may take place from different locations and time zones across communication technology that does not allow people to understand each other easily. The nationalities with the smaller representation are also those who are more likely to have poor access to or back up on the technology that is being commonly used.

On top of this multilayered scenario, fraught with problems and inequities, we have established that the company is probably relying heavily on this team to deliver successfully. This is why we think these teams deserve a whole book of their own. International teams can be viewed as a high risk, high gain way of working compared to working in national teams based in one place. As summarised above, the co-ordination of the workflow and tasks will be much more difficult, the co-ordination and interaction of the team members will be far more complex and pitted with cultural, linguistic and technological difficulties. They can have much higher levels of conflict. As a result, the role of the international team leader is broad, complex and probably almost experimental in companies which are new to this form of management. These teams take longer to reach optimum performance. As companies are trying to achieve so much more with these more difficult teams, they clearly need to be supported, evaluated and trained differently from national teams.

It is of course at this point, an understatement to reiterate that the added complexities and high costs increase the need to focus on how these teams work, just as much as on what they are achieving. This book is to help team leaders and members do just that. Having seen so many international teams underestimate difficulties, crash, burn and come running for help, our hunch is that a longitudinal study on the effectiveness of intervening in international teams would support our experience as facilitators.

If nothing else, good facilitation can prevent international teams from falling out at major milestones.

The pathways of international business history are strewn with the casualties. What is alarming is how slow many companies have been in recognising that being proactive in creating a workable context, instilling best practices and fully supporting these teams is not an option to procrastinate about, it is an urgent necessity. The difficulty is that it demands not only time and expense, but also a considerable change of mindset and refocusing of many associated organisational policies and processes.

In summary, the added risks associated with international teams mean that team leaders and members need to:

- be able to analyse and anticipate the impact of cultural differences on the interaction of the team;
- creatively structure and manage the interaction;
- appreciate the increased number of functional and organisational boundaries that have to be skilfully traversed;
- understand and support the breadth of the team leader's role.

The senior management and other key players in the organisation need to respond by:

- seeing the need to evaluate these teams differently than national teams;
- having clarity on what the overall strategy is and communicating it effectively;
- involving key people up front, especially human resources and information technology, on how these teams can best be staffed, supported, facilitated and trained;
- being clear on the role and responsibilities of the team sponsors, leaders, member and facilitators;
- providing in-depth knowledge and training for the team leader and members on what impact cultural differences and organisational norms will have on the team;
- creating processes whereby internal and/or external facilitators can embed best practices into the team and the organisation, with the aim of making themselves redundant;
- making huge increases in up-front investment of time, money, training and technology to bring these teams successfully up to speed.

The message is surely clear:

Setting up and sustaining these teams is not an overnight task worked out on the back of an envelope.

Most new teams take six months to a year to really get to grips and understand the challenges that they are facing. For now we want to focus on that lonely team leader who needs to act as the bridge between what happens in the team and the expectations and influences of the organisation. One thing we are convinced of is that being an international team leader is not an easy assignment, even if it is a fulfilling and rewarding one. All too often there is a chasm between the espoused intent of senior managers and the reality of international team leaders as captured in the following story:

> After adopting a consultative leadership style, one newly elected international team leader decided that it could only progress if key people from a different department were involved in the team. He rang his sponsor and asked for his support in approaching the other divisional manager. 'I cannot tell my colleagues what their job is' was his reply, 'you are on your own'.

The second section of this book will look at what key organisational players need to do to support rather than abandon such team leaders. The first section is dedicated to assisting the lonely new team leader and the team members to make the decision to go ahead into totally uncharted territory. It covers the understanding and tools that they need to see and navigate the way. It starts with a comprehensive look at how cultural differences will affect the behaviour, communication and expectations of the different team members

Summary of Key Learning Points

- *Companies increasingly need international teams in order to respond effectively in the global marketplace and many depend on them to do extraordinary things.*
- *They have strong advantages and equally strong potential disadvantages. Creating and sustaining them demands full commitment.*
- *The best practices that apply to any team also apply to international teams. However the different cultural and linguistic conditioning of the individual team members adds further degrees of complexity that have to be handled well within the team. The organisational context adds yet more.*
- *Due to lack of cultural mixing, especially at the top of an organisation, strong numerical and perceptual biases can badly affect international teams and lead to exclusion of some team members.*
- *Some functions tend to become international before others and some not at all, which can create frustrations and inefficiencies as the team tries to make headway.*
- *These added layers of complexity lead to frequent communication difficulties in international teams. On the whole, companies are not proactive enough in addressing these difficulties before they create serious and expensive problems.*
- *Generic team skills are a good starting point, but additional training in cultural differences is not enough. The team structure, support, training and evaluation processes need to be tailored to the additional needs created by the broader task, cultural differences and probable geographic distances.*
- *What is needed is not only for team leaders and member to understand how the different layers of complexity play out in their particular team, but also for the organisation to re-examine the mindsets and processes that hinder these teams and mobilise people and resources to support them.*

Chapter Two

Know Your Team

'It is so different to have German vigour challenging Latino American Style.'
Seagram Manager 1996

'Understanding other styles does not entail abandoning our own nor is recognising differences only a preparation to obliterating them.'
A Kaplan 1996

> David thought he should let the meeting flow by simply introducing the topic, asking a relevant question and letting the team members argue out the solution. After a while he noticed that the Hong Kong, Chinese and Japanese team members were never speaking up, even though their English was perfect. He was puzzled.

An international team leader can take little for granted. David can stop the discussion and ask the participants directly why they are not speaking up. However, in some cultures being publicly critical, especially of the leader is not an accepted norm. In order to understand what the problem might be, as well as how to acknowledge it openly and find a solution, David needs to understand the many ways in which cultural differences can influence the interaction within the team.

This chapter gives team leaders, facilitators and members a comprehensive understanding of these key cultural factors. With this knowledge, they can diagnose and so anticipate events like the one described above. A word of caution. We are aware that putting such a comprehensive chapter near the front of the book may alienate those wanting to quickly reach the 'what happens in these teams (Chapter Three) and what do I do about it' (Chapter Four). We therefore advise those in a hurry to read the first page, the bullets and the highlighted learning points within the chapter and return to it for specific issues, as and when they are needed. For others, read on for a deep dive that will show and remind you what is down below as you surface to participate in the team. From our research and experience, we have identified five culturally determined and three organisational factors that we have seen have a marked impact on the performance of international teams.

Five 'Cultural' and Three 'Organisational' Factors that affect the Interaction in International Teams

Cultural factors

1. The degrees of difference or similarity that exist between the cultural norms of the individuals in the team
2. The degree to which individuals might manifest their cultural norms
3. Differences in language fluency, communication patterns, non verbals and who says what when
4. Culturally different leadership styles
5. The different expectations about key team processes

Organisational factors

6. The status of different cultures within the organisation
7. The geographic spread of the team members
8. The similarity or difference between functional, professional and other 'cultures'

Five Cultural Factors

1 The degree of difference or similarity that exist between the cultural norms of the individuals in the team

Culture has been defined in many different ways

In order to understand what a cultural norm is, you first have to understand what is meant by 'culture'. Unfortunately an agreed definition of culture remains elusive*. Rather than defining the 'thing' itself, it is usually defined by the attributes which we recognise it by. These are different 'normal' behaviours, clothes, values, beliefs, traditions, rituals, assumptions and so on. After looking at many definitions (see Appendix 1), it is not hard to see why culture is often referred to as the 'dustbin' concept; throw everything in, especially if you do not understand it and cover it with the lid of culture. It is now common to talk about individual, gender, team, functional and organisational cultures as well as national cultures.

---

*For some good discussions see books and articles recommended in Appendix 1.

It is both an individual and group, internal and external affair

Most people agree that culture is both an individual and group phenomenon. If you were the last person in the world, you would still have a culture. That is, you would still have a particular way of doing things and a particular set of explanations as to why you were doing things that way. People of one culture are presumed to have similar explanations for doing certain key things the same way, the group 'norms'.

Some of the ways in which culture can manifest are inside our minds, eg ways of thinking, values, beliefs, assumptions and others are more visible, such as rituals, clothes, food etc. This leads to a problem when comparing cultures. Some people view culture as subjective[1]. They argue that culture cannot be measured separately from the context of shared meaning and values in which things happen. From this standpoint, it is not *objectively possible* to compare a concept like leadership across different cultures. Other people define culture according to internal and external factors that they consider they can establish as 'robust' concepts. These are concepts that can have meaning *independently* of any one particular culture. From this 'objective' viewpoint it is valid to take a concept like leadership and compare it across cultures.

It is important to keep in mind that while extensive cross-cultural comparison and research may elicit statistical differences across concepts like leadership, power and uncertainty, our understanding of what those differences mean in practice is probably limited.

Some researchers now express the need to include both approaches. The important message is that because we are each culturally conditioned, there are some things we may never understand or see the same way other people do. It is often quoted that the tribes on the southernmost tip of South America did not 'see' Magellan's ship because it was outside any of their frames of reference.

Gaining a reliable understanding of others' values, beliefs and assumptions which are thought to drive their behaviour is difficult

The mix of internal and external, conscious and unconscious features in culture is often represented as an iceberg, a popular diagram copyrighted by several intercultural exponents. The difference is usually in the wording of external observable features marked above the 'water line' and internal, often unconscious features such as values, beliefs and deepest assumptions, marked below. The analogy of the iceberg is used to point out that there is usually much more below the visible surface than above.

One reason that it is hard to access what is below the surface is that there is very seldom a linear connection between one underlying value and one observable behaviour. Ask your team members if they have ever done something that they disagreed with, but did it because their boss, teacher or parents told them to. It is likely that almost everyone will raise their hands. Now ask whether their own personal values were reflected in what they felt or what they did. The chances are most people will opt for what they felt. The question is 'then why did you do it?'

Usually because it was not *that* bad. They were not being asked to kill or perjure anyone, and the difference between what one was being asked to do and what one felt, was balanced by thoughts of losing one's job and not being able to support the family, being seen as unreliable, a coward, a failure etc. In other words, a set of different values. In contrast, the list of things that people imagine they would never do under any conceivable circumstances is usually very short. If values are defined as 'the preferred way of doing things'[2], then one has to add 'in a favourable or particular context'. As the context changes, the results of this on-going evaluation will change 'normal' behaviour. The point being made is that each of our actions is based on a continuous juggling act of weighing different values against each other. This means that:

You cannot predictably assess someone's values and beliefs by watching what they do, and by doing so, assume that you can predict what they might do in future.

It is hard to ask people why they do something the way they do without causing offence. It is often also difficult to fit the reply into one's own framework of meaning.

> Over a period of months, a Kenyan night watchman always agreed to, but never turned up for, dog training and always said 'no problem'. He explained that he wanted to come, but something else always got in the way, so it was no problem. Only if he did not want to do the dog training at all, then it would be a problem. When later the same watchman was asked to join other employees to search for a missing item, he refused. He explained that if he found it, that would mean that he had known where it was all along.

It is almost impossible to understand someone else's internal deliberations. It is easier to label them as being 'obstructive' or 'fickle'. You do need to ask them and prevent yourself from making quick value judgements. A team leader needs to keep an open mind until he or she can create an open discussion.

These difficulties explain our zealous support for an exercise called the 'cultural value checklist' described in Chapters Four and Five. The exercise makes the team member's different preferences and values that relate to the team's interaction explicit, laying them out on an equal playing field for discussion within the team.

Nationality and ethnicity are only rough guides to someone's culture

It has been suggested that people must share a language, live in the same time period and be geographically contiguous[3] to belong to the same culture. It is easy to see why nationality is usually used as the rough guide. Nations have to sort out some kind of common spoken and/or written language in order to function at the nation state level, even if there are numerous different official languages and scripts within the national borders.

One problem is that nationality can be given either by birthplace (eg UK) or ethnicity (eg Germany to date) depending on the policy of the countries involved. Nationality can be a purely external feature, changed by changing passport. To be useful in identifying possible cultural differences in international teams, nationality needs to reflect something about a person's thinking, expectations and underlying reasons for their behaviour. While some nationalities are ethnically/culturally quite homogeneous (eg Japan) others are now ethnically very diverse (eg Malaysia, Brazil, Kenya, Australia). The status of someone's ethnicity or sub-culture in a nation has been shown to affect their perceptions and behaviour[4] while they technically share the same nationality as everyone else. Nationality is obviously a rough categorisation, but using ethnicity and race turns out to be just as problematic.

> *'People like books lose something in translation ... It is the fate of migrants to be stripped of history, to stand naked amidst the scorn of strangers, upon whom they see rich clothing, the brocades of continuity and the eyebrows of belonging.'*
> Salman Rushdie, *Shame*

The original Western categorisations of race by Linneaus in 1758 were on the basis of known geography. They were changed in 1795 when a German called Blumenbach created five categories, Caucasian, American, Mongolian, Malay and Ethiopian, preferring Caucasians* as he liked the way they looked. Amazingly the same arbitrary term is still used today. The American melting pot of 'Caucasians, Hispanics, Afro-Americans, Amer-Asians and East and First Nation Indians' to name a few, can still refer to groups of people with very different spoken and written languages and customs (eg East Indians; Tamils, Gujuratis, Bengalis, Punjabis etc) giving rise to different cognitive, behavioural and cultural norms. On the other hand a child born to second generation Gujurati parents in Canada will most likely have a very different set of norms and language skills to a child born to Gujurati parents in Gujurat. Ethnicity or race does not give more reliable definition of a person's cultural norms than nationality.

*From the Caucasus (Bolshoy Kavkaz) mountains, between the Black and Caspian Seas.

> A team leader has to remember that when anticipating differences based on different national norms, the boundaries between nationality, ethnicity and culture are very fuzzy.

National stereotypes tend to be unhelpful, especially when attributed to individuals

Stereotypes usually come through the media, experience, and jokes. 'We all have knowledge of them, but we do not all act on them.'[5] They can give a traveller some sense of security that they know something about an otherwise totally unknown destination. They can also leave a sense of frustration that instead of being a blank page ready for raw new experiences, one's mind is cluttered with usually negative and certainly questionable, generalisations about large groups of people. Not surprisingly, the ability to look afresh has been found to be more effective in international management[6]. Some interesting findings about stereotypes are:

- Stereotypes are fairly resilient and can be said to have a kernel of truth[7]. People would rather label individuals as non-stereotypical than change a national stereotype[8]. Hence stereotypes often change more slowly that actual cultures'.
- Stereotypes are often double sided[9], 'Americans are friendly, open and flexible, but also insincere, uncritical and shallow'. Similarly, changes in stereotypes are not uniform. Canadian citizens initially described Indian immigrant women as 'quiet, polite and demure' which, based on the same behaviour changed after some months to 'dull, unfriendly and selfish'[10].
- Interaction tends to reduce rather than undermine the biased perceptions that feed them'[11].
- The accuracy or subsequent adjustment of stereotypes depends on prior exposure to correct information or media[12].

It is usually very frustrating to be on the receiving end of stereotypical behaviour.

> A Papua New Guinean top American management school graduate was sitting in his house in Port Moresby playing chess with an American friend. As he was also a local chief, he was wearing traditional dress. Another white person entered and talked to the American in fluent English, switching to pidgin when talking to the management school graduate. The graduate politely replied in fluent American English, yet the visiting white man continued to talk to him in pidgin. His stereotype about people in grass skirts prevented him from 'hearing' the reply.

International team leaders need to be aware of their own stereotypes so that they do not act them out and can anticipate the problems other stereotypes will cause within the team.

The research on cultural norms can be informative, but it needs to be applied with caution

One of the aims of comparative statistical research on different cultural norms has been to create a more objective way than stereotypes of assessing similarities and differences.

> After hearing a presentation expressing the need for cross-cultural work in a UK subsidiary, the Norwegian operations manager banged his fist on the table and exclaimed 'Culture? But we are of one culture'. Presumably he meant organisational culture. The consultant did not wait to find out, but quickly created a survey that showed that the British workers and Norwegian management had very different views of what the problems were. The operation manager fully supported the statistical results.

Statistical work comparing different value dimensions or leadership across many nationalities* has been extremely helpful in persuading even the most hardened sceptics that national cultural differences do exist and can delay, if not wreck, international business ventures and teams.

International team leaders and members need to read the literature (see a sample in Appendix One) that explores the national norms of their team members. The peaks of the normal statistical curves that describe cultural norms in the value research will show which cultures are statistically closer on specific issues and which are farther apart[13]. While reading this literature, team leaders need to exercise caution and remember that:

a   Any individual may fall anywhere within the statistically normal curve describing their culture. If one falls at the edges of a national curve, there is little explanation of how this might modify one's values and behaviour.
b   It may be that Americans and British people consistently score as more individualistic than Japanese and Koreans. However, the way in which they are individualistic may be very different. For instance, Americans are proud to be able to tell you how good they are at something, whereas traditionally most British people believed actions spoke louder than words and were taught not to discuss their achievements. This can lead to

---

*Common value dimensions and further reading on this much used and discussed approach are available in Appendix One.

the British perceiving the Americans as pushy and arrogant and the Americans perceiving the British as ineffectual and underachieving. East Coast Americans are often very conservative in their dress and business behaviour, which differs from California. The way people manifest the measured norms can be very specific to regions and countries.

c   The discussion above demonstrated how difficult it is to link specific values to specific behaviours. Not surprisingly, there is no clear explanation of how *value* dimensions assessed from written questionnaires actually influences *behaviour* in different social contexts. Suppose someone is assessed as highly individualistic on a pre-questionnaire, finds it individually worthwhile to be very group oriented when working with a particular team, but again measures highly individualistic on a post questionnaire. People who believe all cultures are converging into one homogeneous business culture may take it as evidence to support their argument. Others may regard the behaviour as a temporary adaptation and not related to the real underlying cultural values of the participant. Still others may take it as a sign of bi-culturalism or that the individual is highly adaptable across cultures.

So, reading and knowing the literature on cultural norms does not mean you can accurately predict individual behaviour in your team.

Despite these limitations, one interesting use of cultural norms is assessing 'readiness' to work in self managed work teams. In-depth studies have suggested that different countries will embrace or resist this form of work for different reasons[14]. Americans tend to be more individualistic than Mexicans and hence, less team oriented, but are more comfortable with being autonomous. People who have an individually based outlook tend to regard team pay structures as unfair, more than they resist self managed teams per se. One set of findings suggest that there have been some significant shifts in some of the cultural dimensions over the last twenty-five years. America was slightly more collectivist and even less hierarchically oriented than before, suggesting that maybe as new work forms are introduced and team members start to have positive experiences, values can change.

Duncan Crundwell, an enlightened CEO has written a thesis looking at the implementation of self managed work teams in his small dynamic UK based company[15]. As the workforce primarily consisted of American, British and Japanese employees, he came up with the following assessment of cultural norms that would help or hinder working in these teams (Table 2.1).

Each culture is seen as having advantages and disadvantages. In Britain, the strong sense of initiative and willingness to defer gratification, support the ambiguous and slow process of establishing self managed work teams. However, the lack of motivation and short-term focus of management can be a strong hindrance. In Japan the strong team ethic and long-term focus would both support setting up teams, but the hierarchical approach and lack of

Table 2.1: Cultural norms that help or hinder self managed work teams

Country	Cultural advantages	Cultural disadvantages
Britain	Strong sense of initiative Can be hard working Willing to defer gratification	Poorly motivated management structure Low ability managers Poorly educated management Short-term profit mentality Not socially acceptable to excel at business
Japan	Long term investment strategy Strong loyalty Very hard working Strong team orientation	Education system that does not support creativity and abstract thought Very bureaucratic Hierarchical Centralised structure
America	Strongly encouraged to excel in business Free of social class constraints Decentralised structure in business	Lack initiative Expect instant gratification Had it easy for too long Work for personal recognition

creativity will work against the team achieving self management. In America there is much less acceptance of formal hierarchy as people prefer to be autonomous, however, the need for instant gratification can work against the time it takes to get these teams working effectively. The same CEO who made the study found that novelty value made setting up self managed teams in Britain, where management was usually the problem, much easier than in America, where his style was just like everyone else's.

Our advice is to know these cultural norms, and to handle them with care. Looking at the norms may give the team leader and members some common starting points that are not so obviously apparent. For instance, although they may interpret it differently, Japanese and Malawians can share a strong preference for collectivist behaviours with a high regard for the leader. But this is as far as extrapolation from the value dimensions should go. As the Papua New Guinean example earlier showed, acting on preconceived generalities is usually very offensive and ineffective. Once the team has matured, cultural differences and stereotypes can become a source of light-hearted humour as well as richness.

When thinking about the difference between the cultural norms, international team leaders and members need to remember that:

- *Culture has been defined in many different ways.*
- *It is both an internal and external, individual and group affair.*
- *Gaining a reliable understanding of others' values, beliefs and assumptions is difficult.*
- *Nationality is only a rough guide to someone's culture.*
- *National stereotypes tend to be unhelpful, especially when attributed to individuals.*
- *The research on cultural norms can be informative, but needs to be applied with caution.*

2 The degree to which different people may manifest their cultural norms

Concepts of self and personality differ between cultures

Personality and self is understood and defined differently in different cultures. Eastern writers note that Western cultures think that 'every society is composed of individuals and that every culture is created by and expressed in the individual'[16]. They point out that languages like English and French treat each person as if that person exists as a separate independent entity from other people. In Japanese, a 'person' does not have a hard shell of personality or definite identity as an 'individual', even though he or she does have a membrane to separate him/her from people[17].

Most Western cultures currently seem to think of 'self' or 'me' as some kind of insoluble nugget residing somewhere in the brain (or in more current holistic thinking, the mind and body) that needs 'self development' or assertiveness training to achieve what is wanted in life. On the other hand, the aim of traditional Indian Yogic techniques is to dissolve the illusionary web of desires called 'self' by understanding how thought creates it in the first place. As most people are brought up in one culture, it is unlikely that any one person can quite understand how others really think of themselves in relation to other 'people'.

Even without different interpretations of what 'I am', searching for what thoughts and action result from personality and what thoughts and actions result from cultural conditioning is a definitely fuzzy pursuit[18]. Yet again, despite the fuzziness, it does seem intuitively okay to say how someone as a personality has responded to different life experiences, can determine how strongly they adhere to their national norms. The two are linked.

Personality and experience can change the extent to which someone exhibits national norms

It is obvious that people adapt and that cultures as a whole do change for all sorts of internal and external environmental reasons. Personality, experience and the amount someone is exposed to other cultures may lead to them being strongly or weakly committed to national norms. Yet research has shown that international experience is no guarantee of greater international expertise or understanding. It depends on the individual. Not surprisingly researchers have found that people who base their expectations and thinking only around their own culture, are less able to adjust than more open minded individuals. As one CEO expressed it 'people with high ego needs cannot adjust to other cultures'.

People adapt, but 'good' adaptation is often seen to be one way

Extreme adherence to cultural norms is, of course, the source of much amusement in films and stories. Yet even cultural adaptation is riddled with status issues. Many Western expatriates in the richest parts of developing capitals live in luxurious compounds, with servants and swimming pools. Compare this with the shock for managers from developing countries of dealing directly with developed metropolises from a self-contained flat. It is easy to imagine who achieves the greatest learning curve. What is more, 'good' adaptation tends to be strongly viewed as one way by most Western cultures. Westerners who adapt to local cultures are usually derogatorily described as 'going native' while it is considered helpful for those from others cultures to fit seamlessly into Western business cultures. 'Sometimes I even forget that he is Indian/Japanese'. Thankfully, even for Western business people, some adaptation to other cultures is usually essential to success. The question is 'what is it that changes when people adapt to other cultures?'

> One Hong Kong Chinese team described themselves jokingly as bananas ... yellow on the outside, but white inside. When it came to someone being elected or self electing as an observer, the team was in confusion. They finally agreed to play an elimination game using hand signs until one person was left. Nobody wanted to self-elect out of the team and nobody wanted to embarrass anyone by suggesting that someone should be isolated from the team. In American or European teams, a number of people usually rush to select themselves, or names are usually quickly put forward.

People may adapt behaviour without changing deeper values

While people may exhibit adaptable behaviour, deeper values may not change. It will depend on the depth at which the value is held and how entrenched a behavioural pattern is. The way we see and think about the world is deeply embedded in our mother tongue. As such, it is likely that the way we think and process information encapsulated by that language, would probably be the last to change. In thinking about the extent to which a team member may or may not adhere to their cultural norms, international team leaders need to remember that:

Figure 2.1: Role modelling effective international working

- *Personality and experience can change the extent to which someone exhibits national norms.*
- *Concepts of self and personality differ between cultures.*
- *People adapt, but 'good' adaptation is often seen to be one way.*
- *International experience will change some people more than others, it is no guarantee of greater international expertise or understanding.*
- *People may adapt behaviour without changing deeper values.*

So in summary, it is important to understand how different cultural norms are likely to affect someone's behaviour in a team, while at the same time appreciating that they may behave in a totally different way.

3 Differences in languages, fluency, communication patterns, non verbals and who says what, when

Language changes as it spreads

> 'I always thought we spoke the same language, but there are loads of differences. I have ended up having more misunderstandings with my American colleagues than my Japanese counterpart, just because I assumed they knew what I meant.'

'You Brits have sayings that are complete nonsense over here.'
'It's the simple words that trip us up.'

Languages develop in particular environments and often either die out or spread. In spreading, they change. Current 'American' English uses many different words and grammatical structures that are misunderstood in 'English' English. Microsoft currently lists nine 'types' of English in its spell checker. In colonial countries where English, French, German or Portuguese for instance have been imposed and maintained as the language of government and commerce, the grammar and word usage usually reflect the nuances from the original language in those countries. As a result, as the quotes infer, misunderstandings can easily occur.

Some languages are precise about relationships, others imprecise

English is a language that tries to have fairly exact meanings independent of how it is said. Although British suggestions are in fact often direct orders, Arabic, Kiswahili, Japanese and Chinese do rely much more heavily on inflection, pitch, tone, context and non-verbal cues to convey the real meaning of the word. English people tend to expect 'Yes' to mean precise agreement. Yet many languages have short words that mean 'I have heard you', not 'I agree'. 'Hai' in Japanese, 'Acha' in Hindi. These are usually translated into 'Yes' or 'Okay' in English. This leads to countless cases of English speakers getting angry when others 'go back on their agreements'.

> One British manager asked his Finnish colleagues to say 'Yes Yes'; when they agreed to an action point rather than just acknowledge it.

On the other hand, English is very imprecise about relationships. English verbs tend to stress informality and symmetrical power relationships unlike Japanese and Korean which emphasise formality and asymmetrical power relationships.

Korean has special vocabularies for different sexes, different degrees of social status, different degrees of intimacy and different formal languages. Similarly the ending of a Hindi verb will express the power difference, intimacy and level of formality of a relationship. Barely audible small changes express whether 'I will do something,' 'I will have someone do something', or 'I will make someone else do something.' Imagine then getting used to only using an impersonal 'you' in English, rather than showing the level of respect and intimacy, or having to state explicitly that I will have someone do that for me, rather than I will do it for you.

Language deeply affects the way people think and where they will put important information

Many Chinese and Japanese characters were originally based on pictorial representations of reality. This creates a written Chinese script that crosses many spoken languages and is recognisable after thousands of years (most English people need to have Chaucer 1342–1400 AD translated). Depicting reality supports concrete thinking not abstract hypothetical thinking[19]. Not only what information is considered useful, but how it is presented is different. Chinese managers have suggested that they would be seen as 'rude immodest, pushy and lose face for acting aggressively if they put the information they wanted to convey at the beginning of a sentence like Americans and British[20].

> One Japanese manager in Unilever said 'I learnt that I had to put the important information at the beginning or else nobody will hear me'.

Silence and pauses mean different things in different cultures

The pace of speech is also interpreted differently and second language speakers are obviously more likely to speak more slowly. Korean listeners attributed credibility to a male talking at a slow pace (women were found to have little credibility whatever their pace), whereas American listeners attribute credibility to a much faster pace[21].

There is evidence that different cultures have different uses of silence and patterns of overlap or interruption. Silences and pauses in Japan and some Scandinavian countries are a sign of respect for the previous speaker, and that you are absorbing what they are saying. Apparently the Japanese have a saying that goes 'he who speaks is a dumb ass'[22]. When many Americans and British people first encounter long pauses, they are extremely uncomfortable and immediately assume that something is wrong. Silences and pauses in America and Britain usually mean that you are lost for words, 'stonewalling' or ignoring someone. The problem is that silences do sometimes mean respect, but can also be a result of another strong East, South East Asian and African norm of not voicing criticism in public.

> A team leader of one predominantly Finnish team stood up with two other teams present, and said ' we have had great difficulties working as an international team'. The facilitator asked 'do you want to share what they have been?' 'No' was the resounding response.

The impact and use of interruption is different across cultures. Because the important information is at the beginning, interrupting in English usually means only losing the padding. In German and Hindi for instance, the verb is at the end of the sentence. In Hindi, 'kal' means yesterday and tomorrow, only the tense in the verb at the end of the sentence will tell you which one it is.

Many Japanese working in English will wait for a pause before they speak, or not speak at all. However, Japanese teams working in Japanese have very high levels of simultaneous talk. The purpose of it is to show enjoyment of conversing in a harmonious atmosphere by maintaining and supporting the partner's speech[23]. However, American and British speakers for instance, tend to use simultaneous talk to interrupt and cut other people off as the underlying rule is that only one person should be talking at once. As illustrated in the next chapter, interruption patterns play a significant role in who gets to talk in international teams. American and English presenters are often very put off when Italian listeners start discussing loudly between themselves while the presenter is still talking.

Second language speakers will tend to speak less

Most people find that heterogeneous teams have greater communication difficulties than homogeneous teams. In international teams, fluency with the working language as well as different linguistics norms and backgrounds also exacerbate these difficulties even more. Less fluent team members are more likely to be excluded from the interaction of a team. The last four points all contribute to the way in which this happens as illustrated in the next chapter.

Team leaders and members need to actively lower the costs and increase the benefits for second language speakers to speak

When team members have different levels of fluency in the working language, they will constantly assess the cost or the benefit to the team of speaking up. By the time a second language speaker has mentally constructed or translated what they want to say, the rest of the fluent members have usually moved on. The second language speaker is likely to do a quick mental calculation. 'Is what I want to say important enough to bring the group back to the point that they have just left? What will their response be?' If images of angry impatient faces immediately come to mind, then the point will have to be evaluated as very urgent or of much higher quality and importance than what the first language speakers have just said. If an image comes to mind of being met with a smiling ' Yes, by all means' then the personal cost of the second language speaker intervening is much reduced.

If the fluent members have not completely forgotten about the quieter members, they are likely to occasionally assess the cost/benefits of slowing down to ask a second language speaker whose points may take more time, perhaps be expressed in 'painful' language or come out in a strange order with 'muddled' irrelevant logic. Probably if they think they are doing okay with the task, they will carry on with the justification 'well, if X really has something important to say, he/she will stop us'. As illustrated in the next chapter, good teams create a pattern of communication with enough small pauses that people can easily speak up.

When working in a foreign language like English, people can also feel the need to re-affirm certain aspects of their cultural identity that they do not feel the need to do when speaking in their mother tongue[24].

Non-verbal communication differs across cultures

Non-verbal communication is an important aspect of communication in teams. Researchers have found that when using groupware computer technology, the commitment to the teamwork is far higher if the team is sitting together in the same room. Presumably the occasional round of laughter and grunts in response to points being made on the large screen keeps people interested. Grunts and hand gestures have different meanings in different cultures.

> One angry British driver was stunned as a pushy aggressive 'matatu' (a small minibus) driver in Kenya backed off instead of erupting in rage, after being shown a two finger v sign showing the back of the hand. While it is about as rude as you can get in Britain, in Kenya the same sign means 'hey, let's be peaceful'. Making a circle between the first and forefinger means 'spot on' in America, 'nothing' in France, something rude in Israel and is extremely rude in Columbia. Americans feel comfortable pointing at people, considered rude in Britain, like showing the soles of your shoes in Arab countries and India, or passing things with your left hand. There are many examples pointing out the need for care.

On a subtler level, the length of eye contact is also crucial. Looking someone straight in the eye is considered a sign of honesty, determination and straightforwardness in the UK and America. A Kikuyu intercultural trainer would tell of how he had never looked his father in the eye once during his lifetime. It would have been a mark of disrespect. When testifying against an alleged West Indian thief, an elderly British lady said, 'I knew he was lying because he would not look me straight in the eye'.

There are different levels of comfort with demonstrable emotion and physical touching between cultures. While a Turk may display a large show of emotional outpouring as a necessary ingredient to getting a good price, a Finn may signal displeasure with an almost imperceptible raise of one eyebrow. One British manager went to a meeting in Portugal and sat with his mouth open as all the other male managers hugged the Chairman who had come in late, crying. The meeting then proceeded. An American lady was alienated for the rest of the week when the first cross-cultural learning exercise on a week long programme in Germany involved touching people that she did not know well. On the other hand, a Spanish manager declared that if he did not kiss his secretary every morning, she would wonder what was wrong.

We often unconsciously mirror each others movements as a way of tuning in. It is not uncommon to see some small movement reflected back and pass around the team. If one person shifts in their chair or leans back, so does someone else, perhaps to keep them company. At a micro-level, body rhythms associated with the consonant-vowel-consonant patterns of speech and listening are common across all nationalities and languages[25]. Despite such reassuring imperceptible sameness, team leaders and members have to be careful about coming to hasty assumptions about the meaning of each other's ways of speaking and visible gesturing.

There is no one right way to communicate in an international team

Effective or ineffective patterns of listening and interacting based on language use are usually set within the first few minutes and will continue unless something else intervenes. It is important that everyone feels that their contribution has been well received and given proper consideration. Setting good ground rules and having good leadership or facilitation to break up dominant patterns is helpful. That said, there is no one set way that a team should interact to be effective. There are many tactics that teams can adopt depending on what is actually going on in the team.

> In one UNEP/World bank meeting on transport and air pollution, a representative of the automotive industry was determined to give the industry's view at all costs. Initially, his contributions were forcefully stated objections to what else was being explored, which left no room for creative discussion. After a while, the rest of the team met any contribution from this man with a short but stony silence. After the pause, during which most of the team either stared at him or their laps, someone else would carry on with a nod in his direction, but as if he had not spoken. By the second day, he was approaching team members, especially during the breaks, and trying to soften what he had to say in an almost apologetic way. In effect he was asking to be let back in on the understanding that he would be less belligerent and more collaborative in his approach.

Perhaps the team leader could have been more explicit in saying that it was not his ideas that were difficult, only the way he was presenting them. Instead the team communicated through their behaviour, which was effective in the end. At the other end of the spectrum strategically losing your cool can also cut through hours of ineffective talk. However, as Aristotle warned 'anyone can become angry – that is easy; but to be angry with the right person, to the right degree at the right time, for the right purpose in the right way – this is not easy'[26].

When planning how to manage the interaction in an international team, team leaders need to remember that:

- ***Language changes as it spreads – there are many 'types' of English.***
- ***Some languages are precise about relationships, others imprecise.***
- ***Language deeply affects the way people think and where they will put important information.***
- ***Silence and pauses mean different things in different cultures. Second language speakers will tend to speak less (and that does not equate with being less intelligent or having less to say).***
- ***Team leaders and members need to actively lower the costs and increase the benefits for second language speakers to speak.***
- ***Non-verbal communication differs across cultures.***
- ***There is no one right way to communicate in an international team.***

4 Culturally different leadership styles

'I do not know why some of them bother turning up, they don't say a word all meeting.'

'He's so autocratic, he just loves the sound of his own voice, when he gets going I just switch off – he's not interested in my view so I shut up.'

'It's brilliant, she really involves the whole team – if you don't need to go to a meeting or cannot make it – she makes sure she catches up with you later to fill you in.'

As the quotes remind us, this aspect of international teamwork is crucial and is touched upon again in Chapter Seven. Exactly what is appropriate and when, will be dependent on the cultural context and make up of the team. Recently the mostly American quest for a universal effective leadership style has centred on changing autocratic, non consultative, controlling leaders into more 'participative', 'visionary', 'intuitive', 'ethically principled', 'collaborative' 'facilitators and stewards' who are able to handle diversity.

Words like 'equal power', 'mutual accountability', 'equal participation' have also recently taken centre stage in the discussion on effective national or international teams. On seeing the words 'equal power' one French manager leapt out of his seat shouting 'stupid Anglo-Saxon list, there is no such thing as equal power in France'. Even so, as much management theory emerges from America, the usually implied message is that large hierarchies are outdated and cultures still demonstrating high levels of power distance (the extent to which

Table 2.2: Hong Kong Chinese/Australian Behaviours

Hong Kong Chinese leaders	Australian leaders
Tend to lecture subordinates about principles behind policies and instructions	Hover between authority assertion and authority disclaiming attitudes
Expressly invite the contributions of named subordinates	Seldom expressly invite subordinates to contribute
Greater use of open questions and strategies to draw out sensitive issues from subordinates, eg greater use of explicit choices and open ended consultation	Much less open consultation. Instead, use of loaded questions and ritualistic consultation to involve and influence the subordinates towards desired outcome
Warm hearted, paternalistic, condescending	
Similar gate-keeping and facilitatory strategies and appeals to organisational principles applied more situationally	Similar gate-keeping and facilitatory strategies and appeals to organisational principles applied more universally

Hong Kong Chinese subordinates	Australian subordinates
React with ready compliance and ritualistic deference. Will only cover factual non evaluative statements until manager draws it out further.	Query and challenge directives. Self initiated and self sustained pattern of challenging the establishment.
Very few unsolicited contributions.	More frequent unsolicited propositions, show more initiative and are more active in the discussions.
More direct invited and uninvited disagreement with superiors when asked, especially when defending their own proposition, but never self initiated. Fewer 'hedges' and 'disclaimers'	Less direct disagreement with superiors, more use of 'hedges' and 'disclaimers'. Greater range of indirectness.
Engage in acrid exchange and heated discussion	Engage in acrid exchange and heated discussion
Consensus in hierarchical meetings but look to leader for final decision	Consensus in hierarchical meetings but look to leader for final decision

power is distributed unequally) (eg where subordinates still expect to be told what to do and how to do it) are seen as undeveloped and undemocratic. To quote one writer 'even illiterate peasants (in Peru) can use participative management effectively if they are taught to do so'[27] Even if one ignores the condescending tone, a lot will depend on how the word 'participative' is interpreted.

One researcher[28] looked at the interaction between team leader and members in twenty-two Hong Kong Chinese and twenty-two Australian banking teams. The results are shown in Table 2.2.

So if participative leadership means allowing people to speak as and when they want to, then the Australians were more participative than Hong Kong Chinese. If, however, participative leadership means stimulating open-ended unbiased consultation and allowing direct statements of disagreement and criticism, then the Hong Kong Chinese were more participative than Australians. If participative leadership means allowing acrid exchange and heated discussion in the search for consensus with the leader making the final decision in difficult situations, then both Hong Kong Chinese and Australians were equally participative. Clearly one cultural understanding of concepts like 'participative management' is ineffective. The other important message from comparing the two styles is that:

Structuring a team's interaction can increase rather than decrease individual participation and protect minority views.

Making sure your leadership style fits the over-riding cultural milieu of the teams is important. Three operational team leaders in a Hong Kong Telecoms company were American, Samoan and Canadian. The American had been in Hong Kong for twenty years, the Samoan for three and the Canadian for eight months. The accepted 'formal' pattern of interaction of the chair asking someone to speak and then summing up the information before passing on to ask the next person clearly irritated the Canadian when he was a team member of the Samoan's team. When it came to leading his own team, he would ask someone to speak and then leave the conversation to follow a 'natural' flow. Discussions would trail off with him saying 'okay, okay, okay'. A female Chinese finance manager had come to the meeting to contribute and listen to the team's work. She soon fell into the role of summing up the points. Although the Canadian team leader spoke the most in his team, he was the only operational team leader in the study who was not perceived as having had the most influence on the team; the female finance officer was seen as more influential.

On the other hand, one pan-European team in a London-based oil company was led by a laid-back Scotsman. He would stretch his arms over his head and ask 'so what do we want to do?' Although a German counterpart talked more and did his best to dominate the meeting, the Scotsman maintained his role as being the place where agreements were 'ratified' and clear explanations of contextual matters were to be found. The Scotsman was perceived to have had the most influence. If maintaining influence is important, you can afford not to be the pivot of the interaction in Europe, but not always in Hong Kong.

The best way to find out what is expected of you as a leader is to ask the team in a way that puts different expectations on an equal footing. The cultural value checklist exercise described in Chapters Four and Five unearths the different preferences and expectations at the beginning of the teamwork. The team can then, explicitly or implicitly, guide the leader towards the most appropriate style for that mix of nationalities in that organisational and cultural context.

In anticipating what leadership style to adopt, international team leaders do well to remember that:

- **Preferred and effective leadership styles vary across cultures.**
- **Team members will come with different expectations and preferences.**
- **There is no one universally effective style for all teams, tasks and team stages.**
- **The most appropriate style is best negotiated with the team.**

5 Different expectations of what constitutes effective group behaviour

Team members will have different understandings of many group processes. One joint venture team facilitator observed that unlike the Americans, the Germans preferred to build trust slowly based on deeds and to start off in a formal, matter of fact mode where contributions were assertive and conclusive with a high tolerance of silence[29]. They also preferred adherence to a predetermined agenda in meetings, with a centralised 'director' organising the patterns of contributions. While many such group processes are influenced by different cultural expectations, in this chapter we will focus on conflict resolution and decision making.

Conflict resolution and preferred decision making processes vary across cultures

Conflict resolution

Different cultures have very different ways of successfully resolving conflicts depending on the context.

> In one international institute with a dysfunctional director general (DG), both the local African staff and the international staff were agreed that they had a problem with a lack of vision and random management decisions. However, the local African staff were appalled when the international staff asked the DG critical questions in a large group meeting. Speaking out and criticising the boss was not their way of solving the problem.

'There's a couple of Americans on our team who just tell it like it is — sometimes they go too far and a real row breaks out, that wastes so much time.'

Some cultures prefer indirect conflict resolution. A British personnel manager for a Japanese company in London bemoaned the fact that if an employee made a mistake, his or her desk would be moved to the window from the more important

Figure 2.2: Resolving conflict in international teams

central position. The employee would then have to ask a string of people to find out what he or she had done wrong. It would take about a year for their desk to be slowly moved back to the original position. Expatriate managers in South Africa have successfully resorted to using the psychic powers of the local shaman to find the whereabouts of the stolen computers when nobody would own up.

> *'I've realised now that I have to got to deal with things while everyone is in the room. I was leaving it to try to do it one on one, but you can't bollock* someone on the phone too easily without really offending them.'*

Dutch and Americans are renowned for favouring 'straight talking' and getting it 'all out on the table'. However, despite these generally accepted stereotypes, it is the authors' perception that on the whole, American bosses find it hard to deal with criticism. Persisting in order to get one's point heard is seen as 'being so full of anger that you had better see a psychiatrist'. The responses to conflict in many cultures often seem to be based on denial, covering things up to smooth things over, or knee-jerk reactions such as instantaneous dismissal. If mediation is called for, mediators in Norway and Germany are expected to be rational and

---

* An English slang word/idiom meaning to reprimand or discipline someone.

emotionally distant. In America, it helps to be 'warm and supportive', yet in China, mediators are expected to persuade, cajole, haggle and negotiate.

Some of the most detailed work on cross-cultural conflict resolution has been done within Siemens, the German based power and electrical company. In American/German teams, Americans tended to be much less direct than Germans in confronting conflict situations. Unlike the Germans, they took strong argument as a personal attack. Americans are much more ready to use emotional resolution rather than long factual debates and so go through the 'resolution cycle' much faster than Germans. Americans also preferred to focus on the future and the broad picture, while the Germans preferred to start with the detail of 'what is'. In any negotiations, the Germans were looking for a workable compromise of the facts, while the Americans were looking for a good deal and to drive a hard bargain[30].

When these kinds of detail begin to emerge between cultures that are both considered part of the industrialised 'Western' world, it is not hard to imagine how difficult it is for much more mixed teams to resolve conflicts to everyone's satisfaction. In fact in many cross-cultural conflicts, it is evident that people cannot *see* the problems other people are bringing forward, let alone understand how to resolve them. What international team leaders and members need to appreciate is that conflict between cultures is not just about differences in ideas, but often tests deeply held assumptions about other people.

> Suzannah is a brilliant Taiwanese born research analyst in an aggressive American power company. She is posted in London. Two (of many) examples illustrate how she used her indefatigable sense of detail and logic to guide her action and in doing so, unwittingly crossed unwritten rules that caused major problems.
>
> Her boss suggested that she buy the books that she needed to cover her particular area. Being thorough, she bought four suitcases full. That was not what he had had in mind. The hidden assumption that he meant about six or ten was not spelled out. Suzannah had 'taken advantage' of the system.
>
> Because of her status in the UK she did not have a cash card for the canteen. When she asked the personnel manager, she was told that the system could not handle it. Suzannah took the initiative and worked directly with the computer people to change the system. The personnel officer was surprised to see her with a cash card and asked her how she had obtained one when she had been told she could not have one. Suzannah explained how she had sorted out the personnel manager's problem and changed the system. The personnel manager was furious. In her eyes, Suzannah had gone behind her back and undermined her authority. She went on to create many problems for Suzannah who only thought she was improving the system and solving problems. Many months later, Suzannah was still struggling to understand what the real rules were supposed to be and how she would get to know about them without an endless string of misunderstandings.

Unlike Siemens, most companies do not spend a lot of effort on persuading their team members to delve deeper and to admit that they do not understand each other well. People like Suzannah are often left to struggle and become labelled, at best, as 'oddballs' and at worst as a 'smart ass' who wants to buck the system and show how clever she is. In practice, what often happens in international teams is that the less powerful members of the team capitulate to the resolution methods of the more powerful members. However, few people act on decisions which they still quietly disagree with or feel that the method by which they are arrived was biased and unfair.

Decision making

International team members are likely to have great differences, not only about the processes that lead to decisions, but also about who should be involved. The speed of decisions in any one culture will depend on:

- who is expected to be involved with making them;
- how time is seen to work;
- how much any one culture adheres to past traditions that change slowly;
- what kind of information someone believes they need before they can make a decision.

Take time for instance. For some people, time (and the language used to express it) is seen as a linear process that follows a linear pattern of cause and effect and that can be spilt up into meaningful segments. Specific tasks are sequentially laid into these segments. For others, it is more like an open space in which things can happen simultaneously and in which the play of social interactions takes place and will probably determine the next move. Often just waiting means that the missing link will come around and the issue will decide itself. 'Time will tell'.

Not all languages adhere to Greenwich meantime: Nine am UK time would be called three 'in the morning' Kiswahili time (based on the unchanging equatorial dawn and dusk) and mistakes are made switching back and forth between languages. Beyond counting time differently, the amount of importance people give to being driven to make decisions by the Western clock varies considerably from culture to culture. This fact may underlie some of the very different interpretations about what people mean when they say 'yes. I will get it to you soon'.

> *'The Italians say yes, even if they mean no — I never know if the project is really on track until a crisis blows up in my face.'*

When start-up time is not given to creating a decision-making process that consciously integrates these large differences, a few people usually end up very frustrated.

> In a top executive committee of an Italian American 'joint venture' even after two years, the Americans were sure that the plenary committee meetings were supposed to be where decisions were made. The Italian Chief Executive on the other hand was sure, as were the other Italians, that it was just a forum to have some last minute feedback on the decisions he was about to make and which he had already discussed one on one with the 'relevant' people. This led one American to comment that 'These meetings seem to be like play-acting. I always feel that the actual decisions are being made behind the scenes, somewhere back in Italy'.

'We just seem to go round in circles with no-one willing to make a decision. It's getting really frustrating.'

A common pattern in international teams is that team members will initially find that they have a wide range of perspectives on certain issues. Instead of looking at *how* to deal with these different inputs, the team often starts going around and around with everyone restating their own viewpoints in slightly modified terms. In desperation, the majority take sides with others whose views are most similar to themselves. Usually one or two people have stuck to their points and not joined the larger subgroup. A quick vote creates a 'decision' and rules them out. The ones who maintained their positions are left feeling alienated, fed up and as if nobody listened at all to what they thought was important.

This pattern will repeat again and again, until the team realises that having gathered all the different points of view, they need 'time out' to decide on a decision making process that will evaluate everyone's viewpoints and collectively reach some agreement. There are many models and techniques widely available[31].

Team leaders and members need to actively understand the differences and agree workable processes before getting involved in the content

These examples serve only to reinforce the point that each team needs to *consciously* work through each of these processes as and when they need them and tease out the different underlying expectations in the team. By using the cultural value checklist described briefly in Chapter Five, a team can raise these differences in its early stages and set some basic ground rules. In anticipating how to manage the group processes, international team leaders need to remember that:

- ***Team members will have different understandings of many group processes.***
- ***Conflict resolution and preferred decision making processes vary across cultures.***
- ***Team leaders and members need to actively understand the differences and agree workable processes before getting involved in the content.***

Three Organisational Factors

International teams exist within corporations that not only have specific roots in one or two cultures, but also have differing amounts and types of international experience. These organisational features will affect what happens in these teams. We strongly support the view that the benefits or problems that cultural differences give to a company is not just to do with the differences themselves. 'Contextual factors act either to fan the flames of inter-group conflict and cross-cultural polarisation or to encourage organisational members to accept these differences'[32]. The organisational responses to internationalisation described in Chapter Eight are key. A team leader should be aware of the total organisational response and imagine how it will affect his/her team. There are then three issues that he/she will need to look at very carefully.

6 The status of different cultures within the team and organisation

Team leaders and members have to be aware that structural, linguistic and perceived inequalities can be far more dysfunctional than cultural differences per se

This issue was raised in Chapter One and will be illustrated in full in the next chapter. In order to look deeper, it is useful to first distinguish between heterogeneity and inequality. Heterogeneity comes from different kinds of recognisable characteristics per se. Inequality comes from characteristics that affect how we see and respond to someone's social standing[33]. A team of ten with two groups of five from two different cultures is just as balanced, but not as heterogeneous as a group of ten people all from different nationalities. However, if those ten nationalities are intrinsically accorded different levels of importance (eg: we three are from the European headquarters and therefore we automatically understand more than that Moroccan lady who only comes from a small production unit) then inequalities (perceived or actual) will skew the interaction. Three categories are useful when looking at the effect of inequalities in international teams. There are those that arise from having more of one nationality present – structural inequality, those that arise from different levels of language fluency – linguistic inequalities and those that arise from perceptions of power and influence – perceived inequalities.

Suppose there are five people of one nationality and two of another, what happens to notions like equal participation? The most useful thinking on this comes from Rosabeth Moss Kanter who described teams as uniform, skewed, tilted and balanced[34]. A uniform team would have members who are all from one nationality; skewed teams have a token different one or two people, tilted teams have unequal subgroups and balanced teams have equal numbers of different people.

Skewed teams are the least 'balanced'. Token individuals tend to be treated as invisible, excluded or are assimilated into the overriding norms of the group. The extent of a minority's influence in a skewed team has been shown to depend on their negotiation style, the degree to which they differ from the majority and whether the 'zeitgeist' is favourable or unfavourable (eg the real rather than espoused attitude of the company towards diversity)[35].

International teams are by definition never uniform across cultures, but they are also rarely balanced. Skews and tilts invariably exacerbate national and linguistic differences. The impact of structural and linguistic inequalities on international teamwork are demonstrated in depth in the next chapter.

There are no simple solutions for dealing with preconceptions and inequalities in perceived power

A third type of inequality comes from preconceptions and stereotypes about the superiority and inferiority of one's own and others' nationalities. In the late seventies, groups in the International Labour Organisation in Turin were asked to rank countries according to their stereotypes, before working together[36]. 'Members judged as most qualified were always coming from countries which were judged the most developed and economically strong.' The same ranking test was applied at the end of the course 'when people had the opportunity to substitute real experience for personal stereotypes' and no statistical ranking was found. Despite this modification of stereotypes, other important observations created by the imbalance of power were made:

- The phenomenon of 'initiation' will be shorter for the 'foreign worker' as the characteristics of his/her nationality are automatically attributed.
- Aggressive behaviour of an authoritarian supervisor provoked other group members in response to 'discharge' on the 'lowest' national status members.
- Leadership, cliques and sub-grouping will follow the same rules based on national status if no corrective forces are present to modify the trend.
- Rationality plays a much smaller part than the emotions in a person's attitude toward foreigners.

Preconceptions and ignorance about other team member's expertise and usefulness will determine how much each person finally contributes and the general attitude that greets each person's response. These perceptions are usually a mixture of positive and negative and so need careful diagnosis. Each individual in the team is likely to be selective about which parts of someone else's contributions and behaviour they like and which parts irritate and annoy them.

Initial clarity of roles and responsibilities and exploration of different skills, knowledge and the meaning of power sharing can go a long way in levelling the playing field

Despite the alienating and negative effects of perceived or real superiority in international teams, it is seldom addressed in depth. It is usually deemed politically incorrect to raise it as an issue, and so as demonstrated in the next chapter, it is left to wreak its havoc while everyone tries to deny it exists. Balance this against oft-quoted prescriptions for international teams such as 'create equal power' and team leaders should appreciate the need first, to understand it and second to do something about it as suggested in Chapter Four.

In thinking about imbalances in the team, international team leaders need to remember that:

- **Team leaders and members have to be aware that structural, linguistic and perceived inequalities can be far more dysfunctional than cultural differences per se.**
- **There are no simple solutions for dealing with preconceptions and inequalities in perceived power.**
- **Initial clarity of roles and responsibilities and exploration of different skills, knowledge and the meaning of power sharing can go a long way in levelling the playing field.**

7 The geographic spread of the team members

Plot the team's geographical and temporal spread and the different levels of infrastructure and think through the consequences for the team's distant interaction

> 'The trouble is if a problem crops up after lunchtime, it has to wait until the next day as my project leader is in the UK and is at home by then – that does slow things down.'

International teams are often dispersed across time zones and geographical distances as well as across cultural ones. The useful concepts of skew, tilt and balance can apply again. In a tilted team, most of the team are in one place with a spread of scattered 'outliers'. In a skewed team, all but one of the team are in the same place. In a balanced team all the team would be equally spread out.

The challenge in tilted and skewed geographic teams is to keep the outliers feeling as involved as the rest of the team, especially at key points of the task. A small transatlantic team had one British team member. The team relied on phone, fax and courier services to exchange data. As deadlines approached, there was increasing reluctance to involve the UK outlier in anything but comments on almost complete drafts. There was not the time or technology to create ways of brainstorming and arguing through the underlying logic and messages that the team as a whole wanted to portray. This undid any sense of teamwork that may have been established.

Meanwhile in thinking about the geographic spread, international team leaders need to

- ***Plot the team's geographical and temporal spread and the different levels of infrastructure and think through the consequences for the team's distant interaction.***
- ***Follow the best practices laid out in Chapter Six.***

8 The similarity or difference between functional, corporate and other 'cultures' (Ethnic and gender)

A recent survey of 15,000 British CEO's[37] showed 52 per cent to be registered chartered accountants, unlike France, where engineers would be more likely to predominate. Different functions will be held in different levels of regard.

> *'they think that because they are medics that they rule the roost, well they don't know about statistics.'*

In Fiat, the Italian motor company, the staff managers involved in strategic planning, procurement, sales and marketing, and human resources tend to have more power than the operational managers running the factories. Not so in many UK companies, where human resources is often regarded as the function that comes along after the real work has been decided on.

Some authors assert that 'similar educational experiences can erase ideological differences' such that 'those within the same profession tend to espouse similar values regardless of nationality'[38]. Aside from having different standings in a company, different functions can be shown to have different priorities and value sets, similar to individual cultural differences. 'Cultural' dimensions have emerged to measure and describe differences in organisational and functional cultures[39]. A quick study in one Finnish company showed that finance was 'tight' while research was 'loose'. Production was more parochial than sales who emerged as more 'professionally' oriented. The new corporate identity espoused a process/people orientation where most functions still emerged as results and job oriented.

Similarity in other areas can lessen the affect of national differences, just as differences can add to the complexity

One team that was persuaded to focus less on their national differences and more on the fact that they were all statisticians together, stopped arguing and began to set a clear path towards working together. Yet, if an international team is also cross functional, the possible complexity and potential misunderstanding greatly increases.

> *'Sometimes they use jargon that I don't understand – I think it is just to show off and to make me feel stupid.'*

Functional languages based on technical terms, idioms, abbreviations and jargon can be as diverse and as unintelligible to an outsider as national languages. Mice, bugs and viruses in computers, love, charm and quarks in physics are words that bear little relationship to their original contexts. 'ROIs', 'APRs', 'ROEs', 'PL sheets', are abbreviations that roll off accountant's tongues as if everyone automatically knows what they stand for. These differences reinforce the fact that cross-national, cross-functional teams will have an added dimension of differences, especially with different functions also being at different stages of internationalisation as described in Chapter One.

Team leaders and members need to explore all sources of similarity and diversity in the team and understand which ones will be most influential in that particular organisational context

> *'It is great having all the different functions on the team – you realise how much talent there is there.'*
> *'Even though we are all supposed to have an equal role on the team, some of the team members have a "we're better than you" attitude – you see it in the way they miss you off e-mail distribution lists – as if I did not need to know what they are talking about.'*

The relative amount of influence that different nationalities or functions will have on the team dynamics is dependent on the context of the team and what the team members are expected to bring to the teamwork. In thinking about the impact of functional differences or similarities within the team, an international team leader needs to remember that:

- *There are useful ways of categorising differences in organisational and functional cultures.*
- *The results should be used with the same caution as national norms.*
- *Similarity in other areas can lessen the affect of national differences, just as differences can add to the complexity.*
- *Team leaders and members need to explore all sources of similarity and diversity in the team and understand which ones will be most influential in that organisational context.*

Summary of Key Learning Points

The team leader needs to understand these eight sources of similarity and difference in depth in order to anticipate and act on areas of difficulty. They can also use the findings as a checklist against which to try and understand the underlying basis for difficulties within his or her team. To sum up, the eight factors are:

Cultural factors

1. *The degrees of difference or similarity that exist between the cultural norms of the individuals in the team.*
2. *The degree to which individuals might manifest their cultural norms.*
3. *Differences in language fluency, communication patterns, non verbals and who says what when.*
4. *Culturally different leadership styles.*
5. *The different expectations about key team processes.*

Organisational factors

6. *The status of different cultures within the organisation.*
7. *The geographic spread of the team members.*
8. *The similarity or difference between functional, professional and other 'cultures'.*

The important issue is to be prepared, to have the ability to analyse a situation if it does arise, and to know that something quite different may actually take place. It is a bit like scenario planning. You have to mentally imagine all the possible scenarios of what could hijack the team's effectiveness and ensure that, from the start, you establish key patterns of interaction and ground rules that will prevent dysfunctional behaviour. If team leaders and members are not already persuaded to do this by some tough experiences, then the next chapter describes some of the impact of these factors on real international teams.

Chapter Three

The Impact of Inequalities

'The companies which succeed in being global will be those which best understand how to manage diversity.'[1]

The previous chapter explored eight factors that affect international teams. The objective of this chapter is to illustrate the powerful role that national representation, language, stereotypes and perceived and real status differences have in determining who leads and talks the most in international teams. These three types of inequality can exacerbate or diminish the importance of cultural differences and create dysfunctional power plays within a team. This chapter tells real stories and details the research findings from twenty-seven international teams videoed in Western Europe and East and South East Asia.[2]

Cultural differences rarely play out on an equal playing field and this applies to differences in organisational, functional and ethnic cultures as much as to differences in nationality. Differences in power, wealth, economic and educational levels, for instance, often underscore cultural differences.

Minority/majority dynamics often dominate intercultural exchange to a far greater degree than cultural differences in world views, communication and behavioural styles per se.

Differences such as age, job status, gender, length of tenure, motivation, reward, knowledge and skills create inequalities in all teams, including international teams. They need to be managed well to prevent them from being dysfunctional. If you take job status, when Seagram set up its re-engineering teams, one motto was 'leave your stripes at the door'. It was clearly harder for the mostly Japanese team.

'In Japan, the problem is that grading is seen to be a major barrier, therefore in order to overcome this behaviour, I had to tell the junior members to be more aggressive and mostly everyday to enforce that the team is independent, that there are no grades, that everybody is responsible for the results of the team.'

In the operational teams (as opposed to ad hoc training teams) in the in-depth video research, the amount one person spoke was clearly influenced by managerial level.

'What really bugs me is people thinking that they can use the fact that they have letters after their name to pull rank.'

'It was difficult in the beginning to engage the more junior members in the discussion as the more senior members were overpowering them.'

In one meeting to develop strategy, the managers talked the most about overall strategy, while the personal assistants spoke less and when they did, they focused on their operational difficulties and the communication between each other. They kept being reminded by the managers that this was not the purpose of the meeting.

Similarities or different personalities may also sometimes override cultural differences in international teams. In one ad hoc training team, the only apparent explanation for a Turkish man being shunned seemed to be that the rest of the team did not like him, even though, according to him, he had the most experience on the task. His measured personality type* was different from the three dominant team members. Otherwise over the whole video research, there was no significant relationship between personality type** and the amount any one contributed.

So while the same issues of job status, tenure, age, gender, personality will affect international teams as much as national teams (although probably each one in different degrees in different nationalities), there are the three kinds of inequality that specifically affect international teams more than national teams; inequality arising from the composition of the team, inequality arising from different levels of fluency with the working language and inequality arising from perceived differences in power and status. However great cultural differences are, the interaction that is set up by unequally distributed power based on the three factors often overshadows them.

Structural Inequality and Size

As mentioned in Chapter Two, except in the UN, World Bank and a few regional functional teams, very few teams are completely heterogeneous, eg one representative from a wide range of nationalities. Some may be balanced (five French, five Japanese) but not very heterogeneous. A recent piece of research shows that over time, teams of four that are totally heterogeneous, do just as well on a variety of performance indicators as homogeneous teams. Both these types of team do better than balanced but less heterogeneous teams. (eg two US, two UK)[3]. Although the research did not explore it, we suspect that skewed teams (eg three US, one UK) are likely to do even worse again.

It is proposed that the determining factor is the extent to which the team members can create an 'us' and 'them' situation. If everyone is different, it is

---

* As measured by Myers Briggs Type Indicator.
** Again as measured by the four Myers Briggs dimensions.

hard for such in-group identities to form and it is more likely that the team will form its own 'culture' and work well together, just like a nationally homogeneous team. If you have a balanced team of two each, then you are more likely to have two sub-teams with two distinct 'subcultures' that may have difficulty integrating. In a 'skewed' team, the majority of three is likely to dominate the one sole member who will be expected to 'fit in'.

The problem with the above research is that, like much experimental team research, it takes place on courses in business schools where real organisational influences are missing. In an American organisation, as opposed to international business school, if a team consisted of an American, French, Venezuelan and Nigerian, the chances are that the American will be the leader, be perceived to have more power and will, consciously or unconsciously, be expected to 'set the norms'.

In the video research, even when there were three Malaysians and two Dutch, as the company was Anglo-Dutch, the Dutch members assumed control.

So while the numbers of different nationalities in an international team can lead to one nationality numerically dominating the others, the power within the organisation may mean that a minority will in fact dominate. Similarly having more people from the same nationality as the leadership of the company (called here the dominant culture) meant that people from that nationality talked more and were perceived to be significantly more involved and to have had more influence than other people in the team. This organisational dominance often hijacks many international teams striving for 'equal participation', before they even get started.

The message is that the interaction and play of power in skewed teams, especially those that favour people from the same nationality as the leadership of the company, needs to be proactively managed.

Small is beautiful

Much experimental research uses teams of four. Our field research range covered teams of four to thirteen.

The results suggest that small is beautiful if you want to get your point across in an international team.

The most balanced and satisfied teams were of four and five people respectively, noticeably with one or no mother tongue speakers to dominate the airspace. The most balanced team of four was composed of two Malaysians

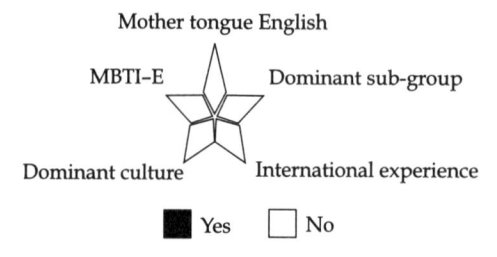

Figure 3.1: Key to the meaning of the stars

and two Dutch (one born in Nigeria). The 'satisfied' team of five was composed of one Australian, one Omani, one Norwegian and Two Malaysians. In both teams, it was discovered that a Malaysian had the most experience relevant to the task.

In the smallest team, only 5 per cent of all the contributions were started when someone else was still talking, in other words, the rate of interruption was low. In some of the larger teams, especially those with more British members than any other nationality, interruption rates reached 39 per cent of all contributions made. In this research, especially in a Western context, the bigger the teams became, the more some people spoke much more than others as Figures 3.2 and 3.3 show.

These Figures represent ad hoc training teams with no pre-appointed leaders and with people of more or less similar level within the organisation. On the left-hand vertical axis is the percentage of total contribution made by each person (a star represents a person). The different arms of the stars show (clockwise):

- if a person is a mother tongue speaker;
- if they belong to a numerically larger subgroup;
- if they have had previous international experience or not;
- if they belong to the same nationality as the leadership of the organisation;
- if they are an extrovert as measured by the Myers Briggs personality test (missing in the middle team).

If an arm is shaded, it means yes, if blank it means no. All five factors were expected to contribute to someone participating more in an international team. Overall, being an extrovert and belonging to a numerically larger subgroup had no significant effect. The other findings are discussed throughout this chapter.

Coming back to size, the closer what we called the 'participation balance' score is to zero, the more everyone contributed the same amount. In the team of four, as second language speakers, they all contributed almost equally. In a team of seven, with four mother tongue speakers, the range is from 22 per cent to 7 per cent. In the team of nine, with seven mother tongue speakers, the range was from 20 per cent to 1 per cent.

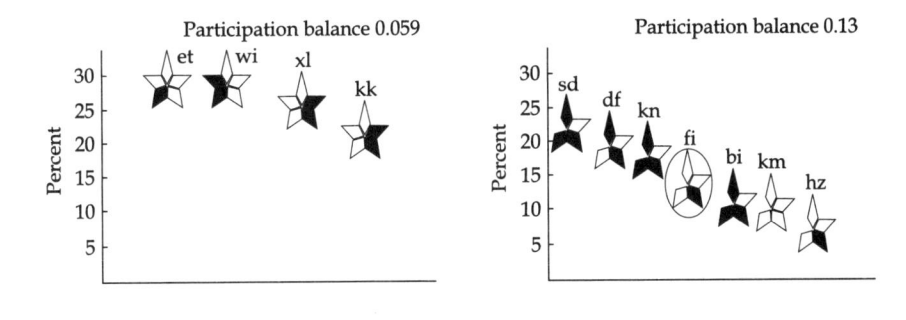

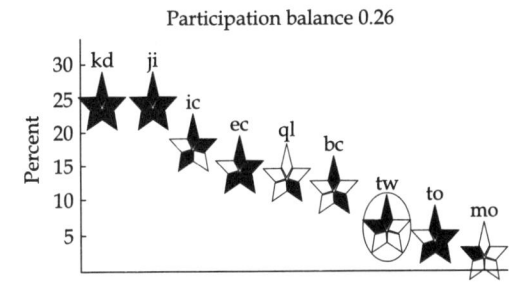

Figure 3.2: Examples of participation patterns in international teams

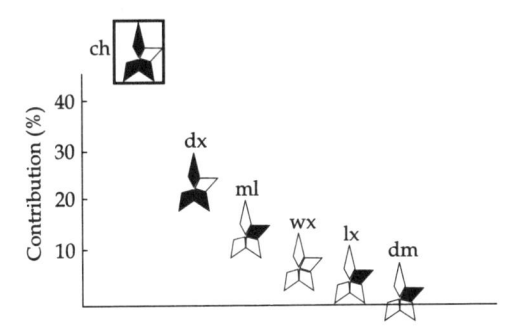

Figure 3.3: Participation patterns in a Hong Kong team

A circle shows the person who was appointed as the team leader after the team started, called the 'emergent' leader as opposed to a 'pre-appointed' leader. It was only in teams of seven and above that an emergent leader was appointed, mostly to manage the process, not the content of the task. Below seven, nobody seemed to feel the need. To sum up, in these Western based teams, the smaller the team, the more they spoke the same amount and the more satisfied they were. However in Hong Kong, less balanced participation did not affect the level of satisfaction.

Figure 3.3 shows an operational team in Hong Kong. The pre-appointed leader has a square. She made 52 per cent of all contributions while a Hong Kong Chinese team member made 1 per cent. The interruption rate was very low, around 1.5 per cent of total contributions. Despite the great difference in the amount people spoke, all the teams in Hong Kong were just as satisfied as Western based teams of similar size. All the conversation was directed by and through the pre-appointed leader (in this case an American) so it seems the formality of this process was accepted. In fact, many Chinese will say 'why waste your breath shouting out'? As mentioned in the last chapter, culturally appropriate leadership is important.

Summing up on ideal size, it seems it is much easier to involve everyone in small teams of four or five than in larger teams, especially when there are more mother tongue speakers. If the team is large, breaking up into smaller groups for key discussion will probably increase the participation of second language speakers. It was noticeable that one or two Malaysians spoke significantly more in the whole teams after they had fed back the discussions of their subgroups. It seemed that being able to share their expertise in a smaller group gave them the confidence to speak up in the larger group.

In order to manage structural inequalities, team leaders need to:

- *Wherever possible create highly heterogeneous teams and avoid very skewed teams.*
- *Wherever possible create small teams of four or five, especially if they are supposed to be self managed teams. If the team is large and the task involves using everyone's expertise to the full rather than gathering bits of information, split into subgroups (that lessen the inequality) at strategic brainstorming points.*
- *Proactively manage the patterns of linguistic and perceived dominance (described below) that are likely to exacerbate the numerical inequalities.*

Unequal Language Ability and Interruption and Patterns of Logic

Choosing the working language

> One international consortium of top HR managers and business teachers started to talk about Japanese appraisal systems. An American academic professor jumped up to explain all about them. After much sign language from the back row, the chairman finally asked the one Japanese company representative to speak. His English was very hard to understand, but he did slowly put forward a few very different points of view. When time is short and expensive, do you let an American talk at speed for everyone (and still call yourself an international consortium?) or do you listen patiently, arrange for someone to translate and access different points of view?

A huge amount of research and skill has gone into the art of simultaneous translation, in being able to translate the intended meaning as well as the words. It is very impressive, necessary and/or often insisted upon in inter-governmental meetings and diplomacy. It usually leads to people making speeches at one another so that all the heated arguments and draft decisions are hammered out in small working groups behind the scenes. Formal translation is too impractical for most operational teams in large companies; especially where humour can play a large part in building comfort zones. With simultaneous translation, one half always gets the jokes when the other half has already laughed and moved on. So the first task of an international team is to decide on the working language.

For most Western based companies and increasingly others as well, this is predominantly English. As one American international team member put it. *'Basically my French sucks'*. In joint ventures, we have seen a CEO declaring in Italian that English is the working language (even though he was unable to speak English). In another, an Italian director (speaking with his eyes closed) quashed a young English manager's desire to learn Italian (because it was not the declared working language of the joint venture). The choice of language can have a very large impact on the outcome of negotiations and decisions. One international group found that their German boss seemed to become much more generous and forgiving when they talked with her in English than in Hochdeutsch.

Declaring, like a small Finnish based marine engineering company, MacGregor-Navire, that everyone must be able to speak in English, is probably only possible in smaller companies and perhaps also those based in countries like Finland and Holland where many people are schooled to be multilingual. Otherwise the reality in many companies is pockets of different languages, the need to translate much company wide information and varying degrees of frustration. When computer interfaces are in local languages, itinerant international managers find that they cannot log on if they have not taken their own PC with them. Thankfully for many, not only have there been some significant recent breakthroughs in Japan with computerised translation technology, but also personal communicators are now becoming the size of mobile phones.

One irony is that although similar languages are easier to learn, they can often cause the most problem as words are translated literally that actually mean something else. For instance 'actualité' in French means 'currently', not 'actually', société is a company as well as a society, fusion is a merger as well as a scientific process, and concretisation is an actual French word that many think must be the same in English. One author recently picked up a prize-winning American book on teams and was lost when it came to 'Japan coming at America', 'they cleaned our clock' and 'team blowhards'. Because they are unexpected, many awkward and funny misunderstandings take place between American and British team members.

Once the working language is decided, offering language training that teaches not only the words, but also the concepts, values, beliefs and norms in which the language is embedded is important. In GEC Alsthom[4] a 50/50 French/English merger, the initial training needs analysis underestimated the ability to listen in each other's language as well as to talk and write. It is often easier to understand than to speak. Sometimes it can work best to run a workshop where for instance, the participants talk in Italian and the facilitators reply in English. Whatever language is chosen, mother tongue speakers have a huge advantage and their communication norms will probably dominate.

> *'English language speakers did sometimes use the fact to their advantage to "wire" a debate.'*

The 'interrupting' English Speakers

Some of the results of video research were gathered by counting how much each individual spoke.

Predictably this showed that mother tongue English speakers spoke more than second language speakers.

Presumably they can think and speak faster in their first language. Moreover, English and Americans often started to talk when someone else was still talking. This can make it hard for others to say what they want, when they want to. One team of peers were all mother tongue English speakers of sorts (British, American, Canadian and Australian). The only perceivable cultural difference was that when Americans started talking at the same time as someone else, they invariably went on to finish their sentences even if no one else was listening. The British team members on the other hand would give up mid sentence.

In one British company, four teams were working to create new aspects of strategy. Each team had more British managers than any other one nationality. They invariably talked more than the other participants did. The overall rates of interruption* were the highest of all teams hovering around 40 per cent of all the contributions made. However, it was not just the British team members who interrupted, the results surprisingly showed that this pattern of high interruption drove *everyone* to interrupt, mother tongue and second language speakers alike. Sure enough, team members in these teams felt that everyone had expressed their views much less than in linguistically more heterogeneous teams, even though this did not significantly affect the levels of satisfaction.

*Technically for interruption read 'starting to talk when someone else is talking'. It depends on how it is perceived by the person already talking as to whether it is an interruption or not.

In these four teams, Indian, Pakistani, and Malawian team members spoke and interrupted as much as the British. This was significantly more than the 'continental' Europeans (Dutch, German, French,) who also rated themselves as fluent in English. Indian, Pakistani and Malawian team members are more likely to work in English as a business language in their own countries, may well have been schooled in English, and so be able to interrupt at speed. In one of these teams, a fluent Dutchman gave up as the pace got too much. Immediately after the team broke up, he cornered the most senior person and animatedly poured out all his frustrated thinking on the topic.

The research also showed that second language speakers with previous international experience spoke more than those without.

As one Hong Kong Chinese man working in a British owned bank in Hong Kong put it:

'When I went to Australia, I had to learn to interrupt or else I would never have spoken at all.'

Previous international experience had no effect on the amount mother tongue English speakers spoke. Presumably they were in any case dominating the airspace as much as they wanted to.

The video research also showed that the rate of interruption increased as the team was about to take a decision and would fall off dramatically once the decision was made and team members were carefully thinking through the implications.

This means that unless the interaction leading up to decisions is consciously structured to include everyone, second language speakers are more likely to be excluded at these key moments.

Americans in the top team of an Italian/American acquisition complained that the larger group of Italian managers would even revert to Italian when decisions were about to be made. The Italians would then politely translate after the issue had been resolved. Needless to say, the Americans felt disenfranchised and like extras 'at a theatre play'.

> A team in a highly profitable telecommunications company comprised of two Finns, Carola and Pekka, a Korean, Mr Lee, a French-Swiss, a Swiss, an Englishman living in Spain and Peter, a 'Geordie' from the borders of Scotland and England. When asked to review their experiences using a team review questionnaire*, everybody wrote that they had enjoyed the four-month project except the two Finns. This shocked some of the other members as the Finns had said nothing.
>
> When asked what was wrong, the Finns replied that the others (aside from Mr Lee, the Korean) had kept interrupting them. This, despite being warned when their team was formed some months before of the dangers of allowing a lot of interruption. Pekka observed that he had protested at one meeting by staying silent the entire meeting, but nobody had noticed. When asked why they had not said anything, they suggested that it was not normal in Finnish culture to verbally complain and hence show others up.
>
> A small study recording how much each person was talking in the team revealed that Mr Lee, the Korean, was saying much less than anyone else, including the two Finns. He was a very experienced senior director, who spoke English carefully and slowly. When he did speak, he made insightful comments, so the team soon learnt to stop and listen to what he had to say. Even though he spoke the least number of times, he was satisfied with his participation because he was listened to and his ideas were taken up. The two Finns however, on average, spoke more, but were constantly interrupted. On the whole, Finnish people prefer an orderly pattern of interaction where you give time to think after each speaker. The pattern of constant interruption set up by the two British people and followed by the other Europeans excluded them.

As facilitators, we learnt three important lessons:

- ***People will sometimes write what they will not say.***
- ***Team reviews need to be done during the teamwork, not just at the end.***
- ***However much you warn a team of the pitfalls of interruption and different communication styles, they do not really get the message until it happens to them.***

There was a short sequel.

*Developed for the session and administered by Claudia Heimer, Ashridge Consulting Group.

> Some months after the team broke up, Peter, the Geordie was surprised when Pekka rang him in his hotel and asked him to go drinking with him. He had presumed that Pekka had taken a personal dislike to him, but in fact no grudge was held and they became good friends.

As mentioned in Chapter Two, Japanese workers also talk a lot at the same time in Japanese, but for different reasons. It is hardly surprising that many Japanese people will wait for a clear pause or even to be asked to speak in international teams working in English. However, when reflecting on the videoed teamwork, it was predominantly the British who criticised their teams most heavily for not encouraging everyone to express their views. Although their own behaviour caused the problem, they did nothing about it at the time. The inability to prevent such dysfunctional momentum is why most international teams need someone to manage the interaction until team members learn how to do it themselves.

Coping with different patterns of logic

Even when the fact that they had talked more and may belong to the dominant organisational culture was taken into account, mother tongue speakers were still perceived to have had more influence on the teamwork and to have been more involved than second language speakers. One strong impression from the video research was that second language speakers tended to be reduced to offering *examples* from their experience and 'bright ideas', rather than driving the underlying *logic* or framework of the discussion. By driving the underlying logic, we mean the person who takes the lead in clarifying with the team what they need to do. It is usually the person who makes the statement, 'Well then, this is what we need to do next' and who intermittently summarises where the team has reached to and again, what they should be doing next. In only one team was this person a second language speaker. She spoke English completely fluently as well as other languages, and had wide and long international experience.

One Japanese writer, Magorah Maruyama[5] has talked about four categories of different types of logic or 'mindscapes'. He then describes how each 'type' will approach management, decision making differently and have different values and attitudes towards cause and effect. As mentioned in Chapter Two, scholars have suggested that the realistic pictorial base of Chinese and Japanese languages makes abstract thinking much harder than for those brought up in more conceptually based languages. While it is not hard to imagine that culturally predominant patterns of logic and thinking will make life hard for some people in an international team, given everything else also going on, it is not easy to demonstrate. Out of all the research, one instance sticks out that invites that kind of interpretation.

> After six hours of teamwork on creating a base case for drilling an offshore oil well, Amin, a Malaysian proposed that the team think about the more expensive newer technology of horizontal drilling. He was met with a sharp retort 'We work on that kind of thing way down the line. Do you understand what we are doing here and how we have to go about this problem.' Eighteen hours later, the course leader came in and asked if they had considered horizontal drilling which by then, everyone had forgotten about. They then worked out that in fact it would make much better use of the excess gas, rendering the proposed gas line unnecessary and greatly increase the productivity of the site. They reworked the figures and technology.

Without more data, it is hard to say whether Amin made an out of place suggestion. Perhaps because he was Malaysian, they did not consider his suggestion important. On the other hand it is possible that because he was not stuck in a pattern of logic that said you have to do 'x' before you can think about 'y', he was able to include an option far earlier in his thinking. It certainly seemed that it would have saved the whole team much time and effort if they had kept his suggestion as a running possibility instead of dismissing it so sharply.

Each language and cultural mindset will determine and to some extent probably mirror, the way problems are usually solved in that culture. You build up a picture around an initial input from a senior member in Japanese. You argue different theoretical positions until you find the 'truth' in German or English.

Many people may be fluent in the *words* of another language, but it is a different level of fluency to also be able to restructure *the way we understand and think* a problem through.

Other languages often do not lend themselves to explaining the different ways of seeing things. The whole feeling and concept behind words like 'Hutzpah' in Yiddish, 'Muzza' in Urdu, 'zeitgeist' in German just don't translate well into English. If finding words to express the whole texture and implications of the pictures in our heads is hard in our own language, then for second language speakers, whole pieces may well be missing. Even though a fluent second language speaker may talk as much as a first language speaker in a team, it may be that often the type of contribution is different, even constrained to filling in with examples and bright ideas. This is an area that needs much more in-depth research. Meanwhile, international teams can probably benefit much from developing creative ways of seeing things differently. Drawing is a good place to start.

The type of task also seems to make a difference. If a second language speaker was identified as having more knowledge on a task that involved calculation, and the pace was slow enough, they were usually rated as having the most influence, even though they had not talked the most. This was never the case in teams working on tasks that needed value judgements and different ways of looking at the problem to come to a new perspective. Yet these are the very tasks where diversity should be the most helpful. In these less structured tasks, dominant groups seem to like to maintain a pattern and type of interaction that stayed within their realms of comfort.

> *'Certainly at the beginning we learned to ask them directly for their input so they could add value at their language pace.'*
> *'The French team member was hard to get out of his shell because of his shyness with the language and adversity to politics. We stuck at it and out came the issue.'*
> *'All team members spoke excellent English so this was not really a problem. The Chinese had a tendency to huddle in a corner and speak Cantonese, which was kind of annoying, but if it was a work conversation, eventually one of them would translate.'*

To summarise, as GEC Alsthom managers discovered, 'lack of linguistic ability is not an indicator of intelligence'. Many mother tongue speakers, especially those unable to speak other languages, tend to forget this unless they themselves have been in the minority situation. In order to avoid the bias brought about by linguistic dominance, predominant communication patterns and maybe patterns of logic, international teams need to:

- ***Slow down.***
- ***Be careful about interruption patterns.***
- ***Remove idiomatic phrases.***
- ***Be aware of multiple or ambiguous meanings.***
- ***Breaking complex ideas down into a series of simple ones.***
- ***Check and recheck understanding, often by asking the same question a number of different ways.***
- ***Seriously consider what seem like off the wall untimely suggestions.***
- ***Ensure that the pattern of interaction and decision making is including everyone.***
- ***Give time out to talk in mother tongues so that people can explore and define what they want to say and paraphrase it back into the working language.***
- ***Use pictures, diagrams or stories to come at something from different angles.***

Preconceptions, Prejudices and Stereotypes

> One team in an Anglo/Dutch multinational* consisted of three British males, Tom, Paul and Gordon, one male Turk, Hakim, one male Omani, Soyul, one female Malaysian, Ashraf and one male Nigerian, Mwenesi. The task was to evaluate the amount of raw mineral available in a certain geographic area. Three minutes after sitting down, Tom, one of the British males asks in a non-specific way 'Are we going to elect a chair? Soyul replies ' Yes you' and so Tom assumes the leadership role without consulting anyone else. He then interpreted his role as explaining to everyone else what they had to do.
>
> After half an hour, Ashraf, the Malaysian woman asks 'Shall we split into subgroups?' Tom replies ' well it would be pretty stupid to sit and watch one person draw straight lines on a graph all afternoon'. Then turning to Paul he asks 'So what shall we do?' Paul suggests that they split into subgroups, each pair taking different parts of a large chart. This they do. Tom makes sure that Soyul and himself take the top half of the chart and Paul the bottom half and he suggests that Hakim and Mwenesi take the middle. Gordon quickly joins Paul working on the bottom half, leaving Ashraf looking over Hakim's shoulder as he worked with Mwenesi. The almost self-elected British leader had made sure that a British person was working on each important end of the chart. Later on, Ashraf asked if they could write up on the flipchart what it is that they want to achieve and how they are going to do it. Tom impatiently retorted that it was easy and counted on his fingers the three things he thought they should achieve. At the same time he starts qualifying what he is saying and so Ashraf starts writing it down for herself, repeating it for clarification as she writes and questioning the assumptions that Tom is making. The course leader later questioned the same assumptions and the team had to rework some of the calculations.

In some other teams, when a British person did not like what was going on or felt excluded, they tended to withdraw. However Ashraf, who all along had been asking pertinent and intelligent questions, stayed with the team despite the derogatory behaviour she received. She progressively changed her tone. She soon opted for beginning her sentences with expressions such as 'what do you think if' and 'is it a useful suggestion if we'. As a result, she maintained her influence in the team. To the British observer, she handled conflict in a subtle and masterful way, even though she vented her frustration in private at the end

---

*It should be stated that both the most balanced, satisfied and least satisfied teams were all found in this company; one of six in the research.

of the session. It was not the amount of participation that led to dissatisfaction, but the way in which her participation was viewed and received.

At no time did any of the team members say, 'because you are a Muslim Malaysian woman wearing a head scarf, I do not value your input as much as my British male colleague here'. However, certainly the impression given to the observer was that these three 'differences' (Muslim Malaysian woman different from Christian, Anglo-Dutch male) were not being treated neutrally. They appeared to consign her to being perceived as less competent, and hence some of her input being treated facetiously.

It would be dangerous to assume that one woman's experience is demonstrating a company-wide prejudice about different nationalities, women or religious beliefs. However, other indications of something amiss came in comments from other teams in the same company such as about Amin, 'He is not bad for a Malaysian, he actually talks'. In other teams there were comments like, 'If we have anything left over, we'll send it to Nigeria' which was followed by laughter from the English and Dutch team members. Having been at odds with the only Nigerian in the team, a Norwegian commented afterwards 'the Nigerian way of repeating every point made by either themselves or others hampered the team effectiveness. This also tends to focus the time and attention on irrelevant details instead of getting the job done'. One Kenyan Asian found that he was spoken to slowly and loudly even after Europeans had heard (but perhaps not listened to) his elegant bi-lingual mother tongue English. In a team with two Dutch and three Malaysians, a Dutch man walked in saying 'I know all the answers and it is very simple'. He then adopted the role of 'teacher on call' to the rest of the team.

Some people might argue that 'lower status' individuals participate less because they are unconsciously fulfilling their own lower expectations. Their lower participation is not because a prevailing norm is being imposed but because of their own low self esteem and so on. There was no evidence from the in-depth questionnaires prior to and after the video research that individuals from non-dominant cultures or second language speakers, expected to participate less than the other members. Ashraf and one other did mark their expectation of being listened to slightly lower than the team average. However, there was no sign that this decreased their attempts at active participation. Perhaps Ashraf was being pragmatic based on her previous experiences.

If allowing prejudices to work implicitly can cause problems, so can their explicit misuse. In four teams where the 'dominant' culture was British, there was a need to establish who was going to do the final presentation. The British members suggested folding small pieces of paper, drawing a cross on one and having team members pick one at random. Malay, Nigerian and Latin American members expressed strong discomfort and concern with this method of selection. In each case, the criticism was dismissed with a joke about this being the 'British way of doing things' and the process was pushed through without discussing any alternatives. When the cross fell to one Nigerian, he simply refused to present. His argument was that the most experienced person would give the best presentation for the team. In the minds of the British, joking about national differences made it okay to push through one particular way of doing things and to override any objections.

Throughout sixty-four hours of teamwork in nine teams in this one company; Europeans made stereotypical comments about Malaysians and Nigerians. Europeans made no stereotypical comments about other Europeans or Middle Eastern members. No Middle Eastern, African or South East Asian members made any stereotypical comments about anyone else.

The way these team members used stereotypes seemed to follow the common ranking of the developed world (eg; Europe) at the top, 'newly industrialised' (eg Middle East and South East Asia) in the middle and the 'developing world' (eg Africa) at the bottom.

Whether they reflect a company wide norm or not, these findings should be setting off warning bells in many Western based established multinationals.

The video research showed that overall, members of these 'dominant' organisational culture(s) within the organisation were perceived to have had more influence on the team than other nationalities, *regardless of the amount they talked.*

For instance, in teams where *all* the team members were second language speakers, the role of keeping a running commentary on what the team had done so far and what they should do next, usually fell to someone from the 'dominant' organisational culture who was perceived to be more influential.

If a sense that one nationality is dominant, regardless of talent, pervades an organisation, then individuals from other cultures will probably recognise that their careers are best served by playing *down* their own national identities and fitting in as much as possible. Individuals from the dominant culture will likewise gain more from reinforcing their own culture rather than trying to empathise or incorporate other cultures. The organisation will not be operating as internationally as a passport count may at first suggest. Only strong messages and actions from the top can change this.

Cross-cultural training usually addresses differences in communication styles and behavioural norms in a light-hearted way to get people to appreciate and work with such differences. However, all our work implies that patterns of dominance and stereotyping can have a much more profound dysfunctional effect on international teams than culturally different behaviours and communication styles. In our experience, differences are seldom perceived as equal.

However, if managers start to talk about inequalities, as opposed to 'neutral' differences, many people become very nervous.

> A CEO described his company as 'international, with the soul of the mother country'. Even so, a senior manager had identified the effect of a dominant culture as a key barrier to the very successful company being truly (and in his mind, equitably) international. He suggested along with others that non-dominant managers were not sure of their prospects and felt undermined when the decision making power kept returning to the mother country. There was talk of a national Mafia.
>
> The opportunity arose to put this down on slides and include it in a presentation to the CEO and Board about key challenges to the company. One non-dominant national bravely wrote the slides and did a practice run with a senior management programme. After he had finished, there was a stony silence. Prompts from the facilitator for comments did nothing. In the end, the facilitator begged for a translation of the silence. One person spoke up suggesting the word Mafia might be removed. Most agreed and after much more silence there was a grudging show of hands that the non national should go ahead having made this modification. The minute the meeting broke up he was mobbed at the door and told that his job could be on the line if he did go ahead. Why, he was wondering, was he bothering to stick his neck out. For a 'non-national' to criticise the dominant culture was perceived, rightly or wrongly, as a threat to his job.

Some companies may be actively working to root out these kinds of prejudices because they are offensive to some sense of meritocracy, mutual respect and undermine international survival. Most others will have presumably recognised that despite the hiccups in South East Asia, the global economy is changing. Only ten years ago, India, China and Vietnam were written off as uninteresting developing countries, now investors are eager to gain entry.

Ashraf's case testifies that unless dominance manifests in recognisable extremes of racist or stereotypical statements, it is very hard to prove or to get people to take it seriously. Senior management as well as team leaders and members need to be proactive in role-modelling the open international attitudes that they wish to see prevail throughout the company and in tackling prejudices head on. Techniques to challenge these stereotypical perceptions and feedback dysfunctional behaviour in a non-judgmental way are explored in the next two chapters.

In order to manage perceived inequalities and prejudices team leaders and members need to:

- ***Be aware of the status quo within the organisation and know their team.***
- ***Role model behaviour that sends a clear message that the organisational status quo will not operate within the team and everyone will be fully involved.***
- ***Demonstrate that differences will be valued.***
- ***Tackle prejudices openly with appropriate exercises and best practices.***

Managing the Process and Interaction in International Teams

Having looked at three important sources of inequality in international teams, the last part of this chapter shares what the video research highlighted about managing the process and what the satisfied teams did right.

Creating reasonably balanced participation

As mentioned in Chapter Two, many authors regard 'equal participation' as an essential ingredient of effective international teamwork. However, the message should now be clear that it is not so much the *amount* that each person participates as when they are able to participate and how their contributions are received. What the research and our experience suggest is that there is a range of useful 'equality' in the amount of contributions. If the individual contributions are very unequal, unless the cultural norms of the situation say that that is okay or expected, then team members tend to be dissatisfied. On the other hand, unless the team is very small, completely equal participation will probably have been achieved by some very mechanical rules being applied to the interaction. This will also frustrate many people. The best range for Western based teams seems to be somewhere in the middle as shown below. If you imagine joining up the stars in the previous Figures, you get a curve. The lines in Figure 3.4 represent the curves of teams with different levels of equal or unequal contribution.

By looking at the amount that each person contributes in a team, you cannot say which person is happy with what they contributed and which person is not. However, counting even for half an hour can be a very powerful feedback tool for some teams.

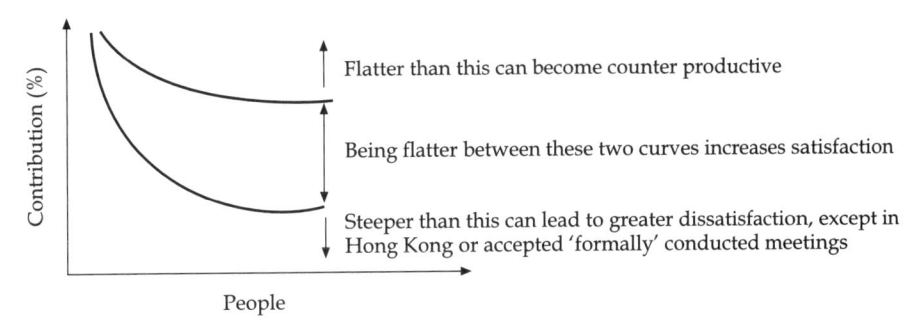

Figure 3.4: Patterns of contribution in international teams

> Imagine a group of HR/training employees on a workshop on facilitating international teams. They have seen the evidence that high levels of interruption can exclude second language speakers. A little later they are given a task to solve. Their interaction is counted and the rate of simultaneous talk is over 40 per cent. All sorts of excuses start emerging, but the message goes powerfully home.
>
> In another team, one member was hardly talking at all and nobody seems to notice. The facilitator again just counted for half an hour, using the chart in Appendix 2. The results are quickly put up on a flipchart and the facilitator says 'this is your pattern of interaction over the last half an hour. Just spend a few minutes looking at it and seeing if you are all happy with it', and then left them alone. No judgements were being made that there must be equal participation, but an opportunity to address any major imbalances was created.

Counting is a powerful, simple tool and most teams are able to laugh about the outcomes and discuss them without rancour.

Questioning the interaction when things are not going well

This is not easy, unless the team is prepared to do it. Neither the most satisfied or balanced teams in the video research ever stopped to question their interaction or review how they were working together. Perhaps, being small, they could get away with it. However, for all the other teams in the video research, the post questionnaires showed that there was a significant relationship between a larger number of different nationalities in the team (regardless of the size of the team), and the team not wanting to work together again and lower team spirit. The team members were not enjoying themselves.

> In one team, a British member started persistently pointing out that they should find a better way of working together that prevented the 'international' managers dominating the 'locals'. At first the other British members gave him a very hard time with retorts like 'if you do not have any concrete suggestions then stay quiet as at least we are getting on with the task'. The response he got was impatience, if not a loathing for, 'soft' issues. He kept going and slowly the team came around.

If this is a typical reaction, it is easy to see why men and women do want not to intervene, especially if the team has not laid any ground rules about participation at the beginning that can be referred back to. It takes courage to stick your neck out to ensure that the end result is good for all ... not just for some.

An outstanding question for managers is how much consciously intervening to encourage participation and good interaction makes a difference to the quality of the outcome. Our experience in real organisations, rather than in research labs, would lead us to say it is often dangerous not to do so and intervening effectively can often make a lot of difference. In Wellcome, teams that asked for facilitation from the beginning said that they achieved things in much less time than they had expected and with much less conflict, whereas those that initially declined often came crying for help when they ran into trouble.

Structuring the interaction and taking up good ideas

Structuring the task well in terms of using and appreciating innovative ideas seem to be two key factors that affect overall satisfaction in teams working on creative and evaluative tasks.

> Two 'identical teams' were created for a senior training programme on strategic planning in a South East Asian Bank. One (Bank 1) was quite satisfied, the other (Bank 2) was not. Both teams were facilitated throughout the four days of working together and received various inputs on project planning, creative thinking and process review. Each team was given a region of the world in which to develop a strategy for the Bank. The different amount of knowledge and different degrees of presence of the Bank in the two regions, the Middle East and Latin America, did not make much difference as the teams went off to look for information on the countries in each region and then returned to make individual presentations. The crisis in each team came at the midpoint after two days, when they had to decide how to *use and structure* the information they had gathered into a well-argued strategy.

> With the walls of their small room covered in flipcharts and information, Bank 1 started a heated argument that began to get rough. One Hong Kong Chinese man suggested that they go down the squash courts and shout out ideas for different possible strategies. They came back with eight possible strategies which they laid out and systematically began to argue them through, using the information and experience that they had gathered in the team. Doing something active changed the whole dynamic in the team and created a much higher energy level. The Hong Kong Chinese team members who had previously been quite quiet, were spontaneously getting up and writing ideas on the walls. The whole team energy was lifted onto a different plane and the excitement at doing something good began to build. In review, although the same Hong Kong man kept complaining that the rate of interruption and speaking was too fast for him, he was praised again and again by the team for his creative lateral ideas.
>
> Bank 2 had no predominant subgroup. They were all very fluent in English and early on felt that they really liked each other referring to themselves as 'the friendly team'. Their enthusiasm quickly translated into all talking at once. Sometimes three or four people were talking at the same time. It did not take them long to realise that they were not listening to each other or getting on very fast. The problem was how to control their enthusiasm without losing it. They appointed a Sri Lankan to be the team leader in order to manage the interaction. He tried to enforce the rule that people spoke one at a time and put their hands up before speaking. He also took his appointment as giving him the right to put his ideas before everyone else's. The energy in the team began to drain away. When it came to having to decide how to build a strategy, the energy was gone and they spent two hours going around in circles. Quite personal arguments started breaking out and they sat wondering what had gone wrong. Slowly they pulled themselves out of it, but never fully recovered the initial enthusiasm.

One difference between the two teams was that, at the crucial half time stage, Bank 1 managed to contain and channel their heated differences creatively, whereas Bank 2 lost it. It may have partly been due to lack of good information on Latin America but also because they never established a communication pattern that enabled them to exhibit high friendly energy, but which was also structured enough to accomplish their task.

One person in Bank 1 was constantly challenging the team on their process and the way that the 'Anglo international' staff members were dominating the 'regional' staff. As a result, the two most 'regional' staff members were asked to make the final presentation to four board members. The most dominant British 'international' manager, who seemed to feel that his global troubleshooting reputation was on the line, was constantly being asked to back off and slow down. At one point a very reserved regional Hong Kong Chinese manager physically put his arm across in front of the international manager to stop him talking. Despite having to manage these strong characters, satisfaction and success came from being able to acknowledge and act upon bright ideas and structuring the interaction so that the team can channel a heated argument into a constructive outcome.

When things go right

What did the most satisfied and balanced teams do? Much went right because they were small, and because second language speakers set the pace. However, they did do some key things:

- They introduced themselves and early on asked who had the most experience on the task. In one of the most dysfunctional teams, members were still asking each other their names after four hours of teamwork.
- They created a slow steady pace of English and unconsciously paused very slightly after every third sentence to take a brief look around that everyone was following. It did not disrupt the flow and gave just enough time for someone to come in if they had a problem or needed clarification.
- When they asked for ideas they made sure everyone had said what they wanted to. One British dominated group squashed a Pakistani's suggestion that they go around one by one and get ideas and suggested people shout out. The Pakistani and Brazilian remained silent.
- When they spilt into subgroups, they consciously spread the skills so that people could learn from each other. In one team it was clear that second language speakers spoke more in the whole team after contributing in subgroups. In two of the least effective teams, the subgroups were decided by the self-appointed team leaders to ensure that they and their colleagues were covering the most important parts of the task, leaving some people hanging.

Light-hearted incidents

Thankfully there are those small incidents that bring a smile to an observer's face. An American lady had been appointed the leader of an otherwise all male team. She had been sick for two meetings and came back in the last meeting as they were wrapping up. Flipcharts covered with writing adorned the walls. She asked if someone could quickly read her through what they had done. A British man started and stopped occasionally to check that she understood what he meant. 'Oh yes' she commented, I understand your verbiage'. At this point the four British men all burst out laughing, none of them noticing the bewildered face of the American woman and then the British man continued. Later again one of the British men joked about their verbiage, again all the Brits laughed and the American woman looked puzzled. Verbiage in UK English means something akin to 'verbal diarrhoea' but presumably simply means 'words' in US English, without the derogatory overtone.

Such events, if they were recognised, can bring the humour back into cross-cultural incidents in international teams. When a team can readily joke about their similarities and differences and *everyone* finds it funny, then the team has matured.

The following chapter outlines what teams and team leaders can do to overcome the difficulties and to sculpt their interaction to fit the tasks over four main phases of their teamwork. It is quite detailed and in-depth. Even so, our impression from our work and research is that even doing a little, such as outlined above, can make a difference to how well team members work together. That said, most of the teams described in this last chapter did not have their company's future profitability riding on their backs. If your team does, like the Glaxo-Wellcome medical development teams, then being very proactive in managing the interaction within the team is highly recommended.

Summary of Key Learning Points

- *Patterns of inclusion and exclusion, the creation of 'them' and 'us' groups and dysfunctional communication patterns are the same as in any team, but often more pronounced.*
- *Three types of inequality, structural, linguistic and perceived inequality based on preconceptions and stereotypes can create dysfunctional behaviour and need to be actively managed.*
- *Leaders need to make sure that an impersonal atmosphere is broken down initially by good introductions.*
- *The speed and pattern of speech should give second language speakers and others who prefer not to start talking when someone else is already talking, time to think and speak.*
- *Leaders need to watch what people say so that stereotypical comments and behaviours that exclude any one individual are diffused and changed.*
- *Brainstorming or collecting ideas and prioritising them needs to be done in a systematic way that consciously asks for everyone's ideas. 'Shouting out' means some people may not participate.*
- *Leaders need to manage the response to alienation should it happen.*
- *Everyone needs to be comfortable with the decision making process or alternatives need to be found.*

Chapter Four

Implementing Best Practices*

The previous chapters have shown that the dynamics of *all* teams will be affected by the personalities, expertise, status, motivation and attitudes of the individuals involved, as well as by team and organisational characteristics and the nature and structure of the task. On top of this, we have established that due to individual cultural differences and differences in the national representation, linguistic fluency and preconceived ideas within the team, international teams are likely to have greater communication difficulties than national teams. This chapter describes the actions that team leaders and members can take to enhance their performance and ensure that likely pitfalls are avoided.

The model used is based on four simple phases in a team's life cycle; the fact that all teams form and then have a beginning, middle and end. However, many teams roll on for long periods of time with changing membership and focus and no clear beginnings and ends. Team leaders and members in these on-going teams need to take an interim point, such as setting a new work plan, celebrating an interim result, reviewing the vision and goals, or introducing a new team member to set the point at which the model would come into play. They will see that the useful things they can do are the same.

As mentioned in Chapter One, international teams are likely to be made up of technical and professional experts who are working with knowledge rather than physical labour. In order to achieve flexibility and responsiveness, many shop-floor teams have learnt each other's jobs through multiskilling, where they transfer technical skills to each other. Because of the heightened emphasis on good process, international team leaders and members also need to be multiskilled at handling intercultural interaction all through the team's life cycle. Team leaders and members need to actively sculpt the interaction in the team to best fit the different stages of the task. Unless the team has a clear model of how to do this, words like 'team processes' usually either get a yawn or a big cheeky grin. This chapter will work through the model from the point of view of an international team leader, but we are convinced that the whole team needs to take responsibility for implementing these best practices.

*Thanks go to McGraw-Hill and M. Berger for permission to reproduce and adapt this chapter from M. Berger (Ed) (1996), *Cross Cultural Teambuilding*, McGraw-Hill, UK.

The Underlying Framework of the Model

Whatever the composition and geography of the team and whatever their task, there is a time before teams interact: phase one. There is a time when the whole team first meets: phase two. There is a period of continuing to work together to get the task done: phase three and a period of completing the task and hopefully passing on the learning: phase four. Team sponsors, leaders, members and facilitators have found this four stage model easy to work with and to develop for themselves. While this model was developing within Wellcome, it transpired that almost exactly the same model with similar wording, but interesting differences, was developed in the human resource department of another large UK pharmaceutical company. This discovery was reassuring that somewhere we must both be stating the obvious, which is usually what works. Figure 4.1 describes the basic model. The model shows how the eight factors, identified in Chapter Two, need to be managed throughout the whole four phase life cycle. There is a lot of emphasis on the work that needs to be done before a team ever meets.

This model is cumulative. That is, the better the eight factors are managed at each phase, the more productive and less troublesome the next phase will be.

Similarly, the more mistakes that are made in each phase, the more likely your team is to fall apart. So the earlier these factors are identified, acknowledged and accounted for, the easier the teamwork will be. This is why Karen has coined the phrase, 3 × 1 preparation for international teams. If it takes you one month to set up a national team, give yourselves three months to set up an international team. Another way of looking at this guideline is, if the team meeting is going to last one day, you need to do three days preparation; for a three-day meeting, allocate nine days of preparation time, probably starting two or three months in advance etc.

Phase one: Start up, Pre meeting

This phase can be summed up as: 'know your task and team'. Wellcome discovered that only 3 out of 42 of its newly established international project teams knew who their project sponsors were. Most of them only had a vague idea of the main purpose of their teams and were left guessing as to the real reason they had been established. They surmised that the point must be to reduce duplication and increase global efficiency, but very few of them thought that these activities were directly linked to the companies overall global strategy. So the first useful step that team sponsors, leaders and relevant managers who will be designing the actual project team can take is to:

Leading International Teams

Phase four: Closing stages
'Review and share the learning'

Phase three: Mid-point
'Work through strategic moments'

Phase two: First meetings
'Start slowly, end fast: agree the ground rules'

Phase one: Start up Pre meeting
'Know your sponsors, task and team: '3 1 preparation'

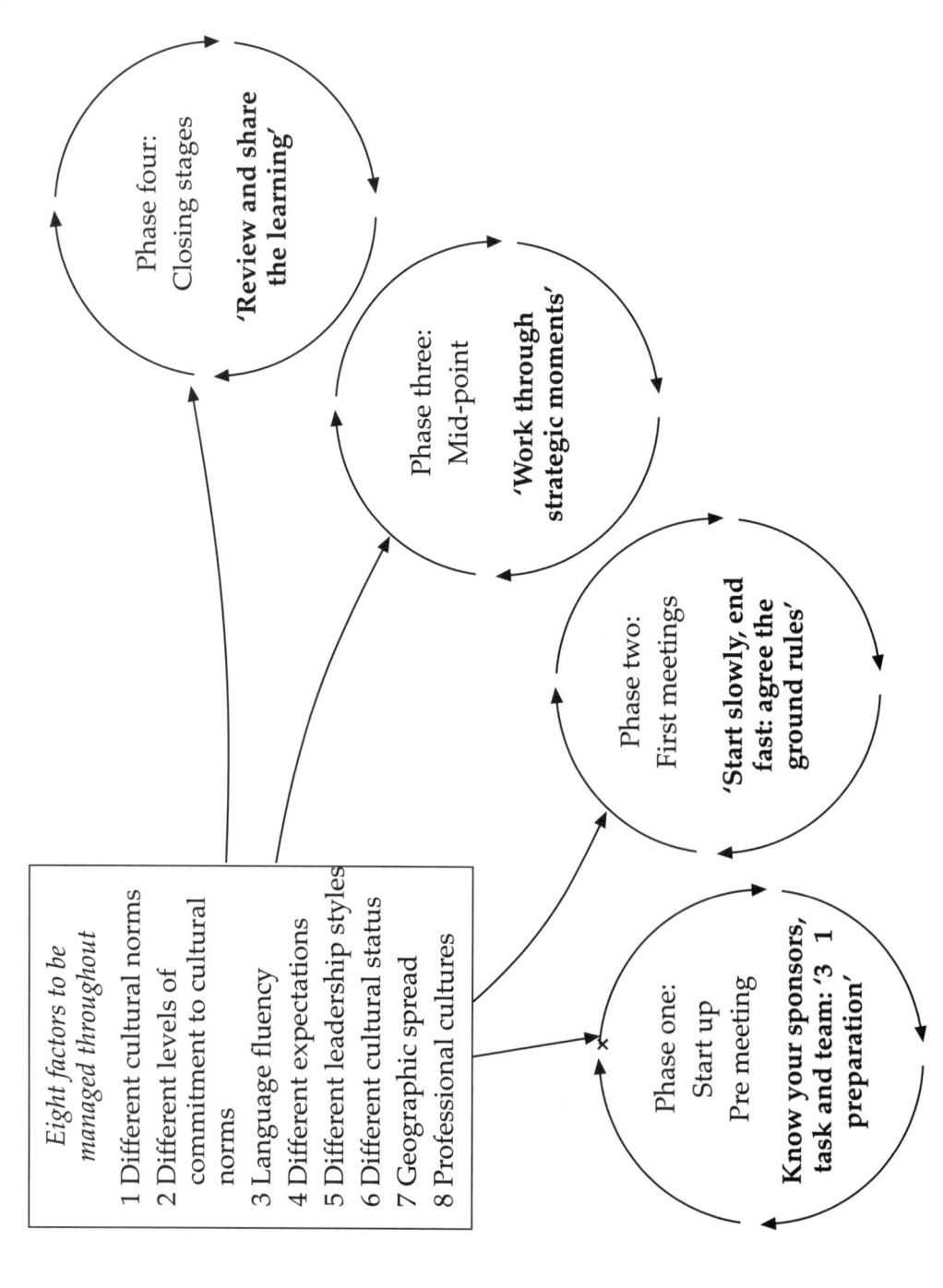

Eight factors to be managed throughout

1 Different cultural norms
2 Different levels of commitment to cultural norms
3 Language fluency
4 Different expectations
5 Different leadership styles
6 Different cultural status
7 Geographic spread
8 Professional cultures

Figure 4.1: An international team's life cycle

1 Develop and agree the purpose of the team with the sponsors

This happens best in one, or a series of, face to face meeting(s), but can be done in a series of teleconferences, e-mails or in a groupware discussion if necessary.

The team leader and sponsor(s) need to painstakingly clarify the mission, purpose, agenda, accountability, time frame, resources available, organisational barriers and key stakeholders.

The team sponsors should lead the session and make sure that all the relevant people are there. Who should constitute this 'project design' team will depend on the context of the team. Suppose a new cross regional team is being set up in a company that has otherwise worked very independently. The relevant country/line managers need to attend some part of or set of these meetings as they are the ones who will need to work out their new relationship to the team members, change the support systems and agree cross-regional budgeting.

2 Select the team members

Once the purpose of the team has been clarified, the next step is to establish the team membership. Quite a lot has been written showing how the purpose of the team will determine the type of staffing, the skills needed and the internal and external team boundaries[1]

The process by which the team members are selected will also have a powerful influence on the subsequent dynamics of the team.

Structured selection processes can overcome organisational biases such as dominant cultures and gender biases. One company found that while introducing global behavioural criteria for internal jobs was fraught with cross-cultural problems, they at least stopped appointing the same sort of person as the person who had just left.

There is also the problem of who should have the main say in selecting team members. This is not the role of the team sponsor. Team leaders often only know who is, or has been, good on someone else's team. Line managers may not want to lose their best people on long-term secondments* or to manage the consequences of overloading their best people on part-time assignments. They will want to create opportunities for training up and coming departmental or regional staff, while the team leaders want experienced people who are already very competent and available. These different perspectives need to be sorted out.

*Especially if they are in charge of a profit centre and paid according to their centre's financial performance.

Especially when different regions are being integrated, specific team roles may have very different levels of experience and standing in the different regions. In Wellcome, the very experienced UK project managers were the project leaders and had a full co-ordinating, negotiating, reporting and advocacy role in the team. In America, project managers were junior staff drawing up schedules and work plans while the project leaders represented and co-ordinated the team. When integrated American/UK teams were created, they were based on the American project model. A whole group of UK professional staff were disenfranchised. When an American project leader was lucky enough to get one of the original UK project managers on his/her team, he/she had little idea of how to use their skills.

So the project design team needs to take responsibility for the full impact of what they are proposing and all the vested interests in choosing who should be on the teams. Senior directors and managers are usually wooed by the strategic advantages that they see coming their way and reckon that the staff will work out how to make it happen. As a result, many companies are making it up as they go along and this can be very hard on international team leaders. Team leaders are advised to work out a clear contract of the goal and boundaries of the work with the sponsors.

Throughout this setting up process, the team leader will be gaining insights into the areas of similarity and difference between the team members and the tensions or points of cohesion that are likely to occur. For instance, if a young team leader has been selected on the basis of having broad project skills, older expert technicians may feel resentful. This insider knowledge is vital. Without it, the team leader cannot start to consider how to make these issues conscious within the team in phase two, nor manage any residual fallout in phase three.

3 Plan the communication technology support

Once the geographical location of the team members is established, the project design team needs to assess what communication technology can enhance the interaction of the team for that particular task. An expert from the information technology or services department usually needs to be involved at this project design phase, especially if international teams are a new phenomena. This is not necessarily the time to design the technology, only to appraise what means of communication currently exist within the company, what is available on the market, what the team can benefit from, how much it would cost, how long it would take to introduce/train the team members and how much budget is realistically available.

As someone once said, 'when you have settled your budget for setting up an international team, double it'.[2]

4 Decide if you need an external facilitator, contract with the sponsors and team and clarify the boundaries of responsibility and the facilitator's role

This is an opportunity to decide what level of facilitation skills is needed for that particular team and whether to use external or internal help. The key issues to consider when making these decisions are:

a   Are the team members coming with conflicting agendas where a neutral person would aid common agreement?
b   Does the team leader need to be heavily involved in the technical detail of the task. Will this make it hard to also attend to process?
c   What is the level of experience and confidence of the team leader in managing an international team with the particular mix of nationalities and histories involved?

In our view, a facilitator's work is *not* to get teams out of trouble. It is to teach teams how to manage themselves from the start so that they can progressively improve their processes and creatively manage differences and stalemates when they arise. There is a caveat to this which is to do with the readiness and openness of the organisation and teams.

We have found that if facilitation and managing the processes of international teams is very new to the organisation, there can be a strong sense of resistance. 'We want to have a go at this first without 'outside' interference.' In this case, it is better to let the team start up in its own way, discover the difficulties and come in about three to six months later. After seeing the benefits, most team members and leaders will invite the facilitator in at the beginning of the next team cycle. On the other hand, if the organisation already has a strong ethic of training and teamwork, often you can go in at the beginning without any difficulty.

Expense should not be a consideration in deciding whether to have a facilitator or not. Good facilitators will pay for themselves many times over if the team would otherwise have difficulties. Many international teams have rejected a facilitator only to have to start again when they have reached a stalemate. This invariably costs the team and the organisation far more than if a facilitator had been involved all along. There is no fixed role for a facilitator and the most effective role will depend on the needs of the team. Criteria to help you consider how to use a facilitator effectively are covered in the next chapter.

It is the authors' conviction through experience that at least 50 per cent of a good facilitator's effectiveness depends on clearly defining the role that the facilitator will play, prior to the teamwork.

Some companies suggest that facilitators should only participate if the team asks for help. This does not work. If the facilitator has had no mandate to guide the team and is then expected to come in when the team hits trouble, it is the facilitator, not the team leader, who gets blamed for the half-baked outcome. 'You know, we do not understand what difference you made', a facilitator can hardly turn around at this point and say, 'but you did not let me make a difference'.

5 Interview the key players

Once the membership has been agreed with the team members, it is useful for the team leader to start getting them involved, prior to meeting face to face. This can be done through interviews or sending out a questionnaire to find out how much the team members already understand about the task, their attitude towards, or historical interaction with, each other and their level of commitment. Some leaders and facilitators find it useful to ask would-be team members to fill in personality tests or team role questionnaires and to process these before the team first meets.

Simplicity and cultural relevance is the key to international teams employing the results as a feedback tool to improve their own performance.

This kind of work is especially useful in organisations where there are high levels of cynicism or uncertainty due to retrenchment exercises or bad management. Team members can unload their frustrations one on one with the team leader or facilitator, rather than bring them, still burning, to the start-up meetings. The team leader and facilitator can then plan in advance how to acknowledge the past before moving on to create a positive feeling about doing things differently. These up front exercises also send the message that each team member matters to the team as a whole.

6 Plan the first meetings

When the above work is done, key team members, the leader and/or facilitator and key sponsors need to go through the agenda for the first meetings. They need to establish who will present what, and check to see that any proposed team building exercises will be new, culturally and organisationally relevant and at the right level of experience. They then need to collate and distribute any necessary documentation and pre-reading, view and book the venue and the social and culinary arrangements.

While the administrative side might seem less important, if it is done badly, it can have a major impact on the start up of the team.

For instance, the timing on the first day needs to take jet lag into account. A Korean coming to Finland may well sleep through presentations on the first evening if he arrived that morning. On the other hand, one French based team would purposefully schedule their meetings for 9.00am Monday morning so that the British manager would always be late and they could make important decisions without him!

It is impossible to stress how important it is for team leaders and external facilitators to get these six aspects of preparation right. The leader or facilitator is the easiest target for any frustration and anger that arises later on. One team decided that 'the facilitators were seeking conflict'. As the facilitators, we thought that the only message we were putting across was the need to integrate the differences between the two corporate and national cultures involved. Because only two key players had been interviewed before the meeting, the pending explosion of frustration, cynicism and anger around confused organisational boundaries, loyalties and trust had not been unearthed in advance. We learnt the need for extensive '3 × 1 preparation' the hard way as the team vented their ire to senior management.

Phase Two: First Meetings

Although it may seem counter-intuitive to action-oriented Americans, British and Scandinavians, teams that plan and work on their interaction first and start slowly on the task usually speed up exponentially towards the end.

If the task was climbing a mountain, then no team in their right minds would set out without carefully planning the route, the responsibilities, the ways in which they were going to avoid major pitfalls and how they were going to communicate, especially if things started going wrong. Most corporate tasks at managerial level are achieved through thinking, reading, meetings, discussion, e-mail and computerised document creation and exchange. For some reason, most people think you do not have to have the same kind of planning. The common misconception is that it will all fall into place as soon as the team starts to climb, as basically everyone assumes everyone else has the same ideas of how it should happen. However, when the team encounters the first crevasse they flounder and start arguing about basic procedures that should have been clear right from the start. Bringing all the different expectations and understanding of processes to the surface at the beginning and planning a common working approach is essential for the success of international teams. The preparation discussed above and best practices outlined below, help teams structure and speed up this process. Moreover we will keep stressing that structuring the interaction is the only way to speed up and ensure participation.

Most of the actions that need to be taken to manage the interaction have been referred to as 'team basics'[3], eg clarifying roles and goals, setting clear targets, establishing interdependent activities and mutual accountability. There are many good books on improving team performance that international team leaders and members can usefully read and that are suggesting useful ways of taking care of these issues[4]. The trouble is that few teams do it well. As stressed in Chapter One, all of the team basics need to be applied in international teams. Rather than go over the same ground, the point is to look at what more has to be done to manage the interaction between different nationalities and across distances. The building blocks for achieving the best interaction to fit the task need to be set in place at this point.

In hindsight, the two most appreciated issues in the start up sessions of Seagram's re-engineering teams were 'creating a clear set of behavioural rules and understanding the strengths and weaknesses in the team'.

Seagram drinks and entertainment company created high profile international teams who had eight months to recommend how to re-engineer the company's processes. Aside from these two 'basics', outlined above, most of the Seagram's team members felt that they developed as a team by working together. If the basics are set correctly at this stage, the team itself will develop the capacity to manage itself in the mid-phase. The first step in putting the basics in place is to make the link between the work of the project design team and the actual project team itself.

7 At the first set of meetings, explain the organisational strategy and policies, putting the purpose of the team in context. Jointly identify, prioritise and agree the mission, purpose, objectives and key success criteria

Companies create international teams to develop the big picture. If team members have never seen it, they are groping in the dark. Research on over 50 transnational teams[5] showed that explaining how the purpose of the team fits in with the overall organisational strategy helps team members to understand why they should go to all the trouble of working across organisational, geographical, temporal and cultural barriers.

Bad experience has taught us this golden rule: First gain commitment to a common direction, then explore differences. Otherwise un-channelled differences can blow up and land in your face.

Once the purpose of the team within the big picture is clear, then the team needs to identify what they want to achieve, how they are going to do it and what it should look like when the team gets there. Not everyone will agree on the words that describe these things*; words such as the mission, the vision, goals, targets, critical success factors, vivid descriptions etc. Keeping the language simple is important.

When it comes to establishing 'how?', the focus is on accessing the different expectations about what constitutes effective teamwork. Once the direction and goals that the team is working towards is agreed and understood by everyone, then the team needs to move onto the next step and build interrelationships face to face.

8 Emphasise building interrelationships when face to face

The most dissatisfied team in one piece of research were still asking each other's names as the team broke up. If the British and Americans rush off into the task, Latin and Middle Eastern team members may well remain silent because the proper introductions have not yet been made. The Americans and British may be culturally informed and yet still come across patronisingly saying 'well, we had better introduce ourselves' while tapping the table with a pencil. Most people agree[6] that trust is best established at the same time, in the same place. It is much harder across a distance.

If humour is integral for some people to establish trust, it does not translate well on paper. British exclamation marks are used to show that you are not serious about what you are saying, but they can be taken very seriously elsewhere. Speaking from British/Australian facsimile experience, exclamation marks can be interpreted as arrogant, conceited, manipulative and totally insensitive when you meant to be funny and to keep it light and open.

Trust is built in different ways in different cultures. Aspiring American presidents usually start poking fun at themselves and deriding their weaknesses in the last stages of a campaign. In Hong Kong they would never get elected. The British feel safe if they can understand each other's jokes, although they will probably tell them to each other standing shoulder to shoulder with a drink in hand, surveying the room rather than looking at each other. For most Germans, the idea of establishing trust after only a few meetings is meaningless. Most will wait to see the steadiness and quality of the work.

9 Consciously explore the cultural similarities and differences and resulting strengths and weaknesses of the team

This is perhaps the most important process of all in international teams ... an in-depth analysis of what you are as a team. Having done this, you can then decide how to best work together. Here we very strongly recommend the use of the cultural value checklist illustrated in the next chapter. It focuses attention immediately on relevant similarities and differences within a common cultural

---

*Especially international human resource and training teams.

framework, creates a common visual display of what the collective results are on each issue and creates a level playing field for an in-depth highly structured discussion. The discussion needs to cover similarities or differences in professional cultures, preferred and expected leadership styles, different communication, decision making and feedback preferences. For instance if some people think that individuals should make final decisions and others prefer group consensus: a discussion of the reasons for the different preferences and a workable team approach can happen without either side feeling that theirs is the right or wrong approach. While dealing with a number of factors, one of the most important aspects of this work is to put in place agreed and culturally appropriate modes of feedback that will enable the team to work through any difficulties caused by cultural differences in the mid-phase.

Apart from ground rules to manage national differences on decision making, feedback and leadership styles, the team needs to develop a strategy for working with different levels of language fluency and other factors that create status differences within the team. As discussed in the last two chapters, setting up rigid patterns of speaking in turn will irritate fluent members. It is better to control the speed of speech and to have someone responsible for checking that each person is saying what he or she wants to say. The same person can also frequently visually summarise and paraphrase where they think the team has reached on the task and keep checking for total agreement. If there is more than one speaker of a particular second language, then giving them time out to check their understanding in their own language and summarise it back for the whole team can be helpful. It gives them a welcome break from the tiring process of listening to and speaking in a foreign language. These are examples of the ground rules that need to be established at this point.

Three things are happening simultaneously during these discussions. First, the basis of intercultural awareness and sensitivity is being established, the team is legitimising and appreciating their similarities and differences and assessing their strengths and weaknesses. By using an equitable cultural framework the team members will later be able to give each other feedback on behavioural issues without getting personal. Second, the team is setting the 'ground rules' for how they will best interact. Third, this process is highlighting which aspects of someone's being, cultural make-up and expected contribution will be considered important and it should keep the salient parts of someone's identity and contribution, often expertise, skill, experience, and discerning ability at the forefront of the teams interaction. Potentially irrelevant issues that can bias the interaction, such as age, sex, ethnicity, marital status can then stay in the background.

Setting ground rules in international teams is important. Our experience shows that however much you talk about and demonstrate the detrimental results of say, interrupting each other, or allowing international staff to dominate regional staff etc, it tends to go in one ear and out the other until these factors become visible in the team. What you tend to get at this stage is;

'Yes yes, we know we should be nice to each other, but can we get on with the task?' Even though it is often uphill work, and some people may only agree flippantly, establishing ground rules:

- Creates workable communication norms specific to that team.
- Creates a commitment within the team that all team members are responsible for generating the best interaction.
- Protects the views of minorities.
- Enables the ground rules to act as a neutral judge when conflict and bad behaviour start to take over.
- Creates a much broader 'field' in which creative and constructive argument can take place.

By the end of this process, which can take two to three hours in a new team, the eight factors described in Chapter Two have been made conscious. Some people are fascinated and others think it is a total waste of time, but even they often begrudgingly admit that if they had taken the pre-work seriously, they would not be encountering many of their subsequent difficulties. *'Oh we thought that was just an exercise for team building or something, not what we were really going to do.'* As the examples in the previous chapters show, if the team members and especially the team leader, lack intercultural sensitivities or have not established clear ground rules, stereotypes and organisational norms will probably prevail and some very upset members are likely to be excluded from meaningful interaction.

10 The final task of the team at this stage is to agree the first set of action plans

At this point, the team needs to agree what will be done, who will do it and by when, before the next meeting. Most importantly they need to agree how they are going to communicate, not only how they will use different technologies, but also the style of communication. Establishing a communication charter should specifically aim at managing any skewed geographical spread. This is where the information technology person from the project design team needs to present his/her findings and for the team to work through and formulate their needs. This process often prompts companies to get serious about establishing global e-mail and standard software packages. The advantages and disadvantages of different technologies are outlined in Chapter Seven.

How long does this first setting up phase last? It depends of course whether supportive systems are already in place or not and whether this is the first team of its kind in the company. It also depends on how well 3×1 preparation has been done, the length of the project and so on. One on-going team spent three two-day sessions over three months completing this part of the cycle. That amount of initial investment paid off eighteen months later when they hit serious interpersonal problems.

The important things to notice are that differences are opened up and explored only after a common understanding of purpose and goals has been established and that the team then works on the 'how' before the detail of the 'what'.

By the end of these first set of meetings, the team should be clear about what it is doing and where it is going. Culturally different norms, different levels of language fluency, different working practices, leadership styles, geographical distances, and status issues should have been made visible and integrated into a workable interactive process that best supports the task and incorporates each team member's individuality.

Phase Three: Mid Point

The mid-phase is often characterised by bursts of activity followed by periods of stagnation and poor momentum in which problems arise, the hidden agendas missed at the beginning can emerge and create what Steve Mitchell, an accomplished trainer in Wellcome, called 'strategic moments'. Aside from working through difficulties and 'strategic moments', the team needs to renew, review and undergo relevant mid-term training. The frequency of strategic moments, the severity of discomfort and the implications of how they are handled by the leader or facilitator all seem to be far greater in international teams than national teams. What exactly are strategic moments?

11 Work through strategic moments

Imagine a team where the Spanish half has been competing internally with the German half. The Spanish from the Spanish production plant do not want to reveal how far they have moved along with the marketing of a brand new product because they are convinced that the Germans from headquarters will steal their ideas and take the best markets. However, they are racing for a deadline with three other competitors. A team meeting is held. A big board is drawn up listing current activities and responsibilities. Suddenly the names of vice presidents and the chief executive are being given for who is responsible, with no names from within the team. The German head of production beckons the Spanish head of sales and storms out of the room. The team has reached a strategic moment. What happens next will make or break the team. If the leader or facilitator knows the history, was expecting the stand off and can lead the team through this moment, the likelihood is that old corporate patterns and years of antagonism and vested interests can be broken down. So while they may be extremely uncomfortable, strategic moments are also great opportunities for changing unworkable corporate habits. In fact, the team will be energised and enthused by the release of all the potential energy that was held in previous dysfunctional patterns. When cultural prejudices, ignorance and stereotyping are included in such a scenario, one can see why international teams tend to go through emotional and traumatic processes and key strategic moments before they start to benefit from their diversity.

In the above example, the facilitator pointed out that two key people had left the room and asked the team what it wanted to do. 'Oh, we want to discuss the product in general.' This was relayed to the two senior managers when they returned. The German head of production suddenly became very 'Spanish' and burst into a fully emotional tirade that if no-one on the team was going to take responsibility, then he was walking out for good. A small Spanish voice came from the back of the room to explain that they had been competing internally. Suddenly the dam burst and everyone was looking for constructive ways of moving forward and stayed late into the evening. It is the leader's or facilitators responsibility to get the team through such moments in the most creative way possible. The form of a strategic moment can vary from highly charged, 'over the top' emotional discharges to complete stony silences that are equally hard to work through. Courage, persistence, humour, and sometimes temporary deviation are all useful strategies that leaders and facilitators can adopt. The strange combination of a personal thick skin and yet high sensitivity to what is going on is also very valuable. For instance when faced with a Finnish group silence, one can insist that due to your cultural ignorance, you need to have the silence interpreted. Emotional outpourings and frustrations can be met by quiet acknowledgement and gentle feedback about someone's perspective and values.

As stated above, if the ground rules have been set tightly and clearly, the team has much greater freedom for creative interaction on the task and particular norms are less likely to dominate. If multiple options and rich pictures have been generated well, the team leader should expect the heat to rise as these options are forged into one path of action at the half time point. The ground rules have to be strong enough to take that heat as all the differences of opinion jostle through a narrow funnel. If they melt as the temperature rises, everything flows everywhere and no product is wrought. Strategic moments can be very healthy indeed. The point is to be prepared for them by having done in-depth homework in the first two phases. This is the time when 'knowing your team', understanding the inequalities and having workable ground rules pays off. The best way of visualising this is to use a concept from Drexler and Sibbet's extensive and useful team model[7] that stresses that teams move from freedom at the beginning of their teamwork, to constraint at the half-time point back to freedom as they have accomplished their task.

In Figure 4.2 after a short early argument the dominant norms either force people to fall into line, or leave the field of play completely. If a certain set of organisational norms or dominant patterns of interaction force the team members onto a narrow path early on, the material gathered will be limited and only a narrow outcome will emerge.

Figure 4.3 represents the participants initially arguing through many divergent points of view. The intense discussion is focused towards a point

102 Leading International Teams

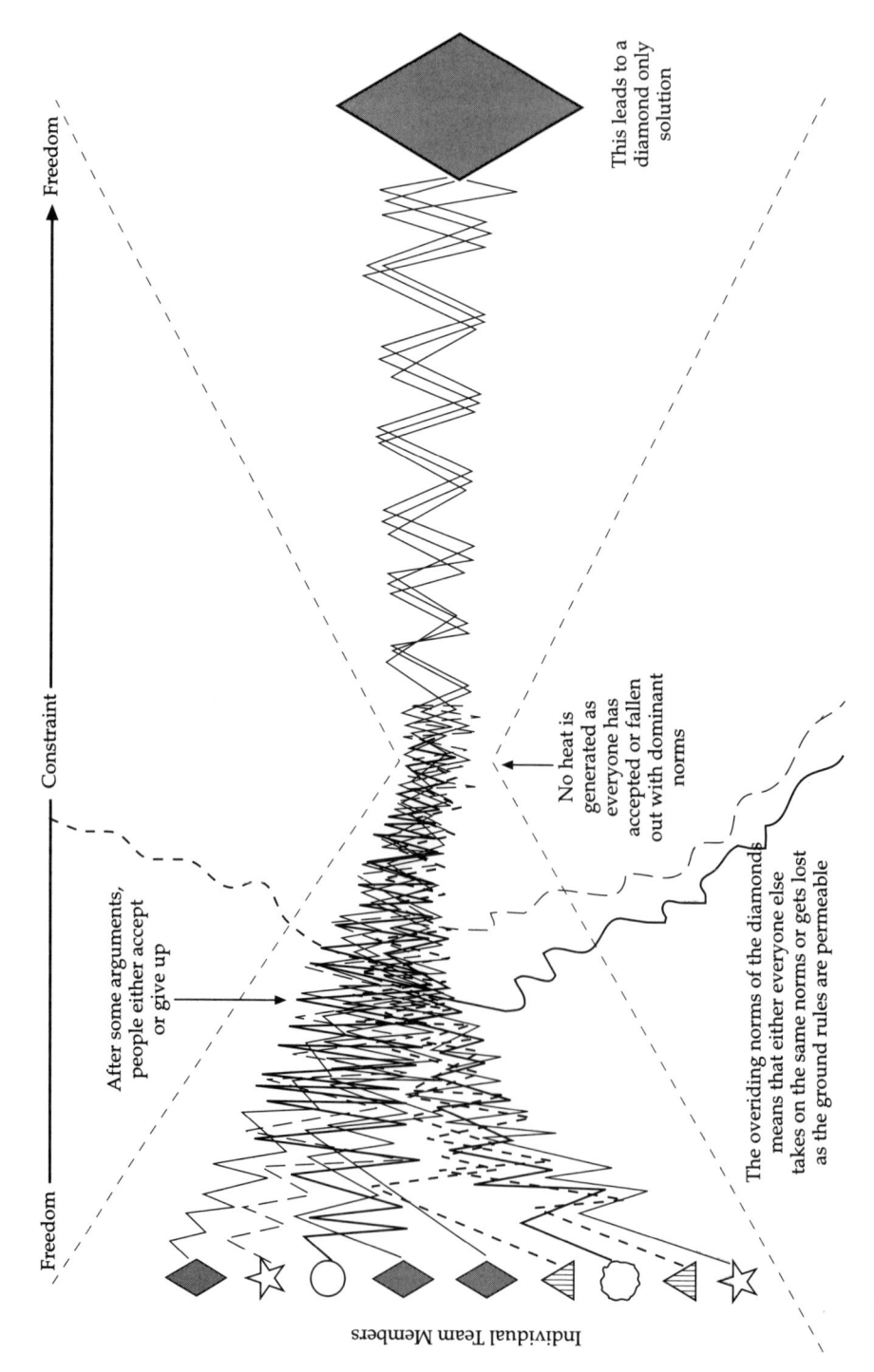

Figure 4.2: Ineffective use of freedom and constraint in teamworking

Implementing Best Practices   103

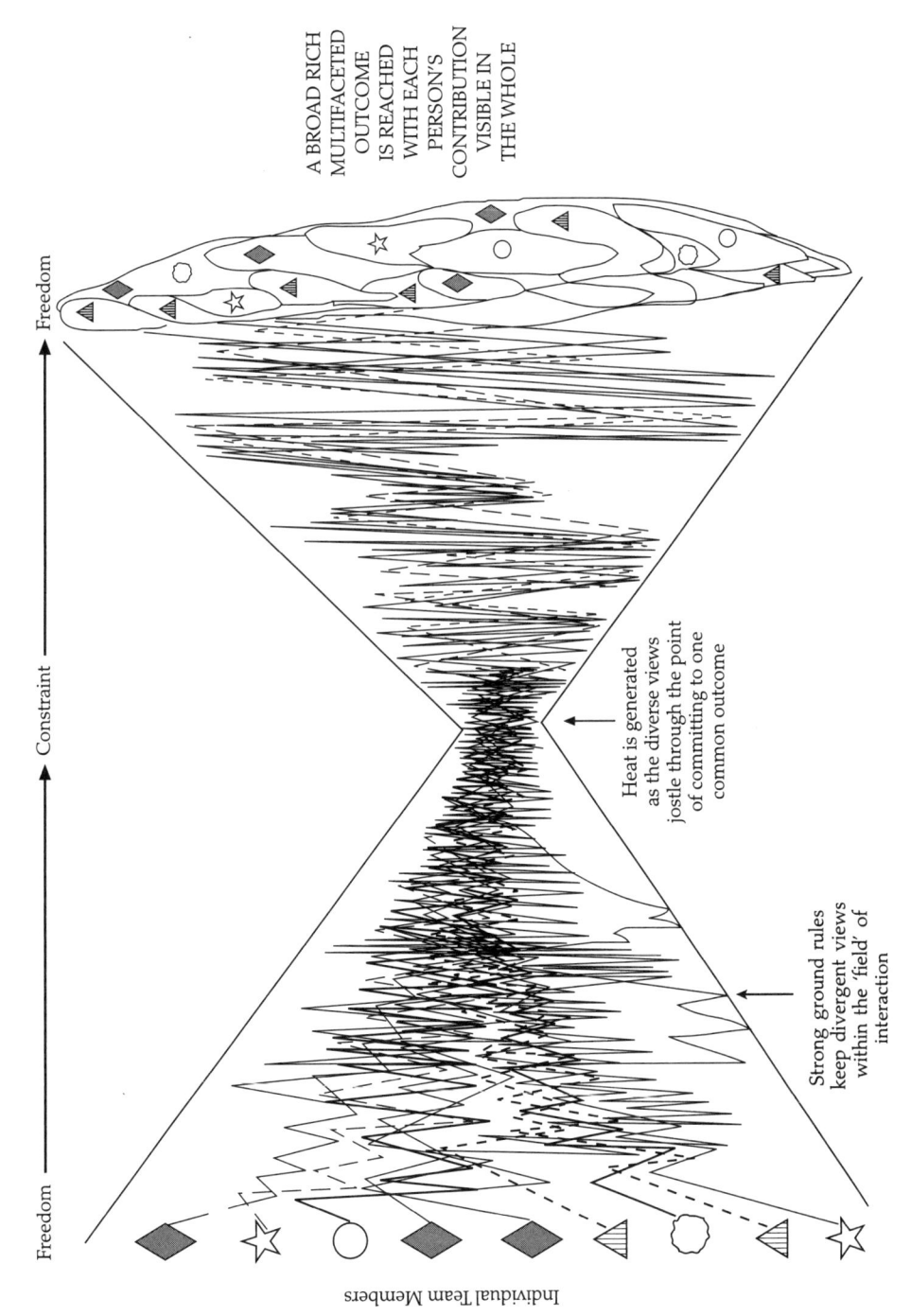

Figure 4.3: Effective use of freedom and constraint in teamworking

of maximum constraint where they have to agree the way forward towards their common outcome. The richness of the initial debate and subsequent focus and decision making allows a broad, rich, inclusive end product to be created. Unlike the 'diamond' only solution illustrated previously, well set ground rules that encompass each team member's preferences of how to interact as well as encourages their input, open up the field of play especially initially and so long as the boundaries are tight and elastic, people and ideas will bounce back into the playing field. Far more options can be created that then need to be channelled through the 'straight gate' leading to a common outcome. That outcome will contain more options, be argued against or supported from different perspectives and already be honed and customised to be implemented in many different contexts. If the ground rules have large holes in them, contributions can wander off track or be thrown out, and the outcome is poor.

We have seen that structured processes can overcome organisational biases that prevent a team from working at high performance. But structured does not mean rigid. It means creating an agreed field to play in[8]. If the temperature does not rise somewhere near the middle of the teamwork, it usually means that the team has not accrued the advantages afforded by the diversity of skills, viewpoints and experience available in the team. Something went wrong, as in the Bank 2 team described in the last chapter. As the team comes under pressure for action and decisions on the form of the final outcome, the potential for strategic moments greatly increases.

A word of warning is needed here. The richness that leads to excellent outcomes can collapse at any moment. Even good ground rules will not be enough. The richness needs to be constantly protected from dominant inertia. For example, one subgroup chose to superimpose an existing model on otherwise rich exploratory findings that might have led to new perspectives. After a heated and rich debate, two report writers chose not to restructure a table that was clearly only applicable to Western markets. Instead they agreed to make a few qualifying statements that most people would ignore. However good your ground rules, the team has to have the will or energy to maintain and use differences. You cannot 'legislate' it into happening. In fact, a lot of problems and poor results seem to arise from laziness, cynicism, inertia, wanting the quick fix, protecting your own turf, or a lack of courage to venture into the unknown or stick one's neck out to change prevailing norms.

Team leaders will often need to inspire, motivate, coerce, negotiate, cut deals, or strategically get angry. It is a tough and emotionally exhausting job.

After working successfully through any strategic moments and channelling heated debates, a team leader needs to make sure of everyone's involvement and the use of the feedback tools previously established.

12 Make sure that everyone is involved and uses the feedback tools established at the beginning

We have established that equal involvement does not equate with having everyone speaking the same amount. The only way to find out if everyone is involved as much as they want to be, is to ask. In fact, it is useful to carry out major 'health checks' every six months and to make mini verbal check ups throughout any face-to-face meetings. The main focus of a review is to establish that the pattern of interaction that has been set up is the best possible type to serve the needs of the task and the individual priorities in achieving that task.

Major reviews are a good opportunity to 'initiate' new team members. Part or all of the original exercises in phase two can be reworked to fine tune the goals, targets and vivid descriptions and to agree a new communication charter and working process to include the new members. They can be shown all the records of the first meetings so that they understand the history and development of the team.

As described in the next chapter, another part of the health check can be detailed observation and video feedback to highlight just how much one or two members are being excluded and the mechanisms by which other people are dominating the process. This is the time that the team leader needs to pay attention to the effects of different levels of language fluency, especially with differences in written and spoken main language abilities and the effect of unequal national status The team leader also has to look for signs of burn out and too much pressure between family and work. Expectations may need to be adjusted and communication patterns and work schedules improved accordingly.

13 Keep a check on the timing, space the milestones and use the time together and time apart to its full potential

It is helpful to spread out the milestones and keep a check on the timing. It is sensible to carry out process reviews in the lulls between bursts of activity on the task. Computer based Groupware technology can allow the exchange and manipulation of data and reports in different places at different times. Using the time apart for such information exchange means that expensive time together can be devoted to resolving difficult decisions and interpersonal difficulties (although sometimes, time apart may allow people to cool down and rethink their approaches). Time together is also useful for 'just in time' mid-term training such as new problem solving and decision making and creative conflict techniques.

14 Communicate what is being achieved and broadcast successes as they emerge

Managing the external boundaries of the team at this point will determine the impact that the final outcome has on the company. This is the time to broadcast interim successes and send out concept papers of what your final results will achieve for the company and individuals alike. This can be done through lunch time briefings, presentations to senior managers, newsletters, team pages on shared databases as well as one on one over lunches. What is important is to package the information in ways that people will read it. Don't send forty-page reports to busy senior executives with no summaries and sit around wondering why he/she never replies.

Communicating successes as they arise can maintain the interest and involvement of the sponsors, enable some interesting feedback and encourage the sponsors to advocate for the team as well as motivate the team members when they see the interest being taken. Broadcasting obviously puts extra pressure on the team members, especially those who feel that their reputation depends on coming up with a final polished product before letting the rest of the world in. But the price of not broadcasting interim successes and priming key stakeholders for the output can be high.

> The transatlantic quality assurance team in Wellcome worked quietly and successfully against the trend of separate UK/American teams, learning a lot about how to span the Atlantic. When two years later the head of their department had the bright idea to restructure the whole of the R&D function into transatlantic teams, nobody came to the original team to ask how to do it. The one regret the excellent team leader had was not shouting louder at the time.

Team leaders also need to do anything that will keep the motivation up at this point, especially celebrate the interim successes. We are not suggesting placing either a Goofy or a Mickey mouse on European team member's desks on Friday afternoons. Nor placing an envelope of bonus money only on the desks of those team members who had been in the team for more than six months (with no explanation to the newcomers). However, publicly acknowledging team members involvement in preparing a team leader's external management review, publishing interim results and highlighting individual and team developments can all help to maintain a sense of ownership and belonging in the team.

15 Leaders sharing control and facilitators reducing their presence

As discussed in the following chapter, our belief is that facilitators are there to teach the team to manage themselves and so need to consciously reduce their presence at this point. Some external facilitators disagree with this view and almost become part of the team. However, if the facilitator cannot pass on his or her skills, how can the team members share their skills with new teams? Moreover, skilled facilitators who can cope when things are going badly wrong are usually in short supply. Similarly, if it is culturally appropriate, leaders should be controlling events as little as necessary by this stage and the team should be becoming self managing and accountable.

Phase Four: Closing Stages

16 Make sure everyone stays involved to the end

There is a great tendency to let team working collapse as deadlines press and especially to decide that the cost of involving distant members in finalising work is too great. This can undo a lot of earlier team building efforts and breed cynicism in those who feel suddenly excluded. This is where Groupware such as Lotus Notes, Novel's Groupwise, Collabra's Share and MS Outlook/Exchange to name a few, can really come into their own and prevent this kind of problem. If it has been introduced at the beginning, the team should be able to customise their work to suit their own needs.

17 Review the learning within the team

This is undoubtedly the most important part of wrapping up. Teams will only be able to work better together in the future if they can learn from their mistakes and share their successes. All the records of phase two and the interim reviews should be available. The performance on the task will ultimately be judged by the rest of the company, but immediate feedback can be actively sought from the sponsors. One team felt it had had a very difficult and turbulent time. However, when they got very positive feedback on their output from the Board, they began to change the way they felt about their difficulties and see them more as bouts of constructive conflict.

The team needs to review its process in a fairly formal way using all the background information to sort out what went well, what could be improved on, and to record specific intercultural problems and guidelines for other teams. Again written questionnaires and checklists can be helpful, as people may write down, especially anonymously, what they will not say in public. This written record demonstrates that as well as the task, the interactive process was something concrete, agreed upon and which developed over time. This is important.

It can be valuable to include the sponsors in the review process as it occurs, rather than collect their views and then feed it back to the team. Many international team sponsors have not been part of an international team themselves and cannot appreciate the peaks of enthusiasm and excitement and the troughs of despair. By participating in the review process they can begin to appreciate the energy and commitment that the team have contributed to the task.

This in turn makes them more able to sponsor future international teams effectively.

If you have worked with a facilitator throughout the lifecycle of the team, it can be valuable for a different 'neutral' facilitator to manage the review process. This enables the team facilitator to contribute to the content of the review and to provide the team with insights from their perspective. It also enables the whole team to be constructively critical about their interactive processes and the role the facilitator has played.

18 Celebrate the success and plan for the future

After their celebrations, the team needs to lay out an action plan of how the results can be fully implemented, evaluated and broadcast through the company. The team also needs to think about what the members are going to do next and if the project was longer than six months, how they are going to be re-integrated into the company and use the network that they have established in the team.

Sometimes new international project teams have no actual status in the company. It is regarded as high profile and good for personal development to be part of one, but often those that have stayed in the management line have gained more power and move up more easily.

19 The team needs to pass on what it has learnt to the rest of the organisation

The team needs to brainstorm how they are going to do this. In fact, this can also be a mid-phase (three) activity so that if there is a large group of new project leaders, they begin to explore ways to share their problems and creative solutions. Large formal gatherings attended by senior management are usually not conducive to sharing the mess ups. These are usually shared informally. Other methods that teams have suggested have included electronic databases, with the attendant problems of how to codify the learning to make it accessible, update it and manage its relevancy. One company set up a best practice office and all sorts of incentives for teams to share ideas. Social events and smaller scale forums are sometimes arranged around the larger formal reviews to which managers are already travelling. Newsletters, electronic white boards, mentoring schemes, a team leaders' network, lunch time briefings all usually figure as suggestions.

One large group of project leaders set up a smaller subgroup to see what would have most impact, was most practical and were then responsible for making it happen. Similarly a team needing to share its learning may need to set up a sub-team to spread the word. The methods chosen will depend on the organisation and probably the main national culture(s). Some cultures socialise easily out of hours, others do not. Some cultures will only take up what is passed on in person, others are happy learning from a computer. The chosen methods need to be multifaceted. Even so, the most concrete passing on should come as skilled team members go on to act as facilitators or proactive team members when they join another team. As we have emphasised from the start, internal and external facilitators should only act as catalysts for a process that then spreads 'systemically' throughout the organisation.

These nineteen practices form the basis of the four-phase model and it is important to note that the largest section is that which covers what needs to be done before the team ever meets. Some people say that nineteen practices are a lot for a new team to handle, which are the most important? As described before, it is an iterative process, so if the preparation is done well, then many problems will be avoided. However, the complete answer to the question of 'which one's are most important for my team?' can only be decided after understanding the model and knowing a specific team's main problems.

When a company is building a network of facilitators to support international teams, the model can create the framework for facilitators to share what they do at each stage and their different tool boxes. The key interventions that we have found useful at each stage are shared in the next chapter, along with an in-depth discussion of how to choose a facilitator and what a facilitator can do.

One of the overall goals of the interaction in an international team has often been described as 'intercultural synergy'. An alluring goal, but there are only vague hypotheses of what it is and how it happens, let alone which mixtures of skills and differences will most encourage it. So far, most people have opted for the 'recommended empathy' approach[9]. This goes something like 'understand your own cultural conditioning first then put yourself in the other person's shoes to try and understand their point of view. Then take the most relevant parts of each perspective and work out something new. This new culture may be reached through 'reconciliatory circles'[10] or through a process that builds on similarities and *fuses* differences' or, 'creates new forms of management and organisation that transcend the individual cultures of their members'[11].

Another common phrase 'integrating diversity', has been defined as 'combining elements into a unified result where the whole is greater than the sum of the parts and as such is synergistic'[12]. Reading such inspiring words can make the team leader feel good, creating the expectation that something truly out of the ordinary may happen in his/her team. However these ideas need 'unpicking' as well as relating to the day-to-day realities of being an international team.

First, no one thing can be greater than the sum of its parts except in very esoteric physics. What synergy can refer to is the process of working co-operatively and combining elements in such a way that the *effect* of that work is greater than if each person had worked independently. Using one main muscle allows me to bend my arm, using other groups of muscles allows me to clench my fist. If I do them in a co-ordinated way, clench first then lift, I can drink my tea. As the diversity in teams increases (cross national, functional, ethnic, gender, etc), more viewpoints, perceptions and experiences are expected to be brought to the whole. The down side is that team leaders need to work harder to co-ordinate and, as described in the previous two chapters, the team is more likely to have communication problems.

These are issues of co-ordination and process. There is, as such, no need to focus on what kind of 'new' culture a team will create for itself or whether this 'transcends' individual culture. We believe that this is unnecessary abstraction. Team members need to consciously share their individual approaches and then jointly weave a co-ordinated process that best fits their particular task and context. This sculpting leaves their individual viewpoints, perceptions, ways of seeing the world and communication styles intact, while also creating processes to access these differences at appropriate phases of the teamwork.

The first part of any sculpting process is a rough, fast and messy affair. Increasing precision is needed as the outcome becomes clearer, then each chisel blow or telephone call becomes more significant and has to be more finely tuned. The first team workshops are likely to be hot, steamy, intense and difficult, but the point is to provide the means for the team to learn to hone its own processes into a fine art. Mistakes and messiness can and need to happen early on.

We have witnessed enough broken alliances, destructive internal competition in loss making companies and half-baked results. Enough that is, to persuade anyone involved that actively doing something to make these teams work is worth it. Not doing anything tends to hurt a lot. Some teams are lucky and stumble across the goal of synergy and weave their differences into a working process that supports the task. However, unless they are skilled at managing their process, they often cannot explain how they achieved it. The best practices outlined in this chapter are the best way we have found to co-ordinate interaction and avoid disaster as well as being able to explain how you did it.

It is obvious that the model is primarily designed to fit a team with a specific task of set duration. As stated at the beginning, on-going teams need to take an interim activity as a starting point. Many companies do not see themselves as organised into tight teams with clear or on-going life cycles. International 'standing' work groups with expertise called in as needed often operate as loose networks. Even so, the key messages remain the same. 3 × 1 preparation for meetings; recognising and acknowledging differences; creating an open atmosphere where problems can be dealt with locally; using a variety of strategies to involve team members, especially temporary members; managing the geographical distance creatively and finding creative strategies to pass on the learning to the rest of the organisation.

Most international networks and teams are created to generate cross-border, cross-functional learning within the company or to achieve greater global efficiency by achieving an outcome that affects many people simultaneously. The dynamic interplay between global aims and local styles, similar goals but different ways of getting there are the sources of the potential energy to be tapped within multinational, multi-ethnic, multicompany and multifunctional teams. The life cycle model only provides the loom. It is up to each team to weave their brightest colours into the finest fabric they can achieve.

Chapter Five

Facilitating International Teams and Key Interventions

The objective of this chapter is to highlight how and when international teams can use a facilitator, what to look for when selecting an effective international facilitator and to highlight some interventions that facilitators use, that have proven to be effective with international teams.

As highlighted in earlier chapters, like any team, effective international teams must have the technical expertise to accomplish the task assigned to them by their organisation. The team also needs the ability to get individual team members from across the globe all working in the same direction. Senior management and HR have a key role in creating a supportive organisational context (see Chapters Eight and Nine), but more importantly, the international teams must actively manage the organisational context within which they are operating. They need to ensure that key sponsors and resource managers are kept well informed.

Chapter 7 highlights the interpersonal skills and attributes required to be an effective international leader, yet many organisations still select international team leaders and members based solely on their technical expertise. They do so despite evidence that technical skills are not the most critical attribute of international team members. As such, many international team leaders and members are often initially ill equipped to manage the more complex interaction within these teams, as well as the team's relationship with the rest of the organisation. An effective international facilitator can help the team develop an awareness of the critical issues they need to attend to and provide the team with the necessary skills to be effective as the following story illustrates:

> ### Facilitators: Providing a different perspective
>
> An international team was established to develop standardised procedures for adhering to new EU regulations. Each European office already had existing local policies and procedures and these needed harmonising into a European wide policy. The team met and agreed what they needed to achieve. However, at a subsequent meeting little progress had been made by the French and Italian representatives. The Swedish team leader was baffled by this lack of progress, as both representatives appeared to be committed to the team goals.
>
> A facilitator from the European HR organisation was invited by the team to come and work with them. The facilitator interviewed each of the team members by phone. She quickly established that team members understood the team's authority to make decisions in very different ways. Both the Italian and French representatives felt that the team could only make recommendations and that the final decision lay with the country general managers. The Swedish, British and German team members expected the team to make recommendations that would automatically be adopted by the general managers.
>
> At the next face-to-face meeting, the facilitator worked with the team to bring the underlying assumptions about critical working practices into the open: practices such as decision making; communication; leadership; performance reviews. The team members were then able to set some ground rules about how they could work together effectively in the future. The facilitator also helped the team to create a map of their key stakeholders and to then develop a communication strategy to influence the critical individuals. This intervention helped bring further assumptions about who needed to be influenced to the surface as well as educated the team members about the cultural differences that existed between different functions and countries within the same organisation.

If an organisation is just beginning to work globally and has only recently created international teams, they often underestimate the level of support needed by teams. Many organisations and teams call in facilitators when team deadlines have been missed, when a team member resigns from the team or when other symptoms appear to indicate that the team is heading for or currently in 'crisis'. The facilitator is sometimes seen as a 'trouble shooter', only to be called on when the going gets tough as the following example illustrates.

> **Where angels fear to tread ...**
>
> A phone call from a team sponsor informs me that one of the critical product development teams is in trouble. The team was established nine months ago and the team leader saw no need for facilitation support. The team sponsor explains that all appeared to be going well until yesterday when two team members arrived in her office and requested that they be removed from the team. After a few phone calls, the team sponsor has established that morale is extremely low amongst all team members. The team has a critical milestone in five weeks. They must deliver. Can I please meet with the team leader and get the team back on track?

This experience is not untypical. Yet this approach to supporting international teams has a damaging long-term consequence for an organisation's ability to operate internationally. If the experience of working on an international team is so painful, staff will soon not be prepared to work on them. Experience shows that when international facilitators work effectively with teams throughout their lifecycles, they can ensure that the 'strategic moments' experienced by the team are crafted into performance enhancing experiences and do not destroy the team's ability to function effectively. As one team member commented to her team facilitator *'we should have used you as preventative medicine rather than accident and emergency – it would have been less painful all round'*.

If a team chooses to work with a facilitator from their conception, they are demonstrating a commitment to ongoing learning – in good times and bad. This is likely to make the team experience more rewarding for the team members, it will enhance team performance and team members are more likely to be willing to serve on other international teams in the future.

What Is a Facilitator and When Do You Need One?

In the simplest terms, the role of a facilitator is to enable an international team to enhance its performance. For some, facilitation is passive and internally focused. In this case, the facilitator observes the interactions of the group and then provides 'off-line' feedback to the group to help them develop their awareness of the way they are working together. The focus, with a passive style of facilitation, is mostly on how the team itself is working.

Yet, as mentioned in earlier chapters, the relationship of an international team with the rest of the organisation is critical for its success and therefore, a facilitator of international teams needs to keep this external perspective clearly in focus.

> The model of facilitation that we are advocating for working with international teams is an *active and externally focused* role

The role of an active and externally focused facilitator could include:

- Coaching individual team leaders and members on working practices to enable them to work more effectively together.
- Supporting teams in managing the organisational context within which they work as this significantly impacts their ability to achieve their tasks.
- Providing skill development to teams as they require it rather than all at once at the beginning of their lifecycles. This enables teams to access skills as and when the task requires, rather than learning skills that they cannot put into practice or have forgotten about by the time they do need them.
- Facilitating meetings of the whole team. This enables team learning to take place that immediately impacts the team's ability to achieve its task.
- Designing process interventions to improve performance of the task.

Some of the advantages of this style of facilitation are:

- It can speed up the performance of an international team as interventions are tailored to the needs of each team.
- It actively develops the capabilities to operate globally as and when the teams require them.
- By watching facilitators role model best practice, team leaders and members can learn fast and the facilitator becomes redundant as soon as possible.
- The facilitators can carry best practice and learning from one team to another.

Whilst we advocate an active and externally focused style of facilitation, the specific activities undertaken by a facilitator are contingent on the organisational context in which the team is operating and the experience, skills and knowledge of the team leader and members. There is no universal formula for success: each international team is unique.

The aim of the facilitator should be to transfer his or her skills in enhancing the interaction and external relationships to the team, so that the team can manage itself. A facilitator can then systematically reduce their involvement. The time scale of this transfer of learning will vary according to the context of each team. If team members are keen to develop their own facilitation skills, this can happen after a few initial meetings, with the team calling on the facilitator for difficult meetings only. Sometimes a facilitator will need to be involved with the team for a longer period of time because all the team members need to actively participate in the *content* of a particular discussion and cannot simultaneously manage their *process*.

The critical issue is for the facilitator not to create dependence. This can happen when the team members are not willing or able to undertake facilitation themselves. An effective international team facilitator constantly challenges and questions a team as to why they feel they need the continued services of an independent facilitator. Thus the use of the facilitator should be built into the reviews of a team's working practices. The exit of the facilitator should be contracted at the beginning of the team's lifecycle and this contract reviewed periodically to ensure the facilitator is still adding value.

In summary, your team may need a facilitator because:

- **The complexities of working in an international team are new to both the team leader and team members.**
- **The team is much more skilled in the technical side of the task than in managing the process.**
- **The task demands that all the members will be exclusively focused on the content or much heated debate and disagreement is anticipated.**
- **Although experienced, the team feels that it could benefit from some alternative techniques and some feedback on how they are managing their process**.

If you have decided that an effective international facilitator is needed, how should you go about selecting or developing one?

Selecting and Developing a Facilitator

The facilitator's role as described is a challenging one – you are working on intellectual, emotional as well as physical levels simultaneously. The role requires a range of skills, knowledge and experience to carry it out successfully. One of the pleasures and frustrations of doing this work is that there is always more to learn. What we are therefore offering to you, the reader, is not a definitive competency profile of the ideal international facilitator that you could use to design your selection process, but rather a number of key areas that you might want to explore with potential facilitators. Some of these areas are skills that can be developed, some are knowledge based that can be learned and some are grounded in experience.

A word of caution is necessary at this point. There are very few individuals who possess all the attributes that will be discussed. One of the most effective ways of working with international teams is to co-facilitate with facilitators of complementary skills and experience working together to meet the needs of the team. This has the added advantage of simultaneously developing the range of skills of each individual facilitator. It is likely that the framework provided here will be used more frequently to develop individuals with interest and enthusiasm for this area, rather than select individuals who already possess all these attributes.

Skills

- Diagnostic and analytical skills
- Conflict resolution skills
- Language skills
- Working with unfamiliar topics
- Possesses extensive toolkit of interventions
- 'Real time' planning and design
- Culturally responsive feedback styles

A number of the skills mentioned here are not specific to international facilitators, but are included in this discussion to demonstrate the range and depth of skill that needs to be acquired before working effectively with international teams.

Diagnostic and analytical skills

An international team's facilitator can use questionnaires and/or interviews to assess the dynamics and needs of a team prior to the initial meetings. He or she will then need to make continual refinements to this assessment throughout the life cycle of the team. The facilitator also needs to be able to make judgements about which diagnostic tools are culturally appropriate for the situation. For instance, by looking at what a person chooses to say, the amount of personal disclosure and how they say it, sometimes open format biographies can tell you an enormous amount about a person, even if you do not get standard comparable information. The facilitator needs to be able to objectively analyse and make sense of the responses. The range of diagnostic tools available to the international facilitator is discussed later in the chapter.

Conflict resolution skills

A facilitator of an international team is often faced with a number of dilemmas – even in her own choice of actions. By adopting a particular approach, she may accommodate some of the team and alienate others. The numerous agendas, organisational and personal, which are often present within international teams, increase the potential for diverse views on a particular issue. If these are not handled sensitively, they can soon escalate into conflict. This diversity can also create undercurrents that make accurate diagnosis difficult. As pointed out in Chapter Three, recognition of the varying expression of conflict by different nationalities is also a skill that needs to be developed. For instance, what is taken to be aggressive behaviour by one team member may well be seen as appropriate debate and discussion by another. Developing culturally appropriate conflict resolution skills is a critical part of an international facilitator's development.

Language skills

In many international teams, English is the chosen working language and most facilitators would need a strong command of the English language to work in this environment. However, the ability to be able to work in the mother tongue of team members enhances a facilitator's depth. It can also be seen as a symbol that the facilitator is credible. A facilitator must take care that if she is fluent in the languages of the dominant cultures of the organisation, that she does not reinforce this dominance. As described in Chapters Two and Three, a facilitator also has to be sensitive to the way a language is used and to the meanings of different silences and interruption patterns.

Working with unfamiliar topics

Often a facilitator will be working with a team whose remit is a highly technical one: eg development of a new global technical specification for microchips; registration of a novel medicine for Alzheimer's; agreeing the project plan for a network of hydroelectric power stations along the length of the Amazon. A key skill is the ability to follow the flow of the discussion, to be able to identify diversions and digressions and summarise key themes without having a detailed knowledge of the topic under discussion. Good facilitators do some homework before the first team meeting. Much credibility is gained by demonstrating a willingness to understand key issues and technical terms from specialist staff.

Possesses extensive toolkit of interventions

This skill is particularly critical when working with an international team. There is a need to have a wider and deeper range of interventions at your disposal in order to accommodate the myriad of cultural preferences present in the teams. Effective international facilitators will examine and experiment with a newly acquired tool or technique to assess its cultural bias as what may work in one culture may be highly offensive in another. 'Does the team fly by the seat of its pants?' may be fine in America, but will confuse most Latin Americans, Europeans and Africans. International facilitators cannot assume that one model fits all. Again, details of types of interventions are discussed later in the chapter.

'Real time' planning and design

Session and meeting design is a fundamental skill of effective international facilitators. Inexperienced facilitators should invest significant time prior to working with the team, by working collaboratively with the client to agree not only the outcomes of the task, but also agreement on the processes to be used. A good design, owned by the client, will provide a solid foundation to work with a team for the first time.

A hallmark of an experienced international facilitator is the ability to 'think on one's feet'. They are able to stay engaged with a team and follow the flow of the discussion, whilst simultaneously anticipating what problems may arise from the discussion and deciding what strategies can be adopted to bring the issue to a satisfactory resolution. They are able to plan meetings thoroughly and yet are prepared to change that plan as issues emerge – sometimes the original design will change many times during the course of the meeting. The skill to 'think on one's feet' is developed over time through working with a range of international teams.

Culturally responsive feedback styles

Developing a range of feedback styles is important if facilitators are going to work effectively with multicultural teams. Understanding that your natural style of feedback is not universally appropriate is a critical early lesson. You can develop this skill by knowing your own personal feedback preferences. You can explore with the team how they wish to handle feedback. Be sensitive to the level of self disclosure that is culturally appropriate for the individuals you are working with. Partnering with a co-facilitator with a different style can be a useful way of experiencing alternative styles of working with teams.

Knowledge

- Knowledge of organisational development (OD)
- Knowledge of business principles
- Knowledge of how to facilitate change in organisations
- Knowledge of cultural norms and intercultural communication literature
- Knowledge of adult and experiential learning in different cultures

There are several fields of knowledge that experienced international facilitators draw on. Some of these are prerequisites to developing the skills discussed earlier, but some are important in their own right. The purpose of this discussion is to highlight the relevant fields of interest – each has an extensive body of literature which readers can access – rather than to discuss the topics in any detail.

Knowledge of organisational development (OD)

An emphatic message throughout this book is that international teams exist within organisational systems and the nature of the organisational system has a significant impact on the effectiveness of teams. For facilitators to work successfully with international teams, they need to understand how organisations function and how to identify the key mechanisms and levers within the system that teams can use to facilitate their success. They need to understand how to intervene in the wider system so that they can coach and support the teams they are working with on how to manage their external relationships.

Knowledge of business principles

Although it is not necessary to have a formal qualification in business to be an effective international team facilitator, it is critical that the facilitator knows the key components of a business, understands the key interconnections between the parts and has sufficient awareness of the key drivers. The facilitator can then appreciate the frequent conflicting demands made on international team members and help the team to put their task into the wider organisational context.

Knowledge of how to facilitate change in organisations

To successfully accomplish their goals, many international teams will need to facilitate change within the wider organisational system. Facilitators need to know a range of models and strategies for how change occurs in organisations in order that they can educate the teams they are working with and provide them with appropriate responses.

Knowledge of cultural norms and the intercultural communication literature

Whether or not they are using them directly, an international facilitator needs to know the detail of and to have assessed the usefulness of the work on cultural dimensions.* They need to have a rough idea of where different nationalities lie on different dimensions and examples of the implications. They need to build up a storehouse of stories and anecdotes that demonstrate all angles of cultural difference.

Both Hofstede's and Fons Trompenaars' work of how different cultures vary across certain value dimensions are readily available for use as common frameworks. The facilitator has to demonstrate expertise, to know the latest work and books that address cultural differences. This knowledge does not replace the experience of having lived or worked in other cultures, but it adds

---

* See Appendix One

important tools and credibility. Anecdotes are important to show the range of the facilitator's experience and also to turn around certain situations. If one nationality is treating another with disdain, a quick story showing that people from that nationality can make mistakes or look stupid, from another angle, can send a strong hint of the need for a change of attitude, before more direct action is needed.

Knowledge of adult and experiential learning in different cultures

International teams often lack the required skills to successfully meet the challenges they have been set. The role of the facilitator is therefore often an educator, assisting the team to learn and develop the appropriate skills as required. In order to be able to do this, facilitators need to have an understanding of the way adults learn in different cultures and to be able to adapt the learning experience to the learning styles within the team.

Knowledge of a wide variety of experiential learning techniques is invaluable. Any tool or learning approach which does not rely on the individual's command of the chosen working language (usually English) is particularly appropriate for international teams.

Experience

- Living through major change
- Engaging with the organisation and the team
- Working with your cultural bias
- Political awareness

Experience is probably the most intangible aspect of an international facilitator's role. What we offer here are observations based on facilitating international teams over many years.

Living through major change

An observation we have made about the most successful international facilitators we have worked with, is that they have all experienced significant personal life transitions and have developed a range of healthy coping strategies. Many have lived for extended periods of time immersed in another culture. This experience reinforces the fact that no one view, including one's own, is right or wrong, only different. It often forces you to re-assess a wide range of values. This can help you realise that you can change much of your mindset without losing your core identity. This flexibility, not to hold or be held to a set intellectual line or approach, is essential if you are going to facilitate an international team.

Perhaps long-term experience in another culture is not essential, major life shifts such as marriage, divorce, redundancy can all teach the same lessons. Good facilitators have often had to cope with upheaval and considerable change and have used these experiences to learn more about themselves. This leads to an emotional resilience that can enable them to remain grounded when the teams or organisations they are working with become dysfunctional.

Engaging with the organisation and the team

Knowing when to accept an invitation to work with a particular international team and when to say no is a judgement that you can develop. As a company internal facilitator, you will already have made the decision to engage with the organisation and your experience should be used to identify where your skills and knowledge can be most appropriately applied to enhance the performance of the organisation's international teams.

You need to learn how to avoid situations when the facilitator's role is inappropriately defined. This can occur when the team does not wish to learn themselves and builds a dependency on the facilitator. This does not develop the capability of the team members to run effective international teams without external support and therefore does not enhance the long-term team and organisational performance. At the most extreme, courage is needed to withdraw from a situation, if it is not possible to influence the view of the client to a more healthy and balanced relationship.

> In one such case, an HR manager of a group of 30 had insisted that the facilitator only observe and give feedback. She worked hard to get clarity that this was what he really meant. The answer was always yes, only observe and give feedback afterwards. During his presentation, the manager stopped in midstream and asked the facilitator to take over. Had she stood up at that moment, he would have lost all credibility with his whole team. The facilitator smiled and stayed seated and hurriedly started to write some slides for him to use. Afterwards the manager said he was unimpressed and did not understand what her role was.

As well as being asked to be a passive observer, warning bells should also go off when the leader wants to use the facilitator to push a certain agenda, or if they are being asked to co-facilitate with someone who has a very fixed intellectual idea of the way things should happen. These are examples of when to consider saying no.

Experienced facilitators working across a range of teams within an organisation can also play a valuable role by observing the patterns and themes emerging and summarise those for the organisation. Giving overall feedback while maintaining the confidentiality and discretion of each team, can help the organisation to identify systemic issues that need to be addressed in a broader context. Resolution of issues that exist in the wider organisation can enhance the environment for the individual teams.

Working with your cultural bias

A facilitator cannot support international teams effectively unless they have recognised that they have a particular cultural lens through which they view the world. Their work is inherently culturally biased. However, as mentioned, effective international facilitators have developed an appreciation that it is only a bias and there is no one 'right' way. It is important to allow oneself to be laughed at when one's bias becomes evident.

Each of us starts with a preferred 'toolkit' that we have developed over time, with which we are most comfortable and find to be most effective. We are not saying that these tools and techniques should be ignored. However, just because something is considered 'best practice' in one culture, does not make it universally applicable. Each time an international facilitator begins to work with a new team, they must use their experience to judge the appropriateness of each intervention, dependent on the cultural preferences of the team. There are no universal answers.

Political awareness

Experienced international facilitators have developed a sensitivity to the *political environment* of the organisation in which international teams operate. International teams are often a microcosm of the wider organisation and issues faced by the team are often symptomatic of difficulties in the wider system. Teams need to recognise these pressure points and leverage them to their advantage. Facilitators are often well positioned to sense these pressure points, as they are not so closely focused on the task. This enables them to work with the team in managing the team's boundaries effectively. They can coach the team to begin to focus externally and to sense what is happening in the organisation, which might impact their ability to do their job. Helping the team to understand the informal as well as the formal organisational system can also facilitate team performance. A word of warning at this point – this organisational knowledge and the insights into the informal system can be threatening to some managers and team members. In one organisation team members became suspicious of facilitators who were assigned to work with them, often referring to them as 'management spies'. It is critical to explicitly negotiate the confidentiality contract with team sponsors, leaders and members to prevent this concern emerging.

Three other critical issues should be mentioned here although they are neither skills, knowledge or experience. However, they should be actively explored if you are either considering becoming an international team facilitator or looking to select or develop one.

Passion

Some individuals have a passion for working with people from different countries and have strong feelings about the negative impact of narrow-minded prejudices. We are not suggesting that being a cross-cultural facilitator is like being a new age missionary – spreading the word of universal brotherhood, as a participant once suggested. However, when choosing a facilitator, if you do not get the feeling that the person you are looking at or developing is not passionate about this work, then look elsewhere. There will be times when the facilitator needs to be fully present with all faculties working, digging and probing for long periods of time. That stubbornness, passion, curiosity, whatever you want to call it, to get to the end of the job whatever it takes, and to enthuse others along the way is essential and contagious. It will win the team's respect.

Physical and emotional resilience

The very nature of the role involves significant amounts of travelling, often alone, and working across several time zones. Even when you are working from your home base, you are working at unsociable hours in order to be able to connect with team members in other time zones. This plays havoc with your personal and social life and individuals need to explore whether this fits with their preferred lifestyle. You have to be able to nurture yourself in far-flung places when the going gets tough, like recovering from having to start the karaoke session as guest of honour when you did not know any of the songs on the record.

Extensive travelling can also take its toll on your health and individuals need resilience to be able to perform effectively even if they have just stepped off a plane after a 13-hour flight. Maintaining some balance and ensuring that you give yourself time to relax and recharge is critical – workaholics burn out and they do not provide the teams with positive role models.

Emotional and professional support

Given the nature of the work, we cannot emphasise enough how important it is to ensure that you have a robust support network – both emotionally and professionally. Working with international teams often means you are uncovering messy issues and working in the shadowy side of the organisation. If you are an internal consultant, this can be a very exhausting place to be. Some mechanisms we have found useful are:

Co-facilitating

Working in partnership with another colleague. This provides you both with the opportunity to observe each other and provide feedback on style and habits. It enables one of you to observe the group's reactions to the other's interventions and suggest how to do things differently if things get stuck.

Supervision

We use this word in the counselling sense. Identify someone who you can meet with on a regular basis to talk through your experiences with the international teams. They should be able to help you to sift through your reactions to the teams and separate your emotional responses from your professional judgements. They should help surface your biases, prejudices and assumptions that are blocking you being effective in working with the teams.

Key Interventions Throughout the Team's Lifecycle

Having explored the key attributes of an international team facilitator, the latter part of this chapter focuses on the interventions that can be used throughout the team's life cycle. The previous chapter outlined a model of best practice for working with international teams and what teams can do at each stage of their life cycle. Facilitators have identified a number of interventions (tools and techniques) which are effective when used with international teams.

One technique which can be used throughout the life cycle of the team and which has proved very successful with a range of international teams, is 'Metaplan'. This is a brand name for a low technology group brainstorming and prioritising technique that uses pin boards, large sheets of brown paper and a range of shaped cards and templates. It is well structured, makes everyone's contributions visual and helps to prevent anyone dominating or being excluded from the process. The use of Metaplan or other nominal grouping techniques can be helpful in bringing out the different ways in which individuals understand the goal and task. It has many advantages for use with international teams as highlighted in Figure 5.1.

Advantages of Metaplan

- Gets people to write before they talk – this plays to introverts and reflective cultures and allows participants working in their second or third language time to contribute fully.
- It keeps in check the extroverts and dominant cultures in a non-confrontational way.
- Gets a lot of ideas contributed in a very short space of time.
- It is simple technology and can be used anywhere.
- It gets participants on their feet which changes the pace and keeps the energy high.
- It brings the group physically together around the Metaplan boards for grouping and prioritising.

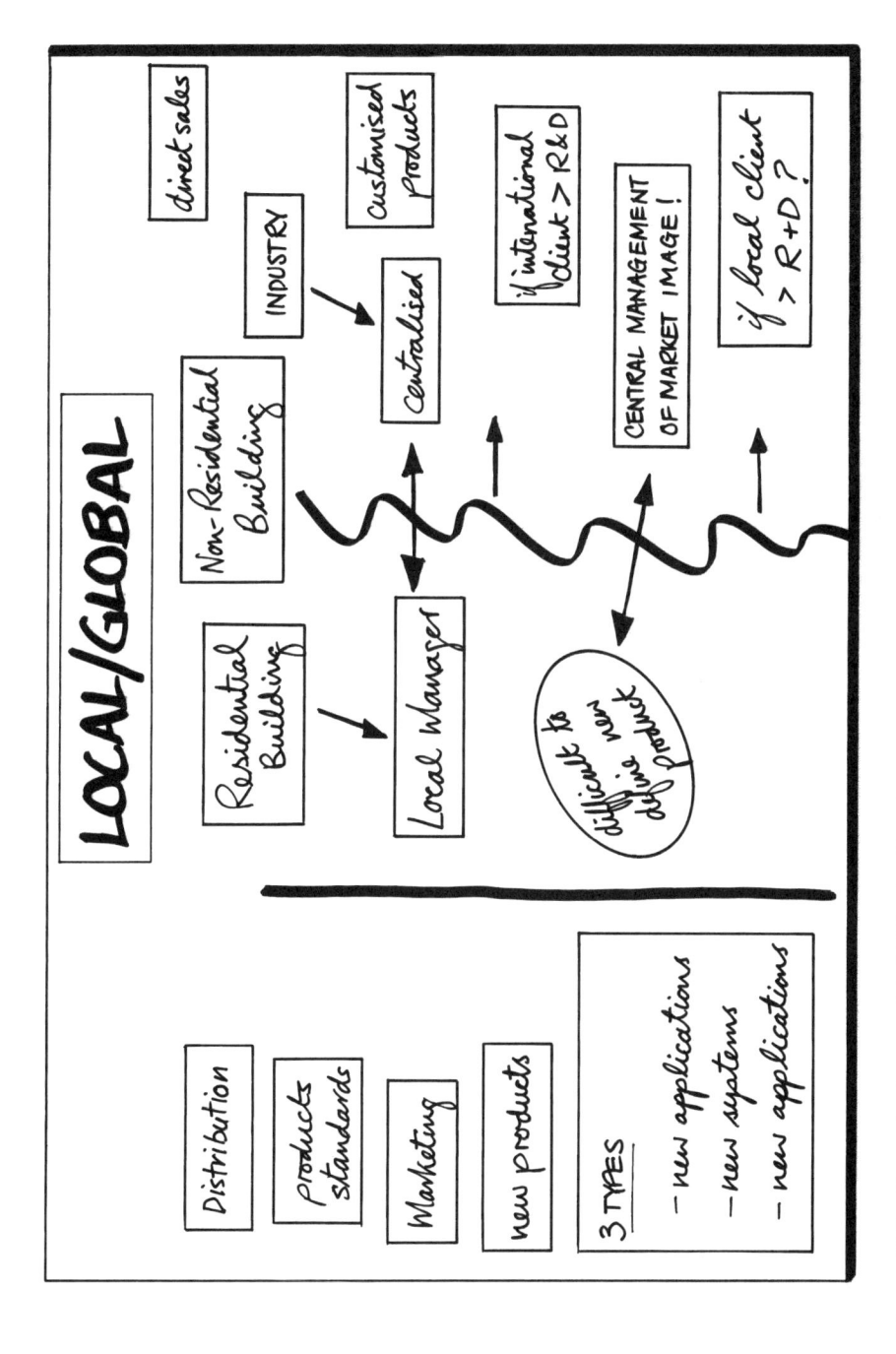

Figure 5.1: Example of a completed Metaplan Board

Phase One: Start up, Pre meeting

Before the first meeting, a facilitator needs to familiarise herself with all the issues that the team leaders have been considering (see Chapter Four) and have thought about the team. The key action here is to get to know the team so that difficulties can be anticipated. The eight factors highlighted in Chapter Two, provide a framework to structure this initial familiarisation process. As noted in Chapter Four, this preparatory stage of working with international teams is often underestimated. Yet a thorough preparation creates significant dividends once the team starts working. If the team has chosen to work with a facilitator (s)he needs to ensure that sufficient time is available for preparation.

This preparation consists primarily of data gathering, diagnosis of the main issues likely to impact the team and designing the first interactions of the team. A facilitator needs to take into account the most appropriate way of gathering this initial information about the team. This will be the first interaction with team sponsors, leaders and members and the facilitator needs to ensure that no cultural blunders occur at this early stage that may adversely impact the ongoing work with the team.

For example, in cultures that value developing relationships as a basis for conducting business it is preferable to do the initial data gathering in person. Face to face or telephone interviews can be used to identify expectations and concerns of all the team members and begin to build trust between team members and facilitators. Some individuals will feel very uncomfortable and even offended if they receive a pack of information and questionnaires through the post, with no previous personal interaction.

Questionnaires, checklists, inventories are all useful tools for gathering data about a variety of topics: personality; work style; leadership preferences; values. The choice of questionnaires available to an international facilitator is extensive, yet some are too complex, culturally biased or too simplistic to use with international teams. Care must be taken about the language used in questionnaires – does it use idioms that are inappropriate for team members who do not have English as their first language? Sometimes simplicity is the key, as the following example illustrates:

> A highly mixed international team wanted to create a middle ground between totally impersonal and over personal feedback. They chose a framework where green stood for people, red for action and blue for ideas, and analysed their preferences. Later on, during the teamwork, 'Excuse me Mr Ho, can you be a little less red and a bit more green' was an inoffensive way for an Australian to tell a Hong Kong Chinese man to stop being so aggressive and fall in line with the team. Even Mr Ho laughed.

Many facilitators from Western cultures may be used to using a range of questionnaires to elicit information about the team members' personalities, work style, learning or communication preferences; values and working practices. This can provide the facilitator with valuable insights prior to working with a team. However, this benefit has to be weighed against the risk of upsetting team members who feel uncomfortable about disclosing such personal information before meeting and working with the other members of the team.

Phase Two: First Meetings

The initial interactions of international teams can take place face to face or remotely. Experience has demonstrated that if teams are going to meet face to face, then they benefit most, early on in their life cycle. This enables the team members to establish strong ground-rules that are workable and understood by all members of the team. During these first meetings a number of interventions have proved to be effective across a range of international teams. These can be done face to face or remotely using videoconferencing.

As emphasised in the previous chapter, the most important first step is to get a shared understanding and commitment to the overall purpose and deliverables of the team by the team sponsors, the team leader and team members. This is no different than working with homogenous teams but can be a more complex and lengthy process due to the range of diverse backgrounds, and therefore the variety of views and assumptions. Teams that rush this task and do not develop real clarity will only find that they are forced to attend to it in future meetings. This is not to say that due to emerging issues, the deliverables may not change over time – organisational reality suggests this will always be the case. However, discussing and agreeing subsequent changes to timelines, resources, deliverables is much easier if team members have at least all started on the same page.

For better or worse, outward bound courses are becoming a popular way of aiming to build this initial trust amongst team members. Unfortunately, or fortunately for some, there is little evidence that hanging off cliffs together helps long-term performance on business tasks. Our experience has shown us that working creatively on the actual task that the team has to deliver provides a much richer environment for learning and ensures that the teams get an accelerated start. All of the interventions we recommend are therefore aimed at encouraging the teams to address the real issues facing them as a team. Some of the exercises that can be used in these team start-up sessions are outlined below:

- Mapping the team life cycle
- Role negotiation
- Stakeholder analysis
- Establishing working practices
- Communication charters

Mapping the team life cycle

Map out the four phases of the team life cycle for the whole team on large sheets of paper or flipcharts (see Figure 5.3).

Get the team to brainstorm what needs to happen in each stage. Then identify and fill in any gaps and discuss how to implement them. This helps the team see the context of the journey they are about to embark upon and highlight where they are going to need extra resources and will need to manage the organisational context.

Role negotiation

Enabling the team to get clarity about who is responsible for what and surfacing assumptions about the way work will get done is a critical early task for international teams. As a first step, team members need to be clear about what needs to be achieved by the whole team and then identify who is going to be responsible for what. At this point, the facilitator needs to ensure that the team is not just focusing on the tangible tasks and deliverables, but also allocates responsibilities for issues like managing external boundaries; communicating with team sponsors; managing team learning etc. This should not all be left to the team leader. One participative way to do this is to have large boards, each one headed with a key role, eg Project team leader, team manager, facilitator and team member. One vertical half of the board is for questions and the other half is for answers. The team then splits into small groups who each take a board and start listing questions about that role. After ten minutes the small groups circulate to the next board and add questions and start trying to answer the other questions. This goes on until each group has written on each board and then the questions and answers are discussed in plenary.

It is particularly important that team members gain a shared understanding about how their roles on the team interact with their roles back in the local workplace. Often international teams are established in addition to individual's existing responsibilities. It is then critical to establish local manager's expectations with regard to their staff participating on this team?

Once roles are clarified, the team needs to work out suitable appraisal and development schemes for team members who are being fully seconded for a longer period. If the team members are part-time members of the team, then the balance of their team work with their line work needs to be worked out and mechanisms for resolving potential conflicts agreed.

Stakeholder analysis

This is one of the most important first tasks that a team needs to undertake. It often needs to happen in parallel with clarifying the team's purpose and deliverables. Only if a team can accurately identify the myriad of stakeholders (often with conflicting needs and expectations) can they be sure they are delivering the right output to the right person at the right time.

Facilitating International Teams and Key Interventions 129

BEFORE THE FIRST MEETINGS

1. SET OUTCOMES
- Draft/agree objectives
- Define and communicate objectives
- Clarify the purpose of the meeting
- Each team member to think about what they want
- Define outcomes
- Clarify success
- Discuss what sponsor/owners want from project

2. PREPARE
- ID stakeholders
- Understand history
- Identify resource needs/constraints
- Agree membership
- Decide who should attend

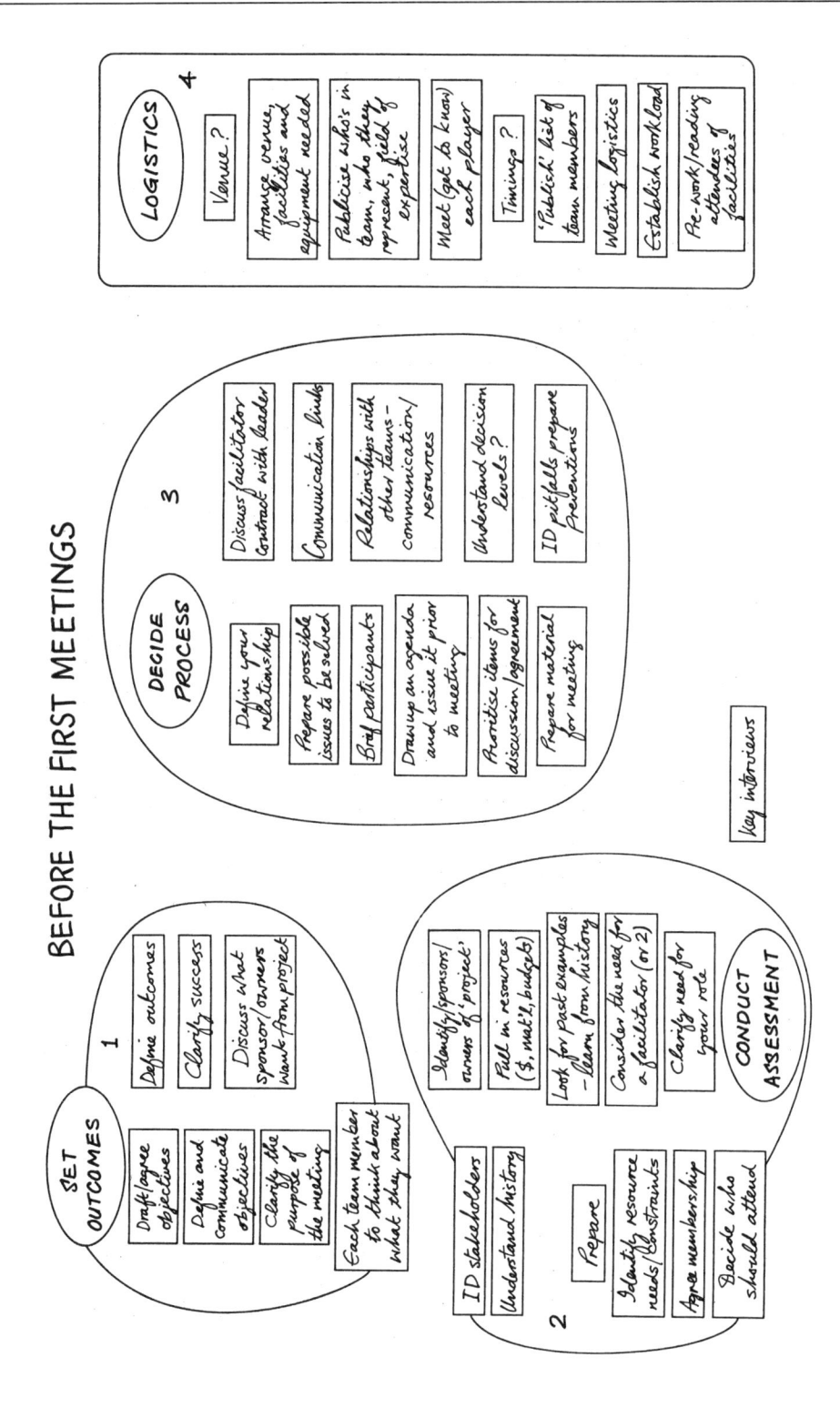

CONDUCT ASSESSMENT
- Identify sponsor/owners of 'project'
- Pull in resources ($, mat'l, budget)
- Look for past examples — learn from history
- Consider the need for a facilitator (or 2)
- Clarify need for your role

Key interviews

3. DECIDE PROCESS
- Define your relationship
- Prepare possible issues to be solved
- Brief participants
- Draw up an agenda and issue it prior to meeting
- Prioritise items for discussion/agreement
- Prepare material for meeting
- Discuss facilitator contract with leader
- Communication links
- Relationships with other teams — communication/resources
- Understand decision levels?
- ID pitfalls, prepare preventions

4. LOGISTICS
- Venue?
- Arrange venue, facilities and equipment needed
- Publicise who's in team, who they represent, field of expertise
- Meet (get to know) each player
- Timings?
- 'Publish' list of team members
- Meeting logistics
- Establish workload
- Pre-work/reading attendees & facilities

Figure 5.3: Example of Phase 1 on Metaplan Board

It is usually helpful to get each team member to spend some time thinking about stakeholders from their local perspective and to share these with the other team members. This will help to surface any differences about who the team member needs to influence to be successful within their local context. For example, members of international teams who originate from some Asian cultures, may have a complex web of colleagues back in the workplace who would need to be consulted or informed before the team member would feel able to make a decision in the team. If the other team members did not understand this process for getting commitment to a decision, they may impose unrealistically tight timelines for decisions. Getting support for international team decisions locally, is critical if the implementation of those decisions is to be successful.

Once individuals have shared their perceptions of the local stakeholders, a stakeholder map can be constructed for the team. At this point it can be valuable to assess the nature of the relationship with the key stakeholders. For example, who has decision-making authority? Who has key resources within their remit? Who is influential in the wider organisation? With team members with differing language skills, visual tools and techniques to create stakeholder maps are preferable.

Once the stakeholders are identified, the team can assess how effective the existing relationship is with each stakeholder. They can then develop appropriate communication and influencing strategies and prioritise what actions need to be taken to develop the relationships for the future. This information is invaluable when the team begins to map out its Communication Charter.

Establishing working practices

Given the range of perspectives usually present in an international team, gaining early agreement on the way to work is critical. Answers to the following questions need to be thought through and agreed:

- How will we make decisions? What does consensus mean?
- How will we give each other feedback?
- How will we evaluate our performance? What constitutes effective performance?
- How will conflicts be resolved?
- How will we design and conduct our meetings?
- How will we communicate our progress?

As we have kept emphasising, a useful tool for surfacing assumptions about the way individuals prefer to work is to use a cultural value checklist*. We have found it to be very valuable with a wide range of international teams. It draws on the work by Hofstede and Trompenaars**.

* See example in Appendix Two.
** See Appendix One.

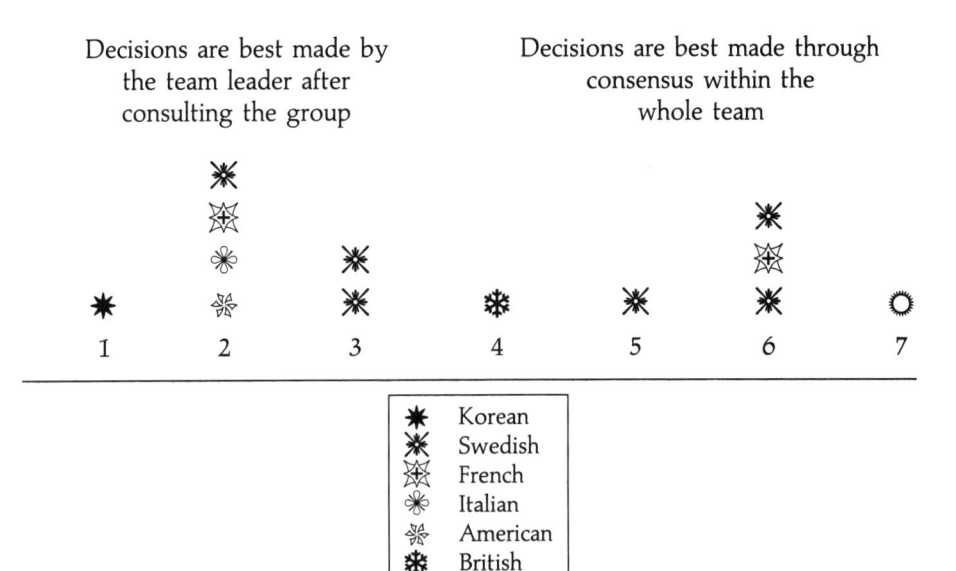

Decisions are best made by
the team leader after
consulting the group

Decisions are best made through
consensus within the
whole team

```
          ✳
          ✵
          ✻            ✳
   ✳      ✵     ✳                ✳        ✳
                                           ✵
                        ✺      ✳   ✳       ✳        ○
   1      2     3       4      5   6                7
```

Symbol	Nationality
✳	Korean
✳	Swedish
✵	French
✻	Italian
✺	American
✺	British
○	Danish

Figure 5.4: Example of a flip-charted cultural value checklist

Once the checklist has been introduced, each participant fills it in individually. If you have a lot of time, the team members can form small groups and discuss why they have put their crosses and circles in similar or different places. The discussion is usually deep and insightful, especially concerning people's different interpretations of the words on the checklist. If time is short and the team needs to move on and set the ground rules, then the two extremes of each dimension with the scale in the middle can be put onto horizontal flip charts around the wall. Each nationality can then be given different coloured stickers to mark their crosses of how they would like it to be above the line and different divisions or teams, depending on the group, can be given different coloured stickers to plot their circles of how they think the reality is below the line. This gives an instantaneous visual picture of the team members' similarities and differences that the team can then discuss in detail, as illustrated in Figure 5.4.

Communication charters

> 'It's knowing who to communicate to and when – everyone moans about information overload and then complains about not being kept in touch.'

Effective communication is absolutely critical to the success of international teams. They have to be more disciplined and to develop a regular and frequent rhythm if they are going to gain momentum and keep motivation high. The team's communication charter needs to identify *who* they need to communicate

Communication Charter for Project Team B

WHO?	TOPIC/ISSUE?	METHOD?	WHEN?
Regulatory	liaise with external regulators re new bill submitted to parliament re conversion	phone and face to face meeting	tomorrow and week next Friday
Clinical	briefing European and Asian colleagues on next actions	focus groups – VC and f to f	before budget submission deadline
Marketing	latest trial data from Japan	written confidential report	before next review
Finance	budget figures for next quarter	fax	tomorrow
Facilitator	design quarterly meeting with sub team Inform team of development opps	video conf and email Bulletin board	by end of month Monthly update
Project Manager	Updates to sponsor update wider network	Face to face email	Weekly monthly

Figure 5.5: Communication Charter

with; *when* they need to communicate with them and *how*, ie what communication method is preferable the beginnings of which are shown in the Metaplan (Figure 5.5).

A useful exercise to do as a precursor to drafting the communication charter is to have team members outline their perceptions of the advantages and disadvantages of the different methods of communication (see Figure 5.6 and also Chapter Six).

Phase Three: Mid Point

As noted in Chapter Four, this is the phase where the teams will be focused on achieving the milestones set in the first meetings and much of the work will be done from a distance. However, teams need to stay connected during this phase and as described in Chapter Four, this is when teams will need to work through 'strategic moments'. Facilitators can really add value to the teams at this stage by helping them work through strategic moments, paying attention to the ground rules the team agreed.

During this phase, facilitators can help teams improve their effectiveness by developing their feedback capabilities and by developing the skills they require to complete their tasks successfully.

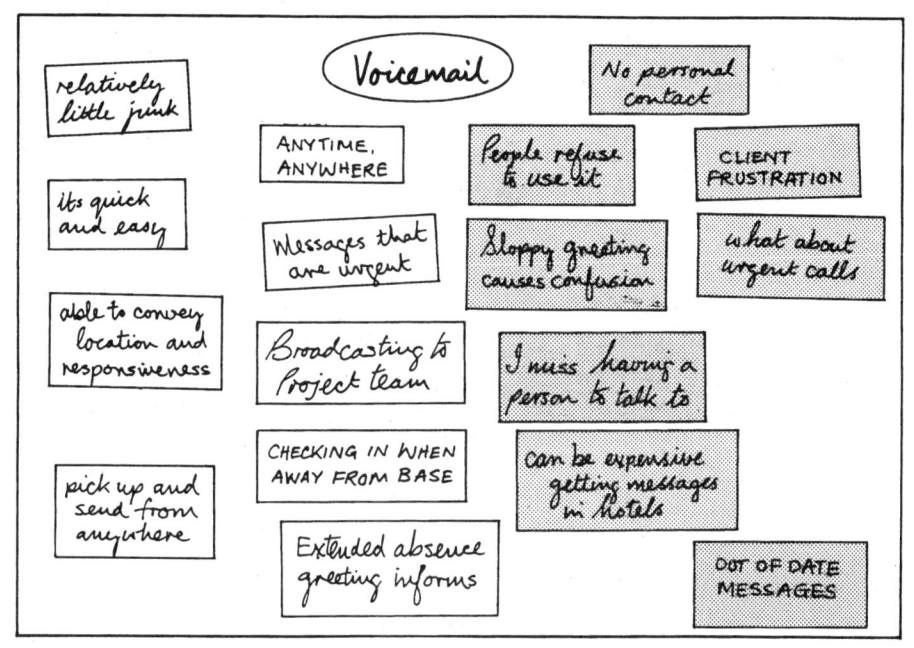

Figure 5.6: Advantages and Disadvantages of communication choices

Develop feedback skills and processes

There are a range of *increasingly in-depth* techniques that can be used to raise the team's awareness about how they are working and provide them with some tools including:

- The facilitator and/or team member observes half an hour of the team's interaction whilst they are working on a task*. They can then feed back the observations to the team and facilitate a discussion about whether the communication patterns they have adopted are useful or if some team members are being excluded or marginalised. A checklist can be used to record the contributions made by each team member. At the simplest level it can be enough to record who spoke, for how long and to whom. When the observers have developed their skills they will be able to consider the nature of the contribution made by each team member – for example, does it build on others contributions? Does it block the conversation? Who is interrupting who? What is their reaction? What is the level of simultaneous talk?
- Designing customised review questionnaires based on the ground rules established by the group**. These can be completed at different stages of

---

*See form in Appendix Two.
**See Appendix Two.

the team's lifecycle to track how they are performing over time. It can also provide an early warning signal if any member of the team is beginning to feel marginalised.
- Videoing part of the team meeting and then replay the video to the team and ask them to discuss what they observed on the recording. Get them to think about the actual behaviours they observed versus the espoused behaviours they aspire to, as documented in the ground rules.

These three modes of feedback can be done in this order so that the team gets slowly used to increasingly in-depth feedback on their interaction. Most teams are reluctant to start with something as real time and 'exposing' as being filmed on a video camera.

As discussed previously, we advocate providing skills development to international teams 'just in time', eg problem-solving techniques, conflict resolution tools. For example, each time a group has brainstormed and need to prioritise their lists, the facilitator can introduce different techniques for prioritisation. The team should review the pros and cons of each technique as they use it so that they develop their awareness of when to use certain techniques.

This requires the facilitator to have an extensive 'toolkit' available that can be accessed by the group as the need arises. We reiterate again (like a broken record) that care needs to be taken to ensure that the interventions selected by the facilitator are culturally appropriate for the group. Simulations can work effectively with multicultural groups as they enable the behaviour patterns to surface quickly and the learning can be very rich.

Phase Four: Closing Stages

This last section will explore what support facilitators can give to international teams to ensure that this final phase is successful. Chapter Four briefly explored the issue of evaluation and emphasised the importance of reviews once the team's task has come to completion. It is this phase where the facilitator's organisational awareness is important: they can help the team to connect with others in the organisation who could benefit from their learning.

Celebrating what was achieved is an important aspect of maintaining morale and keeping staff excited about continuing to work on international teams. However, given the dynamic nature of the workplace, teams can often be disbanded, reconfigured or refocused before they are officially 'complete'. If the team and the organisation are going to gain maximum benefit, it is important that the team is officially ended and a final review of what has been achieved and learnt is conducted. The facilitator needs to work with the team sponsors and leader to ensure this happens. In too many organisations, effective team leaders are quickly allocated to new teams and time is not built in to reflect on their experience.

A word of warning: the first time a team is asked to conduct a project review that focuses on both the task output and the interactive process, the facilitator may need to provide clear instructions and examples to help start the process.

> One team we worked with was given pens and flipcharts and asked to 'draw' their process. Some individuals drew a large round cartoon face with a smile, while others sat with empty pages, staring at the facilitator as if she was mad. For some, there was no concept of the journey that had been taken. The person who had held the team together was the only one to spend a long time drawing a long curving river, with many tributaries flowing in and out of it.
>
> An argument quickly broke out as to whether the task had any meaning or value. Only the river man avidly supported the exercise.

Many people do not have any concepts within which to frame an interactive process. It is something that just happens and you can forget about it once the task is complete.

> One successful team leader was asked by another how her team had achieved the tasks set them, the initial reply was 'We got on well and things just fell into place', which did not help the new leader to learn what he could be doing differently. He tried again, 'Yes but what did you do?' to which he got the curt response: 'Worked of course'.

This is where we come back to the importance of using the four phase model with international teams throughout their life cycle. It gives structure to and demonstrates the reality of talking about 'how' you are doing something as well as 'what' you are doing. As Peter Drucker has said, 'what managers do is the same the world over, it is how they do it that is different'. It is this difference we want to capture in these final team reviews.

Evaluation can be usefully viewed through the lenses of the life cycle model. The relevant issues can be evaluated at each stage as well as at the end. One piece of research[1] found that clarity of mission was the only factor that related to research and development project success across all four team stages. Table 5.1 gives a rough guide of what other aspects of the task and interaction need to be assessed at which stages.

Care must be taken to measure what the team agrees is relevant at each stage. International teams obviously have a lot more in-depth work to do in their initial stages than national co-located teams. If they can hardly ever meet, it will take them far longer to get any sense of being interdependent and well co-ordinated as a team, if they ever do. As will be described in Chapter Ten,

Table 5.1: General recommendations that need to be honed to each specific task and situation

Team Phase	Important Activities for Evaluation
Start up phase	The purpose is clear to all involved
	All involved understand where the team and task fits in corporate strategy
	Sponsors, team leaders and clients have jointly decided what kind of outcome is wanted and relevant
	A sense of urgency has been created
	The necessary personnel, technology and support have been identified and budgeted for.
First meetings	The whole team understands and agrees on the purpose, goals and targets.
	The whole team understands the roles and responsibilities of each team member
	The whole team has been involved in generating the widest range of ideas on the task
	The team has diagnosed its strengths and weaknesses and agreed how to manage its team processes
	The team has agreed its patterns, timing and modes of communication.
Mid phase	The team is clear about its purpose and has narrowed its options to one path to now achieve its goal
	The team is carrying out its agreements and maintaining its scheduling
	The team is ably managing conflicts, inertia, problem solving and decision making
	The team has accessed and is using all supportive technology
	The team has kept team sponsors and clients involved and informed.
Completion	The team has successfully completed its task
	The outcome is effective
	The team members are satisfied with their performance as a team
	The team members are clear about how they achieved that performance and have evolved strategies about how to pass on the learning.

evaluating an international team on the same time scales as a less complex entity can be counterproductive. Such teams need to 'start slowly'. Awareness of the timing of evaluation brings home how important it is for teams to have ongoing objective feedback on how well they are performing on the task, as well as how well they are performing as a team during each key stage of its life cycle. A good outcome can radically change a team's perception of its performance as a team, probably more than good team performance can create an effective outcome on the task.

Although an effective team will have been conducting reviews throughout its life cycle, the purpose of the final review is to take a step back and to look at the project in its entirety. It is useful to give team members a couple of weeks away from the team before conducting this final review to enable them to have time to take stock. Do not leave it too long or they will be sucked into their next task and find it difficult to reconnect.

Get the team members to map the highs and lows throughout the whole life cycle – both for them as individuals and their perception of the team. You can use both formal techniques (reviewing outputs from the team, reviewing communications) to review the deliverables as well as more informal techniques which draw out the richness and less tangible aspects of the experience (drawing, acting, metaphors, telling stories etc). When the process is made conscious from the beginning, the pictures get much more interesting. Unlike the accepted linear pattern of forming, storming, norming and performing, the teams usually draw their processes with large ups and downs, circles and side branches. They often have light bulbs being suddenly switched on or suns emerging when one particular idea or helpful person broke through a thunderously dark cloud and clarified a direction. Rivers, boats, aeroplanes often appear, carrying the teams across the landscape, sea or sky.

Team Review – what worked, what to do differently

Try and make it fun. Some examples you could try with your teams are:

Map the life cycle

You can map out the life cycle of the team once more, as you did in the preliminary meetings and get the team to map out what actually happened in each of the phases. If you have the pictures from the early meetings you can compare and contrast what the team thought would happen and what actually occurred.

Project mural

Prepare some large sheets of paper on a clear wall and along the top mark the timelines of the team. Start with the date the team members were selected and finish with the current date. Ask team members to draw their key moments and achievements that really stand out in their mind. Once everyone has made their contribution, stand back and together interpret the picture you have created.

Project bio-rhythms

This process was developed by an R&D team we were working with. Again map the timeline of the project along the top of the paper and along the side identify all the key stakeholders and participants in the international team. Then for each stakeholder plot their project 'bio-rhythm', ie the highs and lows of the project from their perspective. This process is very useful if you can encourage your key sponsors and stakeholders to participate and plot their own

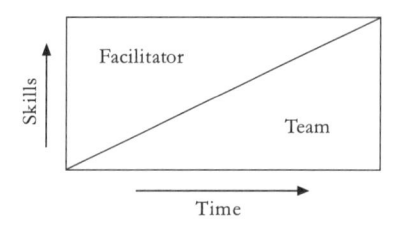

Figure 5.9: Transfer of skills

perspectives. Again once all the perspectives are mapped, stand back and review the story it tells.

This chapter has discussed the role of facilitators in international teams and explored how you can ensure that you are maximising the effectiveness of this role. An effective international facilitator, if used appropriately, can greatly enhance the performance of an international team and embed the learning back into the wider organisation. However, the role of the facilitator is ultimately to transfer all the appropriate skills to the team members, as illustrated by Figure 5.9.

As an organisation develops its ability to select and manage international teams, the reliance on independent facilitators should diminish. Sharing the skills, knowledge and experience necessary to facilitate successful international teams amongst team members is more likely to be sustainable in the long term than trying to develop an elite cadre of 'super' facilitators who are parachuted in whenever a team requires support.

In the early stages of setting up international teams, such a cadre will be invaluable. However, you should take care to staff this cadre with a mix of internal and external facilitators. Not only does this increase the range of skills within the group, but it also means that as the skills are transferred to the team members, you are not in the position of having excess internal resource that requires redeployment.

The tools and techniques outlined in this chapter have been 'low tech'. Our experience with international teams, is that many of them still have not mastered the team basics and 'low tech' interventions are very effective. However, we are living in the midst of a revolution in information technology. One that is having a profound impact on the way international teams can work. Some of the changes and the disciplines these teams need to learn are covered in the next chapter.

Chapter Six

Leading in the Information Space: Teams and Technology

'The systems weren't set up for global working – we can't send attachments – we are still relying on faxes and snail mail.'
'E-mails get lost in the ether.'

The Information Revolution

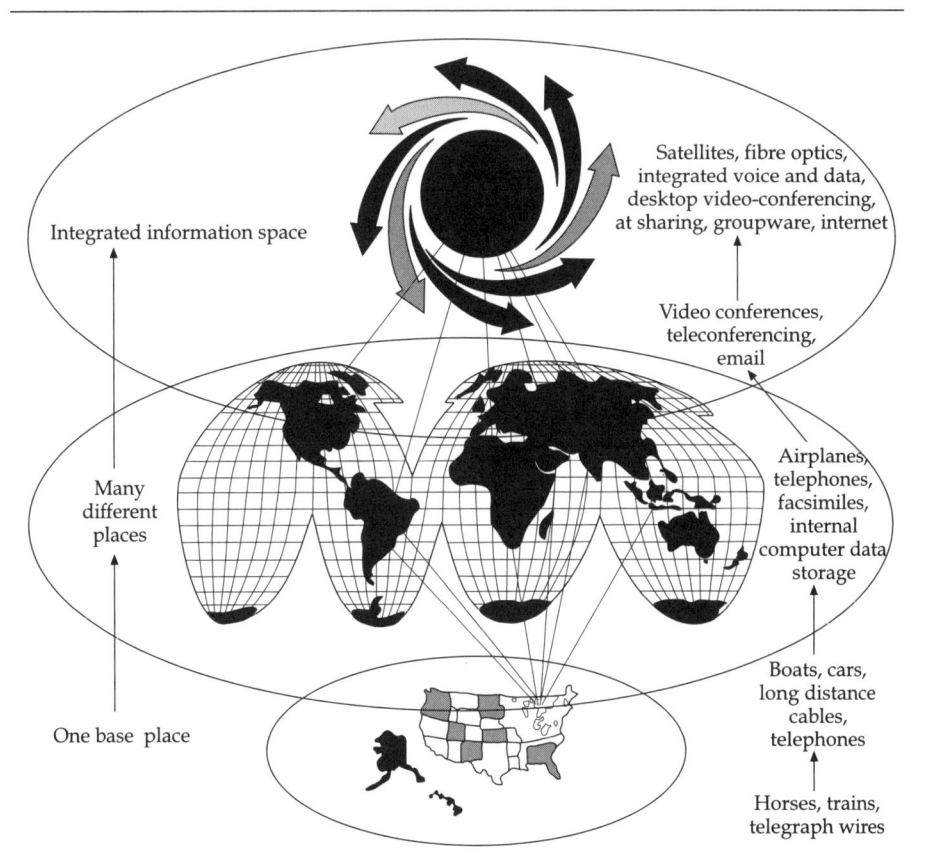

Figure 6.1: The information revolution

The shift towards information as a global commodity and the development of increasingly sophisticated technology are, we believe, major forces in the creation of international teams. Just to survive, companies need to know what is going on in the rest of the world. Lone brains can no longer handle the complexity of processes needed to scan and encode all the available data, or understand all the implications of their decisions and actions. Teams are needed not only to create value from this myriad of information, but also to exploit its value within the swirl of global market forces. It is the evolution from data storage systems into data sharing systems that is creating increased excitement and massive change. Some people estimate that data storage systems never increased the profitability of most companies. The pay off, it is hoped, will come from effectively using data sharing technology.

Computer-based data sharing systems, such as internal networks and e-mail, shared databases, electronic data interchange, Lotus notes, desktop video-conferencing, personal communicators, cyberspace offices, support collaborative organisations and effective team processes. Teamwork takes place increasingly in a 'team information space' rather than in one or more geographic location, due to the shifts outlined below.

- Instead of people moving to the workplace, increasingly the work can be moved to the people, almost wherever they are and in turn, they will be able to contribute to group work from wherever they are.
- Old internal and external boundaries are becoming irrelevant. Integrated cross functional teams with access to a wide variety of different internal and external sources of expertise working within tight time frames have become a reality.
- The role of management and leadership is being forced to change towards supporting and designing collaboration or become irrelevant.
- Integrated visual, voice and data sharing technologies will increasingly enable teams to work faster across distances if these technologies are introduced properly and technical and personal support is provided simultaneously.

These changes in the way people work have allowed dispersed international teams to become a reality. There is already much good thinking on virtual teams, cyber-meetings and knowledge working[1]. Rather than repeat this work, we want to acknowledge these insightful discussions and point readers to appropriate texts. This chapter will instead focus on the ways technology supports or hampers certain team processes and which technologies are good for different tasks and phases of teamwork. International team leaders need to be aware that:

- *Most technologies support but do not initiate or sustain collaboration and effective team processes.*
- *Different current technologies are good for some things and not for others and best practices for using them can usefully be established, especially when working internationally.*
- *However fancy the technology becomes, good cross-cultural facilitation will still be important.*

The Best Uses of Current Basic Technologies

'Since I have been working with the Americans, e-mail overload is a joke – it takes me over an hour a day just to read my inbox, let alone do anything about them – it's getting so I dread coming in – I clear my inbox when I go home and by the time I get in there are a load of new ones.'

Some companies, such as widely spread franchised document handling companies manage an effective global network with telephones and faxes. The key managers meet once a year to exchange ideas, get to know each other, and the rest is based on mutual interest and trust[2]. High tech is not a prerequisite for effective international working. Much can be done with telephones, faxes and e-mails. Whatever the level of sophistication, it is important for international teams to draw up a communication charter of how and when they will effectively use different technologies so as to avoid the type of overload described in the above example. The first step is to work through what each technology is best used for.

The best way to tackle this discussion in a team workshop is to ask small groups of two or three people to work through the advantages, disadvantages and basic ground rules for a specific technology. Our experience of working with teams to create their communication charter has illustrated an interesting dilemma. If you create a table in plenary, using a nominal grouping technique with the whole team of the points made below, most team members ask for the exercise to be dropped – they claim it is too boring and obvious. If you drop the exercise, most will clamour for the list shown below. The fact is that although it can seem tedious, thinking through the use of communication technology is valuable. It certainly helps surface different assumptions about what the advantages and disadvantages of each technology are and highlights that communication technologies are not culturally neutral. The more creatively it can be done, the less painful it will be for any team leader or facilitator.

Current technologies

Telephone

Advantages: Immediate answers or can defer call till later. It is personal. Can choose any language, check understanding, change tone and information half way through.

Disadvantages: Can be intrusive. No record or use of documents unless previously faxed. Variable global quality with echoes, crackles and delays. Long distance. 9–12 hour time differences are always inconvenient.

Basic ground rules: Keep to the point. Note main points before calling. Make notes during conversation.

Tele-conference

Advantages: Involves large group. Can impose disciplined communication. Don't have to book like video-conferences yet they give you immediacy of response and the nuance of reactions missing in e-mail and fax.

Disadvantages: Difficult to keep the whole group in mind. Have to select one language. Second language speakers cannot use body language to interrupt or show confusion. Underused in global working.

Basic ground rules: Fax agenda before, elect facilitator to keep time, stop wafflers, involve everyone. Need to make time for second language speakers.

Facsimile

Advantages: Now widespread. Can be computer to computer. Very cheap but insecure when sent over the Internet. Can be good for accessing less developed countries. Some people will act on the written rather than spoken. Can send specifications, designs, pictures etc.

Disadvantages: Cannot edit while sending. Frustrating if intermittent power failure, switched off or paper runs out. Needs good connection.

Basic ground rules: Stick to facts. Good for small amounts of urgent data. Can be sent and received direct from computer.

Internal e-mail

Advantages: Excellent for short encouraging personal messages and sorting out details. Can set up internal interest groups as well as broadcast progress and achievements. Can reach a selective or wide audience. Participants can choose when and how to respond and can edit and interject into received messages. Time for second language speakers to hone what they want to say and can act when it suits you. Cheap excellent tool using local servers in developing countries where phoning and postal mail is unreliable, prohibitively expensive and slow.

Disadvantages: Usually confined to text unless participants have identical packages for sending attached files. Often lose formatting from word

processing files. Not good for controversial difficult announcements. Can be hard to set up the architecture between disparate sites and companies. American standards tend to dominate. Can be ignored. Overload. Overused. Even then, messages get lost and go unanswered. If too many questions, some tend to go unanswered. Loses intonation and subtlety. Do not use for urgent messages that need a reply. Phone or walk to person's office.
Basic ground rules: Use the priority and action codes. Give clear headings indicating the subject. Keep points clear and succinct. Avoid philosophical debates. Create company etiquette for expressing emotions and negative responses. Train newcomers in company idioms and slang. File and delete as you read. Make an address book of regular mails. Use very specific mailing lists for specific issues and keep them updated. Avoid general mail outs.

External e-mail

Advantages: No need for company to invest in own Local Area Network (LANs) and architecture. Great for informal chat at low cost. Can access wide range of resources at low cost.
Disadvantages: Loose formatting or attachments become scrambled in different codings. Viruses can be carried on attachments. It is insecure.
Basic ground rules: Same practices as above. Use filter for junk mail. Still seems to be more of a problem in America than elsewhere. Remove attachments before sending replies.

Internet

Advantages: Can access a wide range of information at relatively low cost. Teams can create websites to stimulate interest in suppliers and customers not on internal architecture.
Disadvantages: Can pick up viruses. Time consuming especially if surfing is non-specific. Companies can limit the usefulness by insisting all mail is vetted to stop surfing on their time.
Basic ground rules: Update company access to latest web search facilities. Keep website graphics, colours and logos to a minimum. Limit or log connection time and probably access to certain sites, especially if offices are still closed door.

Group decision support systems

Advantages: Increases quantity of participation from all participants, not necessarily quality. Can dramatically cut meeting time. Focuses 'discussion' on task.
Disadvantages: Anonymity may not suit all cultures. Does not help to mature interpersonal processes. Has more impact in teams of more than eight people.
Basic ground rules: Facilitator must be both technically and process able.

Groupware products such as Lotus notes

Advantages: Allows teams to jointly consolidate contributions into one document. Allows preferential editing/reading access. Enables point to point on-line screen shows.

Disadvantages: Can have problems setting up and maintaining the technology, especially between high and low level infrastructure sites. Very large investment in training and on line coaching is needed to make full use of it. Need good in-house people who can create customised templates. All users need to be in All-Lotus desktop environment to take advantage of team computing capabilities.

Basic ground rules: Be selective about edit, read only and access options. Create process and chat files alongside technical and data files. Teach the team how to customise their own files.

White boards/shared database

Advantages: Excellent record of team activities.

Disadvantages: Can be hard to file and index so that information is accessible. Somebody has to maintain relevancy which may lead to reduced usefulness.

Basic ground rules: Need disciplined up dating and sending of information. Information needs to be usefully packaged. Someone needs to be responsible for editing the site.

Group video-conferencing

> *'Getting to the video conference facilities is impossible – people are block booking and then not turning up.'*

Advantages: Can see more than teleconferencing and can all be looking at the same written text, so greater reliability and relevance can be assessed.

Disadvantages: Unspontaneous, formal. Delayed actions due to small bandwidths. Many people say that this is not much better than teleconferencing, except when simultaneous data exchange is also possible. Size of room and access may differ between sites. Needs booking. Still expensive. 'Looks like University Challenge'*.

Basic ground rules: Need advance planning, agendas and preparation, clear outcomes and process facilitator, eg speak one at a time, not more than two minutes; clear bulleted decisions and actions. Have a technician on hand for new teams.

*A British TV quiz where university students sit in straight lines to answer questions.

Desktop video-conferencing

Advantages: More spontaneous. Adds personal immediate dimension, more able to interrupt and change input in response to visual cues. Do not have to travel or gather at specific sites.

Disadvantages: Still not as rich as face to face. Still expensive to set up, but transmission costs will be far cheaper. Technology has still not reached global industry standards and reliability and will demand good infrastructure to be effective.

Basic ground rules: Depending on type of exchange, will have same ground rules as any good meeting for preparation, keeping focused, perhaps agreed signals for strong feelings, summarising and following up. Will need to prioritise questions so as not to bother other people unnecessarily, eg could they answer an e-mail in their own time as well?

Virtual offices

Advantages: Meeting rooms, simultaneous desktop visual and data exchange. As close as one can get at the moment to sitting down in the same room with a group of people. Will soon be able to split up the screen, focus in on people. Move camera etc.

Disadvantages: Expensive, few standard, industry tested reliable products. Weak national infrastructures cannot yet support necessary data flow.

Basic ground rules: All the underlying best practices and disciplines of other 'meetings' technologies will still apply.

Each team needs to explore their current access to each technology, what their agreed best practices on each will be, what they will use each one for and which ones they think they should invest in. While much can be achieved using simple technologies well, when they are used inappropriately, they send strong negative messages as the following example illustrates.

One director in a hurry to fly was on the verge of sending out a company wide e-mail announcing the very early date of replacement of his deputy director. The outgoing deputy saw it and pointed out that she could sue him for breach of the three-month notice ruling. He left the date open and sent out the e-mail, which created much disquiet in the rest of the organisation, as nobody was able to question him about why a popular and effective person was suddenly resigning. Perhaps it was a good move on his part, to avoid the embarrassing questions. Yet it also demonstrated the communication problems that were forcing the resignation.

The Future Possibilities

Some new technologies are focusing on replicating the richness of same time, same place, face to face as much as possible (eg desktop videoconferencing), others on allowing manipulation of two dimensional and three dimensional design objects or even humans in surgery at a distance (integrated modelling with voice and data) and still others on having an instantaneous flow between individual and group work, again across large distances (many kinds of virtual meeting options and groupware). As this is not a book about future technologies, here we point you to other resources[3]. One good source of thinking about future meeting technology is *Cyber meeting* by James Creighton and James Adams. They highlight the following technologies as being close or future possible realities.

- Multimedia presentations/modelling/simulations
- Immediate access to databases
- Software agents that carry out assigned tasks such as scheduling meetings
- Meeting room video-conferencing with participation of multiple parties at several sites
- Voice and written interface with the computer
- Whiteboard technology/PC linked projection screens
- Wall size PC-linked projection screens/systems
- Thin film deposits on walls
- Modelling/holographic projections
- Remote viewing headgear
- Translators
- Expert systems

The emphasis is on anyone, anywhere being able to link up to meetings in fully supported meeting facilities where all the wall space is linked to individual computers, can be drawn on and can be recorded as part of the team memory.

The Cross-cultural Argument

The research into the impact of technologies on dispersed national, let alone international, teams is still limited. Huge increases in productivity are anecdotal and company specific. Academic research has focused on group decision support systems (GDSS). An example of GDSS is Ventana Corp's Group systems V where everyone has a computer terminal in the same room and types in their ideas that are then displayed on large computer screen. These ideas can then be prioritised according to agreed criteria. Group communication support systems (GCSS) refers to the 'different time, different place, at a distance' technologies such as e-mail. Some of the research findings are as follows:

- Electronic brainstorming facilitates the generation of ideas in larger groups (eight and over) more than in smaller groups (less than eight)[4]
- GDSS increases the depth of analysis and increases task oriented communication and clarification efforts[5], but not necessarily the quality of decisions.
- GDSS increases the participation of group members and decreases the domination by a few and seems to reduce the amount of team conflict.
- Unlike GCSS, GDSS seems to increase the consensus between team members on simple tasks. It seems that audio- and video-conferencing lead to quicker consensus than face to face and then same time, same place computer-conferencing achieves it even quicker.
- GDSS seems to increase the confidence and satisfaction of the team members towards the decision. However, while GCSS increases the quality of the decision, it decreases the confidence of the members in the decisions and did nothing to increase the interpersonal characteristics of the team.
- The benefits of using GDSS or other technologies accrues over time as the group assimilates the technologies into its working processes.
- Common figures for shortening meeting times using 'same time, same place' GDSS are halving the procurement time in Chevron, saving $5million on a $100,000 investment and creating 91 per cent–95 per cent drops in meeting time in the American army and IBM. (The mind boggles.)
- The level of commitment and motivation on GDSS falls if participants are separated into different rooms[6].

Most of the research has compared groups using GDSS with groups not using GDSS rather than the different responses from individuals from different nationalities. Without this information, one has to look at some of the surrounding issues.

Some writers[7] go to great lengths to show how the Western keyboards are hard on writers of other scripts. The cursor moves from left to right, the Qwerty board is illogical (and designed originally to slow people down), ideographic scripts such as Chinese and Japanese need completely different ways of thinking about typing and there are relatively few symbols that attribute vowels compared with Arabic scripts. So, argue some people, the very keyboards themselves demand a totally different way of thinking for some second language speakers. In 1995, *The Economist* reported that only eight per cent of top Japanese managers saw computers as critical to their jobs. It is hard to say whether this was a cultural preference or reflects the fact that computer keyboards and software have been primarily designed for English speakers and American patterns of logic. After failing to make much impact in Japan with Windows 3.0, Microsoft customised 3.1 for the Japanese market. They sold over one million copies.

Some researchers have found that[8] GDSS that provided automatic translation demonstrated that, despite poor grammatical accuracy, 98 per cent of the

148   Leading International Teams

Figure 6.2: Global communication

discussion was understood. Thus if language is taken as the major barrier in international teams, this can be seen as a major step forward. However, especially if idioms are used, then currently translation into one language and back again is much less reliable and will not be good for technical detail for some time to come.

It is true that Microsoft converts menu names, command names and instructional files into local languages and builds in the logic to understand different calendars, keyboards and currency symbols. There are multilingual spell checkers (not always with the correct spelling). It easy to imagine that it is within current computer capabilities to make minor cross-cultural adaptations such as adapting preferred forms of address, reversing American and European dates and editing UK English into American English. Using virtual reality for cultural awareness training of specific cultures is already on the drawing boards. However as yet, there is no computerised cross-cultural facilitator to register and adjust differences in values, perceived power, expectations, behavioural and communication norms.

American researchers are putting forward the notion that anonymity, automated record keeping, parallel communication, translation and time to think in a second language without being interrupted all mean that GDSS and other Groupware services are a first-class tool for multicultural groups. What is

---

*On the wall the last sentence says 'the facilitator has superb legs'. The man from Paris is exclaiming 'My God, I have pressed the wrong button. Where is delete? Quick quick.'

more they will counteract the dominance effects outlined in Chapter Three. One Japanese writer[9] warns that it is not that simple. He agrees with the huge benefit of not having to interrupt to get a point across. However, he points out that while Americans place emphasis on the exchange of words and specific explanation of ideas, the Japanese depend very strongly on the context of the discussion, facial expression, postures and tacit understanding, all of which are lost in GDSS. Some Western writers suggest that this kind of need for physical interaction can be accommodated in the breaks, if they are working on GDSS face to face, obviously not if the team are using GDSS apart. Clearly there is a lack of understanding of the importance of these signals for Japanese at key decision making moments. These observations fit in with research on different decision making preferences. Americans prefer deduction and logic that suit the use of GDSS, while the Japanese prefer intuition and analysis to validate their thinking.

Again the message to international team leaders is that while technology may take away some aspects of cultural dominance, it is still an imposition of one way of doing on top of different sets of logic and preferred ways of communicating.

What we find slightly suspect is the very strong preconception that the more sophisticated technology becomes, the more it will be a great equaliser, such that cultural, linguistic and perceived inequality will fade away and become irrelevant. The fact is that however fancy the technology becomes, most meetings will undoubtedly be run in English with all the misunderstandings of idioms and the use of 'American', versus 'British', versus 'second language' English. People can write things directly onto the walls, but there will still be a need to ensure at each stage that everyone is understanding the same thing. And mistakes will be made.

Some people are bound to be more active than others. Some will be more comfortable with computers and familiar with the kind of conceptual and logistical sequencing of the task. Even if a Japanese person is hooked directly into a 'team wall', he or she may still wait for a space in the activity to make a contribution. What is projected from individual computers is technically anonymous. However, in an international team that knows each other, it is soon easy to ascribe 50 per cent of the inputs accurately to individuals. The recognisable differences lie in what they say, which words and idioms are used, grammatical errors, the type of humour and the tone, especially if meetings facilities include being able to get up and move items, similar patterns of perceived influence and linguistic dominance will occur. The leader or facilitator of the meeting will still have to be sensitive to cultural differences and to be proactive in ensuring that different views, bright ideas, and less dominant members contribute. We envisage that a human cross-cultural facilitator will continue to be useful until a team can manage its own internal biases. Karen has also been finding that the greater the reliance on technology, the far harder it is to be subtle about intervening when things aren't quite right. You cannot quietly go up to someone and ask what is wrong or use body language and room positioning to shift the dynamics. Facilitation is still useful for all the same reasons as in face-to-face meetings, but harder because you need to be more blatant.

A sensible question for an international team leader to ask at this point is 'are there different cultural preference for using different technologies?' The problem is that attempting to answer this question can lead to grossly misleading generalities. If one is looking for generalities, then we have had the impression that different cultures seem to take both the spoken and particularly written word much more seriously than others. There are famous cases of Middle Eastern business men shaking hands with Americans, and then dropping out of the deal insulted when the Americans have said 'and now I will call in my lawyer'. Finnish and German people seem to take what they say much more seriously than some other Europeans. They tend to only speak when something is well thought through and to work more from the written word than from a telephone call. Something that may be true of many second language speakers, where reading gives them time to think. The upside of this seriousness is a strong sense of reliability once something has been agreed. Any such cultural generalities should only serve to remind a team leader that they have to explore each of their team members' comfort and response to different technologies when drawing up a communication charter.

It is also our experience that personal style and 'what you grew up with' play an enormous part in any one person's comfort with different technologies.

> During extensive interviews for a research project on transnational teams, in one international team based in a British company, all but one of the team expressed great satisfaction with the communication in the team. The only woman, who was also quite junior, said that although the team members sat only a few yards from each other in an open plan office, they hardly ever spoke to each other, instead they used e-mail and shared databases to communicate. This in her opinion led to unnecessary misunderstandings, delays and a general feeling of unfriendliness, i.e. poor communication.

What international team leaders need to remember is that there will be different preferences and that once they are expressed, they should not ignore them but instead use them to open up a creative discussion.

Technology is not yet good for emotional exchange

> *'Effective messages have to be both plausible and useful in the sense that their recipient will consider them to be substantially true and relevant to his/her circumstances.'*[10]

I was once videoing a team led by a Hong Kong Chinese woman with two other Hong Kong Chinese men, an Australian, a British man living in Beijing and a Filipino woman. They got into such a deep emotional hole that even my stomach was churning with emotion. After a while they asked me to stop videoing and come back later. When I later watched the video, my stomach did not churn. In fact, I was struck as to how difficult it was to pick up any empathetic feeling of what I knew, from experience, they were going through. It then dawned on me that perhaps this lack of tangible 'vibes' from celluloid, television tubes or digital data is the reason why all but the best television and film directors resort to so much overt sex and violence. Viewers find it hard to 'feel' small subtle gestures or overtones.

Communication technology is not allowing us to understand and read any more data about each other than we can pick up face to face. It usually transmits much less. We cannot, for instance, read each other's non-verbal cues to understand someone's complete emotional state at a glance. Richness, in terms of interpersonal cues and emotional messages (and hence confidence in ambiguous situations) diminishes across the different technologies as shown in Figure 6.3:

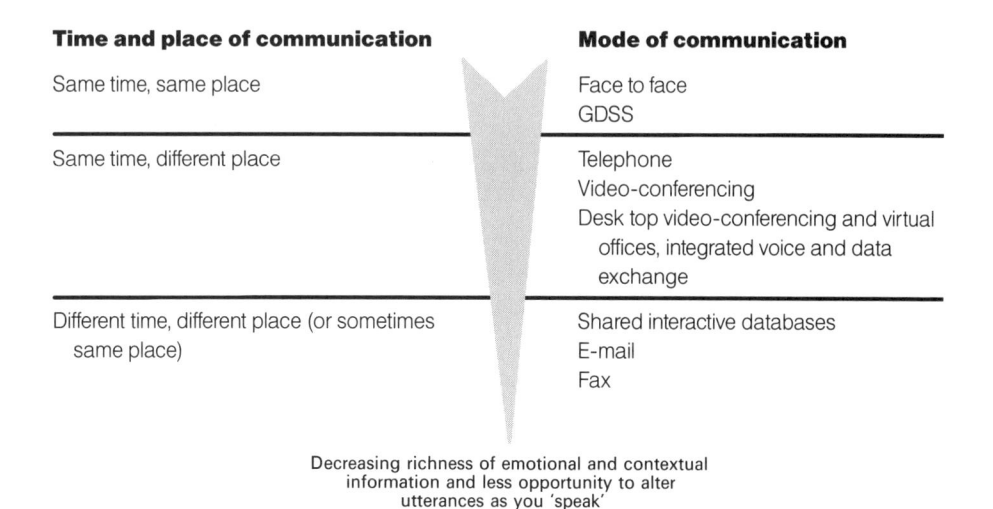

Time and place of communication	Mode of communication
Same time, same place	Face to face GDSS
Same time, different place	Telephone Video-conferencing Desk top video-conferencing and virtual offices, integrated voice and data exchange
Different time, different place (or sometimes same place)	Shared interactive databases E-mail Fax

Decreasing richness of emotional and contextual information and less opportunity to alter utterances as you 'speak'

Figure 6.3

While richness decreases, in each operating mode, the amount and possible diffusion of data has increased dramatically. So far technology has expanded on quantity and handling complex data at a distance, not on emotional richness. This paucity of data in electronic interpersonal interaction has led one team expert to suggest that 'the current technology does not support teamwork'[11]. Other researchers[12] have posited that electronically mediated exchange can only effectively substitute for face to face interaction when:

- the identities of the individual's interacting are not important;
- the circumstances at hand are certain and unambiguous;
- the resulting actions needed are standard and routine;
- ongoing interaction does not depend on a robust structure of relationships.

In other words suitable for routine, bureaucratic impersonal processes that do not involve emotional exchange. These suggestions are certainly not supportive of the flexible, high risk creative teamwork needed to achieve extraordinary targets. Software sellers will also surely argue that these suggestions mirror early day, old fashioned conservatism of what can be done with technology once people understand how to use it creatively.

Nevertheless, a recent book[13] has pointed out how emotional intelligence is as equally crucial to success as intellectual intelligence. A large part of emotional intelligence is being able to correctly read and empathise with what someone else is feeling. Something that gets increasingly hard across communication technology.

> I was once trying to organise a piece of work in Perth, Australia over the fax from London, UK. I put a British exclamation mark after my normal fee to show that I was joking and appreciated that an academic institution could not afford this. I asked them to tell me what they could afford. I had also been asked to write to two separate contacts in the institution, which I did. Dark clouds gathered and when I arrived the friend trying to help me was very upset. 'How could you be so arrogant and pompous demanding such fees and then playing off two departments that are just down the hall from each other? You have some serious apologising to do'. Needless to say, despite apologies, I never worked there and it still leaves a bad taste. I wished I had picked up the phone despite the inconvenient hours from London. Fax, I discovered, is the worst medium through which to start a business relationship.

Being out of 'emotional sync' can seriously hinder progress in any interaction. Some of the conditions of being a high performing international team include reaching a point of emotional maturity, where humour is strong, feedback is not intended or taken as personal and physiologically, nobody's stomach is tight or wobbling for emotional reasons. A good facilitator can feel when this mature pattern of interaction falls into place and know that now the team is ready to take interpersonal risks that they had previously carefully avoided and sidestepped. This maturity can sometimes happen after working through a strategic moment.

One of the main features of a strategic moment, as described in Chapter Four, is that everyone is focused on the same issue at the same time. The tension is held open. Communication across electronic media is sequential. It is hard to imagine how teams will go through these sudden transformational changes* without being face to face in the same time and place. In fact, given the current technology, the only way to be very confident that you are 'in sync' (if the task demands it), is to see and feel it face to face. One network group that was discussing personal issues and emotions spent the first half-hour or so of meeting face-to-face hugging and touching each other. It was as if they were putting into place the missing parts of their previous computer exchange.

In international teams, there will be the added complexity of measurable cultural differences in the extent to which people expect to be involved with someone else as a whole person, at work or not[14]. As explored in Chapter Two, people from different cultures express emotions in different ways and it takes experience and sometimes many years of getting to know someone to be able to empathise with what they are feeling. Even when you have reached the point of being able to ask someone directly, emotional and physical sensations and actions are often explained and interpreted in different ways. Cultural and contextual differences mean international team members will get out of 'sync' and stop collaborating much quicker than most national teams. In other words, they need to meet more often. Teams will need to meet less often if team members understand each other's contexts and how they are likely to interpret messages. In MacGregor Navire, a small Finnish marine engineering company, the top dispersed team met at a different European site each month and usually spent an extra day visiting that site and familiarising themselves with what was going on there. Their future edicts are much more likely to be seen as relevant.

'Trust, discipline, communication and team spirit are the four things that allow us to work as a dispersed headquarter's team.' The CEO of MacGregor Navire, Ulf Hedberg, described trust as knowing that his colleagues share the same business values and were not running separate businesses on the side. It had been long in the building. Despite their long personal acquaintances, it had still taken them a couple of years to achieve the discipline and rhythm of communication needed to manage a top team based in four different countries.

To sum up, values, stereotypes, prejudices, self esteem, respect, and strong personal beliefs and opinions usually come heavily laden with emotions. In our experience, this makes discussion, decisions and difficulties that involve these issues very hard to conduct, make and resolve across electronic media unless the parties involved are willing to give each other a lot of emotional latitude and benefit of the doubt. Very occasionally it has been worth flying all day, just for a lunch, if gross misunderstandings have been put to rest as a result.

---

*Analogous thinking is Connie Gersick's punctuated equilibrium and catastrophe theory.

To Meet or Not to Meet?

> 'Getting to meet face to face has been difficult – some of the managers won't authorise the budget and only using e-mail and phone over this distance is just asking for trouble – they leave so much room for misunderstanding.'

A senior Ford manager who had hardly landed between airports for three months after the initiation of Ford 2000, asked the 'do teams need to meet?' question. Two thoughts seemed uppermost in his mind. 'If everyone does this, we won't make any profit' and 'I am not sure that all this running around really achieved anything substantial'. I was brazen enough to suggest that maybe he was running around for the wrong reasons and wasting a lot of time. Perhaps the team was travelling only to share information, which could have been done more effectively by other means and after all, the atmosphere in most airports, aeroplanes and five star hotels is not usually conducive to doing much serious or creative thinking. It is worth looking very carefully at the reasons why a team should meet, especially in its start-up phase.

Deciding whether to meet or not will depend on what the team needs to achieve and how much money is available to travel and install appropriate technology. One of the first questions is whether the team has worked like this before. If the answer is yes, they are more likely to have established a shared mental and procedural context in which to work together, a 'team space'. There is then less reason to have to meet except as a form of review, renewal and clarification of goals, roles and commitment, a re-affirmation of that shared context. This would still be time and money well spent if it is available. If the answer is no, then, assuming that the necessary technology will be provided to work apart effectively, team leaders and sponsors need to ask the following questions.

1. Is the purpose of the team to share/collate information or to solve complex problems and come to difficult decisions?
2. Do the team members know each other?
3. Are the cultures involved similar or very disparate and how many are there?
4. Is the team working across large or small geographic distances and time zones?
5. Is the team familiar with appropriate technologies for working apart?
6. Does the team have similar or disparate functional expertise?
7. How routine, unambiguous, low risk are the tasks?
8. How much organisational learning or change are the outcomes expected to create?
9. How much impact will a good outcome have on profitability?

When working through the above questions, each team leader or sponsor may want to put a weighting on some questions, depending on the task, the team composition and organisational reality. A widely cross-national, cross-functional team, working around the globe, unfamiliar with technology and each other has both a high probability of failing *and* high costs of getting together. So, focus on the teams who are expected to significantly impact the profitability and learning of the company. Spend the money to get them together to agree the goals and how they are going to work together and to support them with appropriate technology. The processes described in Chapters Four and Five are specifically aimed to speed up this face-to-face orientation work on goals, understanding each other's perspectives and agreeing a common working process. As one ABB manager pointed out, leaving the decision of who and when to contact to human nature is risky.

> *'The fact is there are three types of relationships. There are some people you make friends with immediately, others you do not mind as colleagues and others that you never want to have to talk to again. That affects when you do or do not pick up the phone and who, in the matrix, gets which contract.'*

Support for other teams, such as looser networks for information sharing, routine work and less diverse low-profile teams, can be supported cost effectively through newsletters, on-line, by having a key person to phone, and using teleconferencing.

Another reason to meet is to build accountability across the group. As pointed out in Chapter Four, clarity of mission and goals is one of the top ten factors that leads to project success or failure. Dispersed teams who have never met, may well agree on the business objectives of their common goals. However, whether or not the different underlying personal agendas of each team member are tied in with these goals, is almost impossible to work through over e-mail, phone and faxes. If the team is in a highly political environment, nervousness will remain, misunderstandings will happen. If it falls apart, which is likely, a bad taste or bewilderment is left. A picture or stereotype is then built up and it becomes hard for those people to contact each other again unless they meet face to face. There are many types of trust and many ways it can come about. Most of them involve personal face-to-face communication.

Given the need for contextual understanding, emotional synchronicity, trust, confidence, accountability, it is foolish to assume that introducing sophisticated groupware technology into high risk, high potential teams is an alternative to travel budgets. Communication technology is *not* a cheaper replacement of expensive face-to-face work. It is creating a *new* broader form of interaction that demands higher initial investment and should yield *new* types of results. Massive reduction in time scales, simultaneous launches or registration of products in many countries, a large reduction in faults and inappropriate cross-national specifications, very significant leaps in production outputs, huge cuts in inventory, the ending of seasonal delivery schedules and log jams in pan-European distribution systems, these we have seen. Cuts in most travel budgets should look insignificant in comparison to such gains, especially when to start with such cuts may defeat the whole exercise. However, the reasons *why* people travel should become much clearer so that the travel itself has far greater impact and is used to greater effect than before. To complement this, part of the high initial investment must be used to teach people which technology is best used for what purpose.

Setting the Rhythm of Working Together and Apart

Most teams need to meet face to face when they start in order to create the discipline and interpersonal relationships needed to survive the rigours of working apart. They then need to create the rhythm or 'drumbeat' of working together and working apart.

One transatlantic team in Wellcome that was to run for at least three years met three times for two days within the first three months of being set up. The first meeting was to collectively create a vision for the team, the second meeting was to define the goals and targets and who was going to do what. At the third meeting the team members worked through different questionnaires so that they could appreciate their differences, understand what each person had to offer, how each person might react in certain circumstances and what kind of common language they could adopt to successfully sort out interpersonal problems. After these initial start up meetings, they decided to meet face to face once every quarter with a telephone conference after a six-week period between the face-to-face meetings. Not all the meetings happened on time, if at all, but the underlying rhythm was there.

Rhythm or 'drumbeat'* in distant communication is crucial. It drives home the extent to which you are slipping so that the pressure builds up to catch up however you can.

Taking all that we have discussed and the research on transnational teams[15] and video-conferencing[16], certain underlying principles for working together and working apart have emerged in our work.

Working together

- Agree the overall vision, common goals and interim targets.
- Work through and integrate personal agendas.
- Lay the ground rules within which working trust and working relationships can be developed.
- Form personal aspects of trust, appreciation and understanding of different communication preferences.
- Work through difficulties, conflicts of interest and interpersonal problems.
- Argue through differing viewpoints and make important decisions, especially on value laden, complex, non-technical issues.

*Mary O'Hara Devereaux's term in 'GlobalWork'.

- Evaluate and review overall progress.
- Jointly undergo some training.
- Introduce a new person or aspect of the work.
- If necessary, change values, policies and targets.
- Agree the patterns and styles of communication at a distance.
- Celebrate successes.

All these factors are concerned with underlying values, principles, building relationships or reconciling differences, things loaded with emotion. They are guiding generalities that will not always be true. One researcher recently found that many managers liked to finally resolve conflicts that had emerged face to face, over the phone afterwards[17]. The 'less rich' medium of the telephone, seemed to allow them to apologise, and compromise without, literally, losing face. The breakthrough of groupware technology is that almost everything to do with information and ideas can be done at a distance.

Working apart

- Establish a disciplined and regular system of communication.
- Share output of face-to-face meetings.
- Have regular tele/video-conferences.
- Update everyone on progress, eg weekly e-mail, establish chat files as well as technical files on Lotus notes.
- Send each other motivating messages and comments on each other's work.
- Clarify goals and make suggestions.
- Implement agreed actions.
- Reach consensus on purely technical issues.
- Find, share, collate, edit information.
- Co-create documents, co-design products.
- Meet in subgroups.
- Prepare for face-to-face meetings in advance.
- Anticipate colleagues' questions and needs.

No international teams should ever spend expensive face-to-face time digesting, commenting on or re-editing information that they could have read before meeting. Packages like Lotus Notes, with their replicative facilities, controlled editing/reading and the freedom to design documents/files and databases as you choose now give companies *no excuse* to perform any of those tasks face to face. One Swedish based team commented 'When we do get together, we seem only to get as far as sharing small parts of information, the time frame does not allow for more'. The time frame did allow more; they were using the time for the wrong reasons.

The adage, 'start slowly, end fast' is even more true when training teams to work apart effectively. When technology is painstakingly introduced so that the team can own, customise and integrate it into their work and innovate with it as they go along, the payoffs are seen much faster. Our experience has shown us that team performance is non-linear and exponential. Teams that are going to end well, *make* and *take* the time to play and streamline up to half time. After half time, the processes they have created and the way in which they structure the use of technology to support those processes must be focused exclusively on the finishing post. Ongoing teams, such as top teams, can create their own milestones, upgrading their creative use of technology in each repeated cycle.

Rotate meetings

More sophisticated 'groupware' technologies such as Lotus notes, can do much to alleviate these kinds of problems when they are set up and used well, and these are discussed in more detail in Chapter Ten. Teams usually have to meet from time to time to maintain their sense of joint work and mutual co-ordination. With skewed and tilted teams, it is usually the outliers who have to travel to save on expense. This means that they always meet in the main group's home environment, usually tired, and the main group may never get a 'feel' or understanding of what the outliers are facing on a day-to-day basis. Budgets allowing, it is always a good idea to rotate the meeting sites according to the team members involved.

Establishing horizontal communication

> 'There is still too much allegiance to the "home" country line manager rather than to the project team, so if there is a conflict of resource a team member invariably goes against what the international project leader wants.'

A short example illustrates this small but crucial point. When one American team member was offended by the style of a UK missive, instead of picking up the phone for an explanation or being told to do so, he complained to his boss. His boss complained to his boss who finally picked up the phone to his UK counterpart, who told his subordinate who finally interrogated the UK team member, who then had to explain himself in a teleconference with four managers breathing down his neck. The managers should never have become involved as it was not a major affair, only a misunderstanding of style, so common across faxes and e-mails. The managers' actions diminished the opportunities for the team to learn to trust each other and sort out their own affairs and enhanced the 'them' and 'us' attitudes that the team was designed to overcome.

Work to involve and assist outliers

Technology can also overcome some of the temporal differences, but only to some extent. The fax machine does allow anytime communication, but there are still things that need to be discussed on the telephone. This means that often either someone has to stay up very late in the UK to catch the Australians as they come into the office or get up very early before they leave. Time zone differences often means that there is increased blurring between home and office hours, sometimes for one or two team members more than others. Build the distances and infrastructure into time frames.

Assisting outliers

As mentioned in Chapter Two, international teams are seldom equally distributed across the globe. There are often a few people working together on one site, and a few others spread out. It does not take much for these 'outliers' to feel left out of the main action. When thinking about assisting these outliers and introducing new technologies for dispersed international teams, there are first a few practical realities to take into account:

- New technologies such as desktop videoing, automatic translation and software agents are available, but not yet robust, reliable or constrained by industry standards. It is usually better to wait until the bugs have been sorted out, especially if they are to be used in far-flung places.
- Countries have different import requirements and regulations.
- In some countries, as in most African countries, finding useful software support for latest technologies can be difficult if things go wrong. This is usually not for want of enthusiasm to help, but for want of experience.
- Getting a clear tone (let alone digital and wide bandwidth) telephone line as and when you want it is a luxury of a few countries in the world (and some 'developing' countries such as Mexico have leapfrogged other countries like Japan and the UK on this one). Free access to leased international lines is consciously limited (in Myanmar unlicensed logging on can mean 15 years' jail![18]) or restricted by poor communications infrastructure. If you get a connection, it may be for a very short time. This means that there should be no non-essential graphics such as fancy website logos, the most important information should be upfront without having to go back and forth to many different pages, and data should be as compact as possible. On e-mail, original messages and attachments should be removed or heavily edited before replying.
- Many countries do not have reliable power supplies, satellites can have glitches and (as Canada learnt recently), weather conditions (droughts, floods etc) can play a large factor in working conditions.

As a result of these factors, new technologies will probably be first tried and tested between teams located in industrially advanced countries. It is better to keep technology as simple as possible, the more a team extends into poor communications infrastructure. The cost in time and money of regularly including those battling with lack of basic resources and unfamiliarity with the software will probably exclude them unless companies are very dedicated to getting them up to speed. We are not suggesting that international teams only think about the developed world. Only that they need to get creative and go back to some basics.

Having matched the technology to the realities of the infrastructure available, core team members can assist outliers by a few consistent behaviours.

- **Work out an initial time schedule that is inclusive and sets realistic time frames for turning around documents and includes the time to set up compatible technology as far as possible.**
- **Send regular information updates on what is happening within the core group.**
- **Lay the ground work for what needs to be discussed on the phone by previously sending faxes, e-mails and other written text.**
- **Ensure that fax machines are on and working 24 hours a day and e-mail systems are compatible for attached documents.**
- **Have direct lines (definitely not automated receptionists) and arrange key convenient times for calling.**
- **Inform secretaries that long-distance calls from developing countries take priority and phone back when you say you will.**
- **Sound pleased when an 'outlier' gets through.**

Leading Virtual International Teams

Here we refer to virtual teams as teams that never meet face to face. Such teams are no more different in substance to international teams than international teams are to national teams. They have added dimensions of complexity to handle with fewer options of interaction. When teams never meet they will have to do all the things that are described in Chapters Four, Five and Six, but at a distance and in a slightly different way. Creating a unified 'teamspace' with technology is the ultimate triumph over physical distance. But the paradox is that, at least for the moment, the leader may be more tempted and in fact need to revert to playing a dominant 'strong' role.

Like all team leaders, virtual team leaders will need to:

- Establish the purpose of the team.
- Clarify goals, interim targets, success criteria, roles and responsibilities.

- Create a working communication strategy that clarifies the linkages between team members, takes cultural and contextual differences into account and establishes a workable rhythm.
- Establish and harmonise what technology will be used for what purpose and how often.
- Agree good communication and 'meeting' habits.
- Agree on decision making, problem solving, conflict resolution and feedback processes.
- Establish developmental and learning mechanisms.
- Log the learning so that other teams can learn from this experience.

On some of these issues, the team leader can solicit for preferences, experience and ideas. However, it is likely that the team leader will have to put in the first inputs and then ask for suggestions and changes. One option is to share out the responsibilities for creating first drafts on the different bullet points between different team members.

The second major challenge is being creative about team building. If the team is still using simple technology, it is worth sending pictures and fun resumes of each other even through surface mail. Otherwise scanning photos into e-mails, creating team rooms or extra files where the team shares photos, chat and extraneous items can be important. It is unlikely that many team leaders or members will have the technical knowledge to set up a team room, or even format process templates on groupware. If the team has important work, even if the team is short lived, it can be worthwhile hiring a team facilitator who can design the templates, co-ordinate the communication and who again has to understand and accommodate cross-cultural and contextual differences. Especially in virtual teams, having a facilitator can lessen the temptation to resort to being an authoritarian leader when frustration and long silent gaps set in. I heard of my first leader of a dispersed team of home workers six years ago, because she had had a nervous breakdown. There had been no support to deal with all the ambiguity and uncertainty of what was 'really' going on. Facilitators can help leaders chart this unfamiliar territory and act as moral support.

The third issue is checking understanding at every step of the way. Teams that meet can check at the beginning that they agree the purpose, goals, boundaries, sponsors, clients, roles, responsibilities and working practices when they are face to face. Virtual teams need to send out a questionnaire immediately they feel that these are agreed in order to check that everyone has understood the same things. Again questionnaires have to be carefully worded to avoid dual meanings and idioms.*

If this makes it sound easy, it isn't. In our personal experience, dreams are seldom realised quite the way you thought they would be. Someone gets stuck on the plane in Warsaw and misses the teleconference. It is not possible to catch

---

* A good source book of virtual worksheets and questionnaires is *Virtual Team* by Steve Rayner. http://www.whidbey.com/rayner. Fax: + 1 360 331 2047.

up the next day, because they are already on a flight to America. Atmospheric conditions have disabled the Internet connection between Kenya and America. When they return, their computer system has a virus and is not downloading documents. Brief e-mails get through and messages are left on answerphones. Days turn into weeks. At some point decisions have to be made just to move forward. The leader may have to take more power over final decisions than expected or wanted.

One of the paradoxes of effective virtual teams is that the more disciplined the team is about every aspect of its work together, the more democratic and consultative the processes can be. Absolute clarity of team purpose, goals, and contribution, roles and responsibilities, of agreed working processes, especially to manage boundaries and 'meetings' is vital to allow all the members to be consulted and participate in major decisions.

Much can be done by putting established best practices on to e-mail and intranets. Many of the interventions suggested in Chapters Four and Five, such as cultural value checklist for agreeing working processes and team review health checks, are ideal for setting up on conference and on-line questionnaires. What should not be forgotten is that virtual space is full of paradoxes. Handling conflict illustrates this.

Virtual conflict

In contrast to audio and visual technologies, cues about social context are missing when communicating by computer on e-mail, and so people worry less about how other people evaluate them. Researchers notice that people seem to be more honest and direct, displaying uninhibited emotions and perhaps waste less time on posturing and social niceties (and more on social chat). This lack of inhibition has led to the occurrence of 'flaming', pouring scorn and anger, in response to relatively insignificant levels of provocation, into the computer keyboard, as nobody is going to directly answer you back or hit you. Dispersed teams often suffer from sudden flare ups that come 'out of the blue' as all the cues about the build up are missing. So paradoxically, you have less inhibited emotions, which more sophisticated desktop videoing may come back to inhibit, and on the other hand, you have only part of the information that allows empathetic feeling, especially if you have never met face to face.

As Nohria and Eccles point out, their four criteria for electronic substitution of face to face interaction: unimportant identities, routine tasks, unambiguous circumstances and no demands on the relationships' were the truths of hierarchical, bureaucratic and market organisations. They are the opposite of what is now being demanded of team members in unpredictable but responsive 'network' or 'cellular' organisations and self managed work teams. Hopefully the qualifier will turn out to be 'at the moment'. We will no doubt come up with the pressures, technologies, suitable attitudes (such as 'what was so great about meeting face to face?') and processes that will move working in the 'team information space' through the same iterative changes that have happened to physical organisations. Before long it will seem natural and normal, especially to those who 'grew up digital'.

Identify Effective New Processes Before Buying the Hard and Software

Team leaders need to assess what technology they need before investing millions on hardware and software that does not get used. New technologies seldom completely replace old technologies. Companies still write letters, produce annual reports and send faxes. Each new technology adds a different dimension and usually speeds up a previous process. However, in deciding what to invest in, we advise team leaders to be pragmatic and support the view that:

> 'First understand the processes (that need to happen) and then see how technology can enable those processes.'[19]

If a team needs to collaborate often on creating written reports at a distance, then investing in a replicative database facility such a Lotus notes is essential. If a very high profile dispersed team needs to work on very contentious issues and change core processes within the organisation, then setting up a fully supported meetings facility with immediate access to company data and home offices will be worthwhile.

Our sense is that, even at this moment, most international companies are making do with the basic toolkits of telephones, with conferencing services, voice mail systems, faxes, some group video-conferencing facilities, internal e-mail, internal networks, shared databases and increasingly interactive databases like Lotus notes. We believe that few international companies so far have *widespread* use of computer supported group decision making tools or desktop videoing, virtual offices and high (modem) speed integrated digital voice and data facilities. We also believe that because of the way that technology is often provided instead of introduced, most technology is under-utilised (eg using Lotus notes for e-mail only instead of concurrent document building[20]).

Research is beginning to back up many people's experience that there is a much better uptake and usage of communication technology if the technology grows with the people involved. British Petroleum Exploration, for example, set aside a large sum of money to support a virtual teamwork project. Led by a 'non tech.' who had already demonstrated his passion for organisational change and teamwork in Alaska, the project's aim has been to entice the organisation with pilot projects that showed spectacular results in productivity. Planned over a few years for experimentation, consolidation, spreading of critical mass and becoming profitable, part of their task has been to provide proactive help and coaching, not only on technical support issues but also on attitude change. Super coaches challenge managers and employees on a one-to-one basis, to think through how the technology is changing the way they work and how it can improve the speed and quality of their work. They are using some very sophisticated technology.

Of course there needs to be a dynamic interchange and growth between both the new technologies, the expected increased productivity and people. Even so, the message to over-excited information technology departments is experiment, tickle the rest of the organisation and demonstrate the effectiveness of new products. Do not impose them.

Whether teams meet and work apart or never meet, responsibility for the success of company-wide technology rests with team members and leaders, with creative IT departments and imaginative support mechanisms and with senior management. Wellcome senior managers insisted that all team leaders and members had open diaries on their e-mail to ease transatlantic scheduling. They then decided that they themselves should be exempt so that they could personally decide what to do with their time.

> *'The process (of establishing effective technology) should be viewed as a dynamic interchange between the intentional changes designed by management, the ongoing and developing organisational structures, the emerging and newly created interests created through the technical system and the capabilities and constraint of the system technology.'*
>
> F. A. Dubinkas

Summary of Key Learning Points

- *Understand the best uses of current technology.*
- *Enjoy reading about and fantasising on future technology.*
- *Realise that many of the same cultural and contextual differences and inequalities will apply, however sophisticated the technology.*
- *Understand that technology is not good at conveying emotions and so does not readily support trust building, establishing robust relationships, or making value judgements and difficult decisions.*
- *Think through the criteria of whether to meet or not.*
- *Set a firm rhythm for working together and apart.*
- *Do not expect technology to cut the travel budgets. Look for gains in extraordinary results.*
- *Create horizontal communication to break the dominance of 'national' vertical channels.*
- *Assist geographically dispersed outliers.*
- *Understand that being a virtual team leader has its own issues.*
- *When choosing technology:*
    Work out the processes that you need to support and then buy the technology – realise that technology cannot create good collaboration;
    Pay attention to how the technology is introduced;
    Work on the changes in technology, team members' skills and work habits and productivity simultaneously.
- *Create informal channels alongside technical and task channels.*
- *Start with pilot studies where technology will make a dramatic difference to routine tasks and decision making, and anticipate international problems.*

Chapter Seven

The Role of International Team Leaders

The previous chapters of Section One have focused on the key issues facing international teams and are therefore valuable reading to anyone working with an international team irrespective of their individual role. This last chapter of the section focuses on one role explicitly, that of international team leader, and explores in detail the responsibilities of that role. Whilst primarily aimed at potential or actual international team leaders, the discussion will also be valuable for team sponsors and members so that they can see how their roles support and reinforce that of the international team leader.

The expectations individuals and organisations have of international team leaders are high. They are expected to:

- decide the nature of the team's task, terms of reference and devise a realistic workplan;
- navigate the organisational and political context in which their team operates;
- manage the interface of the team with the organisation;
- create a motivated and cohesive team across countries and time zones;
- ensure that the skills and resources required for the task are available and allocated effectively;
- balance conflicting interests and bridge cultural preferences in the team;
- lead with a style that takes account of their own preferences, strengths and limitations;
- deliver a result that satisfies the multiple stakeholder demands.

On top of this, they are usually also expected to be experts at what the team has to do, and be willing to live with a heavy travel schedule. If this reads like the job description of a superhuman being, it is. So, how do managers of international teams really cope? What do they really have to be good at? Unrealistic expectations derive largely from a lack of role clarity in many organisations around international team leaders. Previously suggested desirable competencies for international managers have ranged from 'marked telepathic and intuitive sensitivity', 'a helicopter view with a sense of reality', 'cognitive complexity', 'boundary spanning', 'geocentric', and 'creating a matrix in the mind of managers'. It is not surprising that organisations and individuals can get confused.

Technical Knowledge or Leadership Skills?

One of the first issues to resolve is whether the international team leader needs in-depth technical knowledge of the subject or needs highly developed leadership skills. The fact is that for most technical experts, once an expert, always first an expert, and second a manager, even if they have been a director of an important international research organisation for over a decade. It is very rare to meet a brilliant scientist or technical expert who has either the desire or in-born skill to lead a complex team, let alone enjoy administrating as this quote from one team leader illustrates:

> *'There are so many reviews and committees — all I am doing is writing reports — when am I supposed to get on with the real work?'*

Yet the previous chapters illustrate that much of an international team leader's time will be taken managing external boundaries, co-ordinating the work flow and the people, and accessing necessary resources. Leader or expert: whatever the decision, it is critical that it is clearly communicated in the organisation, particularly if the decision is a departure from previous practice.

> One R&D organisation had always promoted staff on technical and scientific merit, when it introduced international teams it decided to select team leaders for their leadership and interpersonal skills. This decision to focus on non-technical skills led to resentment among some older, more experienced scientists who felt they had been passed over for younger, less knowledgeable people to whom they now had to report. The requirements of the new role had not been properly explained.

So where should the balance lie? There is no single right answer. It has long been established that the answer to 'should a leader have at hand the answer to any question asked by their employees?' will create very different statistical norms across different cultures[1]. In Sweden and America the answer tends to be no. In Japan, Indonesia, Italy the answer tends to be yes: 'if you do not have knowledge, you will not gain our respect'.

Given this diversity of views, what can international team leaders do to resolve this dilemma? Wherever possible, it is best to ask the people concerned. For example, in one international research institute, a division of sixty people from many different countries, spent an afternoon using a nominal grouping technique agreeing the criteria that they wanted used for the selection of their project leaders. The top criteria were honesty, integrity and fairness as previously people had felt the selection of project leaders had been based on favouritism and nepotism. With that out of the way, they thrashed out the technical versus leadership balance they felt they needed. Everyone agreed that the ensuing transparent process had been fair.

Where it is not possible to ask the future team members, then it should be clear that no one person can sanely handle both the necessary technical depth and the co-ordination of the team. If the team leader is the technical expert who will get deeply involved in the technical discussions, then he or she needs to assign the role of managing the process to another person. If the team leader's main role is perceived as co-ordinating the process, then they will need technical experts on the team. This idea of shared responsibility is discussed in more depth at the end of this chapter.

Changing the Leadership Style to Meet the Needs of the Team

Aside from the expert/leader dilemma, the other difficulty that international team leaders face is that many organisations don't consider the range of leadership styles required. There is no single style with which to lead an international team all of the time. Aside from responding to cultural differences, as highlighted in previous chapters, the team leader's style needs:

- to match the strategic focus of the team;
- to respond to different types of tasks;
- to respond to the different stages of the team's life cycle.

Matching the style to the strategic focus of the team

As highlighted in the next chapter, there are three primary strategic foci that international teams contribute to: global efficiency; local responsiveness; and organisational learning. Depending on which focus is most critical to the team will depend on what type of leadership will be most appropriate.

Three leadership approaches have been identified:

- The **advocate** who represents the team to others inside and outside the company and maintains the legitimacy of the team.
- The **catalyst** who inspires the team to do more than they thought was possible.
- The **integrator** who is able to integrate the disparate facts, ideas, perceptions and behaviours into a workable outcome.

Research on transnational teams (TTS)[2] showed that while none of the above three approaches was specifically related to global efficiency, being a catalyst and encouraging individual initiative and action was correlated to teams focusing on local responsiveness. Being an advocate, on the other hand, was correlated to teams focusing on organisational learning. This suggests that when teams are in this learning mode, it is more important for the team leader to effectively represent the team and to anticipate and plan for change, than it is to encourage members' individuality and initiative.

Responding to different types of tasks

Cultural differences are more likely to play a stronger role in tasks that require making value judgements based on knowledge and experience than on mechanical, computational and co-ordinating tasks where the task is, by its very nature, more structured and is not necessarily demanding so much intellectual input as pointed out in Chapter Three. These more complex types of tasks are increasing.

In highly structured tasks, the leader can usefully act as a facilitator of the structured processes, a mentor to team members and as coach to develop skills. As the task becomes less structured and based more on integrating different viewpoints the team leader will also need to play a stronger, but not necessarily more authoritarian role, in structuring the process.

First, the team leader must be able to anticipate some of the difficult dynamics that may arise from different perspectives, backgrounds and power sources as highlighted in Chapters Two and Three. Then, as Martha Maznevski[3] points out, the team leader will need to inspire commitment to the team and the task as well as the confidence that the team will be able to understand each other's differences and integrate them successfully into a rich solution. The team leader will then need to role model the ability to actively take the different viewpoints into account. They also need to demonstrate that when conflicts arise, they are dealt with by explaining the factual differences between the different viewpoints, and seeking common ground, rather than suggesting that one side is right or wrong. Finally the team leader will create the focus for the team to find and develop a shared view of the outcomes and some agreed behavioural norms of how to get there.

Responding to the different stages of the team's life cycle*

Different leadership styles are also needed at different phases of the team's life cycle. The transnational team research (TTS) mentioned previously showed that advocators, entrepreneurs and visionaries are helpful for envisioning the possibilities and bringing into being what an international team can achieve.

When the teams first meet, it is more important for the leader to emphasise active inclusion of differences and individual initiative. The focus here will be on rewarding team members for generating and implementing ideas. As the team evolves the team leader's focus needs to be on integrating the differentiated activities of the team members and focusing on the common outcome. As the team matures, the team leader needs to maintain the individual initiative while

---

*The team life cycle model is described in full in Chapter Four.

maintaining the focus and ensuring that the outcome is well known and has legitimacy in the whole organisation. In other words, he or she will need to be working across all three roles simultaneously. Often team leaders are stronger in one role rather than in others. Some entrepreneurs and catalysts can find the integrating role tedious and mundane. As a result, some teams have opted for a change of leadership as the team begins to evolve and mature.

- **The team leader needs to match his or her style to the focus of the team, the type of task and the stage of a team's development.**

Our attention now turns to the key responsibilities of an international team leader, which span three main areas:

- Managing boundaries: internal and external.
- Providing direction, focus and closure on the task.
- Facilitating the interaction of the team.

Managing Boundaries: Internal and External

> 'Some of the international project leaders have not realised how important it is to keep senior management informed.'

International teams are embedded in the wider organisation that created them. They do not exist in a vacuum, nor can they perform effectively without interacting with colleagues outside the team. The international team leader has a critical role in ensuring that the team does not become too insular and fails to manage the expectations of its sponsors and stakeholders.

Creating the fit with the rest of the organisation

The team leader needs to understand how the team fits into the strategic thrust of the company. If the teamwork is spread over several years, it is very important that from the beginning the team leader has established a rapport with the team sponsor who can help anticipate and advise on strategic shifts and changes in the environment. This means that the team leader must find a way of succinctly keeping the sponsor and key resource managers informed of progress and difficulties within the team.

> 'You do not go to the quarterly progress review committee meetings with any surprises – not unless you want to get cut off at the knees.'

In Wellcome, senior managers commented that team leaders who managed the external relationship well, in particular with key resource managers, tended to have fewer difficulties when negotiating changes to forecasts and plans and were able to get additional resources. In Seagrams, the Canadian food and drink company, fixed-term international project teams were used as the main drivers for re-engineering. The teams were used to develop and create strategy. Four were focused on customer fulfilment in different global regions, two regional manufacturing teams, and four business sector teams covering duty free, finance, management information systems and business planning. It was the team leaders' job to sell the end product to the senior management.

A very important role for international team leaders is that of external advocate.

It is important that when undertaking this advocacy role, leaders are seen to be acting in the interests of the whole team. Some leaders of the Seagrams' teams were criticised for placing too much emphasis on the corporate reaction during the team work, agreeing too much and in one case this was perceived as the team leader positioning himself for re-entry after the end of the project teamwork. Yet, selling the team's work both up and across the organisation is important. The difficulty is knowing how much information to broadcast to whom:

> *'It is so much better than the old system – I know what is going on across the whole portfolio, instead of just parts of it – and that helps when we are reviewing stuff at the quarterly review meetings.'*
> *'It is knowing who to communicate to and when – everyone moans about information overload and then complains about not being kept in touch.'*
> *'There are so many people who claim they need to know – the distribution list for our minutes has over 200 people on it.'*

One simple guideline is to make short, one page summaries for team sponsors and key stakeholders. As electronic shared databases or home pages become established, they will help in creating the ability for people to pull up the information they want rather than expecting team leaders to push it to them.

One way to include team members in this advocacy role is for the team leader to take different team members to different meetings and to include and acknowledge their contribution in preparing reports. This way, team members can assess external responses for themselves and can then actively assist in devising persuasive strategies. This encourages the team members to take more responsibility for how their work is being perceived within the organisation. It also avoids the criticism that the team leader gets and takes all the credit for everyone else's work.

The other side of advocacy role is the expectation that the team leader will minimise external interference and hindrances. He or she is expected to be a 'bureaucracy buster'. Support systems may not have been changed to handle the cross boundary pattern of work of the international team. Senior management may not understand the importance of certain bits of technology or the need for extra travel expenses at certain times. It is usually up to the team leader to cajole, haggle and push for things to happen.

Negotiating resources

Most international projects will cross functional boundaries. This means team leaders need to liaise and work with many different line managers. If the team is composed of part-time members who are also members of other teams, the team leader has to negotiate hard with line managers on the required level of skills and potential timeframes. Sometimes they will get it wrong:

> 'The trouble is that good statisticians are in short supply and they end up on multiple projects — this is good news as far as sharing best practice goes, but can be a nightmare for timelines.'
>
> 'My project leader does not understand the significance of what my department does — she is always involving me too late and then it is expected yesterday. It is not making me popular with my line manager.'

Any department will be made up of some effective, experienced people, and some less experienced people. International team leaders will talk to each other about the experienced people and want to have them assigned to their teams. Good people can easily become overloaded if it is left to team leaders to allocate resources. However, they may feel completely dis-empowered if all staffing decisions are left to the line managers:

> 'I do not get a say about who is on my team — yet I have to manage them and still deliver — that has got to change.'

Team leaders and line managers need to have very frequent contact and negotiations on these issues. That can be hard when they are on opposite sides of the globe. If the timing of the project is crucial then the relevant line managers need to be involved in the team design discussions.

Carrying the weight of success or failure

International team leaders of these often cross-functional, cross-hierarchy teams seldom have clear designated power within the organisation, yet they are still held accountable for the success or failure of the team. One of the big questions for international team leaders is, 'Who carries the weight of successful implementation and performance?' The answer depends on:

- the legitimacy the team is given within the organisation;
- the extent to which the team has control over its own resources;
- the kind of task.

The following examples demonstrate the impact of these three factors.

> The authority of the international project teams within Wellcome was less than clear. While they have a high level of legitimacy within the organisation, the team leader had relatively little control over who was selected onto the team and how many resources he or she had access to. Also the success of the task (to take a potential medicine from molecule to marketplace) was not entirely within the team's control. It is purely chance as to whether a team leader is given a compound that turns out to have serious side effects or not.
>
> So in many ways it is unclear the extent to which a team leader can be held responsible either for the total team performance or for a successful or failed outcome, i.e. a new medicine on the market. Much depends on the factors outside the team's direct control like the compound itself or the willingness of key resource people to allocate the resources the team requires.

> Before the international project teams were set up in Wellcome, one team in Quality Assurance had decided that they should be working together across the Atlantic Ocean if they were to be more effective. They self-started an international team with the support of the British head of R&D. The head of the R&D department of the American subsidiary did not think their output would be useful until there was international production facility. He tolerated the UK led team but was not actively supportive.
>
> The visionary British team leader was liked and respected by the whole team. She gave the team direction and focus while enabling them to function if she was not present. While this team had no external legitimacy, its sense of pioneering was very strong. The leader felt that they were only allowed to do it because quality assurance had a low profile in the wider organisation.
>
> This team chose itself as a team and so had control over staffing but not much control over its own time and budget. Its successes were exploratory and should have been better publicised by the team. By choosing to self start, all the weight of successful implementation and performance lay with the team itself as a whole, although the skills of the team leader were clearly visible.

As stressed in Chapter One, these two examples demonstrate how the weight of success is determined by the way a team is created, its task and the amount of control it has over its own resources. In general, the more control a team has, the higher the motivation to perform well. Success as well as failure will land squarely at the team and team leader's door. It also involves the whole team in learning how to manage those resources. Not all of a team leader's power will be predetermined by the above factors. It behoves any team leader to work though all the different types of power that relate to the role and to explore which ones he/she can use to best advantage.

Providing direction, focus and closure on the task

Closely aligned to the need to manage the boundaries of an international team, an international team leader needs to be able to see the goals clearly, communicate them, keep the team focused and bring about timely closure. These aspects of the team leader's role can be seen in many organisations where international teams are rewarded primarily for their ability to deliver a particular output. Previous discussions have highlighted that this is only part of the picture, but a very critical part nevertheless. For example, in Seagrams, international team leaders were praised primarily for the task-focused aspects of their work:

- developing and managing a realistic workplan;
- providing direction;
- creating clear goals and standards of performance;
- clarifying roles;
- holding regular meetings;
- good planning and communication;
- constantly questioning the logic, pushing new thought processes;
- ensuring the team was fact based;
- reacting strongly when the process appeared to be off line;
- monitoring progress;
- bringing closure at the end.

This set of actions are very much the same whether the team is international or not. Bringing people with varied skills together to achieve what they cannot achieve alone is the whole raison d'être of teams. The key, as we have stressed in this book is in the co-ordination of those skills. That co-ordination needs to be constantly focused and refocused to be successful.

Facilitating the interaction of the team

The third area of responsibility is the one that historically has received much attention from researchers and practitioners. It has been covered fully in Chapters Four and Five. Certainly many of us carry implicit models about teams and team working that inform how we expect teams to operate and therefore how we expect the team leader to behave. For example, in the Seagrams' teams, on top of what we have already mentioned, team members were sure that their leaders should at least:

- effectively manage personal hardships;
- be available, willing to listen, give direction and take constructive criticism;
- listen to team members and participate in discussions as an equal;
- recognise that some team members need more support than others;
- ensure that the team had some fun along the way.

Of course what constitutes 'fun' could be different for every team. One team leader gained a lot of respect from his colleagues with an impromptu meeting:

> *'We had had a really bad week. Three pm Friday afternoon, our team leader called a meeting held at a local pub with one item on the agenda: How much of the company's money could we drink? Great tension reliever.'*

In some organisations and cultures, such a gesture would have destroyed the leader's credibility. It all comes back to the message in Chapter Two – know your team.

Choosing a Culturally Appropriate Leadership Style

We have established that international team leaders need to actively create inclusive patterns of interaction. Leaders also need to gain the respect of their teams by discovering what they expect of them as a leader. A national team leader may not do this and get away with it. Many team members might share the same expectations of leadership. As pointed out in some depth in Chapter Two, this is not so in international teams.

The variance on this issue will be larger, the more diverse the team. In order to get started, the team leader needs to open up the widely different expectations about what he or she should be doing. Some awareness of potential cultural differences is important in choosing the most appropriate leadership style. The following examples illustrate how values and behaviours are seen differently by various team members.

> The reasons why people respect each other differ in different parts of the world. In America, people tend to respect you for what you have gone out and done or built yourself. Failing and going bankrupt is not a serious social indictment, so long as you tried and are willing to try again. In the UK and Japan, a lot of weight is put on what school or university you went to. In the UK, engineers, ie those studying applied rather than pure science are not held in high regard, the opposite is true in France. In Germany, respect is given after proving your reliability, steadiness and ability to solve technical problems. In Kenya, so long as you are not white or Asian, being rich and displaying it, counts for a lot. Other cultures will give a lot more respect to the wisdom of years than others.

> In one quite recent international survey, the question with the largest national variance was about who wanted to be left alone to get the job done. Australians, Canadians, Swiss, French and West Germans wanted to be left alone, while Egyptians, Omanis, Singaporeans, and Venezuelans expected to be supervised[4]. Some people still prefer and presumably work best with a leader who guides them as much in how to do something as in what to do.

> In some countries with long histories of dominant or colonial rule, waiting to be told is a way of keeping a distance, a self respect for your own way of seeing the world and demonstrating lack of support for the status quo. This often, almost unconscious, non-violent non-co-operation is often interpreted as laziness, backwardness or a reluctance to take responsibility. New young American managers desperate to 'empower' staff so that they can take more responsibility are often met with quiet bemusement.

Making sure your leadership style fits the over-riding cultural milieu of your team is important, however much you may like or dislike doing it. The best way to find out what is expected of you as a leader is to ask the team in a way that puts different expectations on an equal footing. The cultural value checklist exercise described in Chapters Four and Five unearths the different preferences and expectations at the beginning of the teamwork. The team can then,

Figure 7.1: Cultural leadership

explicitly or implicitly, guide the leader towards the most appropriate style for that mix of nationalities in that organisational and cultural context.

Other Aspects of the Role

In addition to these three key areas of responsibility, international team leaders need to acknowledge four needs that will underpin their ability to perform the role in the long term. Some organisations omit to acknowledge some of the more practical aspects of being an international team leader who is often travelling across time zones and needing to make decisions in very ambiguous situations. One obvious need to prevent physical burnout is to have good physical stamina. Some managers have taken time out and realised that they had to start going to the gym or quit the job.

The second need is to have either strong supportive relationships at work and at home that can take the strain of separation, and/or a strong emotional resilience and understanding how to nourish oneself while alone in distant places. It is sometimes sad to see the number of business class managers who feel the need to get drunk and then pass out on any flight longer than four hours. A better example of sustainable leadership is demonstrated by one peripatetic manager, who always schedules an extra day on arrival and after the end of the work, just to rest, get his clothes washed and recover so that he was in good shape to do the work and to arrive home. Few are given or feel they can take the luxury.

The third need is to be able to assess the limits of one's own ethical boundaries in line with those of the company, in many ambiguous situations. It is important to have clearly sorted in one's head what you are willing to compromise on and adapt to and what you need to adhere to. With some experience and reflection, most managers see that they can acknowledge and adapt to different communication styles and different eating habits and can be flexible about how and to a lesser extent when, work gets done. Many will find that they cannot compromise on corporate and ethical principles of doing good business.

The fourth need is to be increasingly comfortable influencing, motivating and communicating across a wide variety of communication technology, as illustrated in the previous chapter. More and more correspondence is e-mail based and most managers are replying to their own e-mails, perhaps because many people write private stuff which they expect the recipients to be editing and replying to themselves. Solving interpersonal problems and making major decisions without the visual clues of being face to face is not easy.

So, even in organisations that have defined and communicated the international team leader role effectively, it is still a very challenging position, as this quote from a team colleague highlights:

> *'Our team leader should have split himself in 30 different ways. That would have helped.'*

However, in our experience to be effective, international team leaders do not have to be superhuman or heroes. Leadership in an international team requires attention to such a complexity of factors that an individual will invariably not be able to attend to all of them. In fact, many international teams, particularly when geographically dispersed, or when part of a wider network of teams, perform most effectively with shared leadership by various people in the team.

Sharing the Many Facets of the Role

Shared leadership and the support of facilitators are not a sign of weakness, they are a vital part of making international teams effective.

Not only our experience of working with a multitude of international teams has brought us to the conclusion that aspects of the leadership role can and should be shared amongst the wider team, it is also supported by research evidence.

> In the video research, almost all the 'leaders' in the training teams were appointed during the course of the teamwork to manage the process of achieving the task rather than structuring the content of the task itself. They were seen as; 'someone responsible for product delivery and who should make decisions if the group reaches an impasse'.
>
> In many teams, although these 'process' leaders contributed well, they were not perceived as having had the most influence on the team. This was usually reserved for the person who took the flipchart pen and structured the content of the outcome or presentation. The one exception was where the person chosen as team leader to manage the process, was also the person most experienced with the task. He structured and summarised all the ideas as the teamwork progressed.
>
> In the operational teams, all the team leaders were pre-appointed, mostly by virtue of their positions within the company. What was striking was that except for one occasion, the Western based team leaders hardly ever tried to alter the 'natural flow of the discussion' by asking someone in particular to speak. This was very different in Hong Kong where the team leader often structured the conversation by asking people to speak in turn.

This research enables us to highlight implications for international team leaders. A common theme is that because the interaction processes in international teams are more complex then in national teams, it is difficult for one person to manage the process as well as the content of the task. The research findings imply that in organisations imbued with Western cultural norms and practices (wherever they are based), the team leader will not lose much influence if they appoint someone else to look after the process. For instance to manage:

- timekeeping;
- setting agendas;
- making sure everyone is fully involved;
- summarising and checking for understanding.

The team leader can then concentrate on structuring the task. Eventually these process tasks should become second nature to the team members so that the role can be exercised by everyone or rotated between team members.

However, evidence from the video research also suggested that unless this role of process facilitation is given a proper framework, the person taking it on may have a hard time and even perhaps lose influence in the team.

'Look, if you are not clear how we should be doing it differently then be quiet, let's get on with the task.'

The receiver of this sharp barb was trying to point out that a few international managers were dominating the local managers, but was not yet able to formulate the problem clearly. This is typical treatment of someone trying to change unhelpful interaction without the recognised permission or ready language to do so. Typically, unless the role is well formulated and appreciated, the team leader can have difficulty getting volunteers. Again, however, it is important to remember that in certain cultures, sharing out the leadership role may not be considered a good thing to do[5]. So the choice of how to divide the role must be culturally appropriate. Whether there is individual or shared leadership in an international team, it must be acknowledged that it is rarely a glamorous task. It can be among the hardest and most stressful jobs in the career of a manager:

'Since taking the job I have had a separate line installed at home – I get so many calls in the evenings because of the time difference – it was the only thing to do – at the beginning I wasn't leaving the office until gone ten and that couldn't go on.' 'If anyone asked, I do not think I would recommend it – unless of course, you do not want a home life!'

and at the same time, it can be highly rewarding:

'I cannot think of a time in my career when I have had more fun, more influence or learned so much in a short space of time. It has been great.'

Summary of Key Learning Points

- *Clarify and manage expectations.*
- *Decide on the balance of technical vs leadership skills and communicate it.*
- *Match leadership style to the needs of the team.*
- *Balance all three areas of responsibility: managing boundaries, task and interaction.*
- *Pay attention to your own needs.*
- *Share the responsibilities amongst the wider team in a culturally appropriate way.*

Section Two

What the Organisation Needs to Do to Support These Teams

Introduction for Section Two

Welcome to Section Two of Leading International Teams.

- If you are a senior line manager or HR professional, this is probably the first part of the book you have turned to, which is great as it has been written specifically with you in mind. You are thinking about setting up international teams in your organisation, or you already have and you want to know what you can be doing to make them successful.
- If you are an international team player, you have probably already read Section One, so you know what it is you need to be doing, now you are curious about what support you could be getting from your organisation. Read on.

Our experience and research has demonstrated that the organisational context into which international teams are introduced plays a key role in determining their effectiveness. There are a number of preconditions for organisations wanting to develop a multicultural outlook and thereby be able to sustain effective international teams:

- valuing and widespread acceptance of cultural diversity;
- low levels of prejudice;
- positive mutual attitudes among cultural groups;
- sense of attachment to larger system.

Creating this context is not a quick fix. It is a long-term commitment. Organisations need to take a systemic view of operating globally rather than simply create international teams in a vacuum and assume everything else will remain unchanged.

Introducing international teams brings into sharp focus the way an organisation operates and this can act as a catalyst for a fundamental review of these practices. If these wider repercussions are not foreseen by senior management, there could be resistance. Many managers do not appreciate the impact that working internationally will have on their roles. The subsequent resistance to the changed way of working can mean international teams operate in sub-optimal organisational contexts, which in turn impacts their effectiveness.

The next three chapters are going to focus on this critical issue of creating an organisational context where international teams can thrive. Recent research with international teams in organisational settings, rather than academic laboratories, has shown that according to international team members, organisational factors have a significant impact on their ability to be effective.

This section of the book will explore the organisational factors that impact international team effectiveness most significantly. Chapter Eight will focus on the role that the senior management of an organisation can play in creating the appropriate organisational context. In particular it will explore how senior managers can assess the readiness of their company to undertake the organisational change associated with creating international teams. The key factors that will be explored are highlighted below:

Senior management

Align strategy in action with strategic intent

- Different strategic foci.
- Clearly link purpose of your international teams to the corporate strategic intent.

Create a supportive infrastructure

- Organisational structure: barrier or enabler?
- Implement team friendly operational policies and practices: HR, Technology and Facilities.

Role model best practice

- Be actively involved with the international teams you create.
- Demonstrate that global working can be human.
- Actively seek to create diverse top teams.

Assess organisational readiness

- Pilot or 'big bang'?

Chapter Nine will then explore specifically the role that the Human Resources (HR) function has in supporting an organisational context where international teams are successful. The key elements of this role are highlighted below:

Human resources

Align HR with strategic Intent

- HR as a strategic partner.
- Developing an HR strategy for supporting international teams: selection; development; performance evaluation and reward
- Taking an organisational effectiveness perspective.

Act as role models

- Creating an effective HR structure.
- Be a high performing international team.

Facilitate change to a team based organisation

- Case study.

Given the importance of the key HR practices in contributing to a supportive organisational culture, Chapter Ten will explore these in greater depth, providing you with examples of best practice from a range of companies. It will take the key aspects of an effective HR strategy (selection, development, performance evaluation and reward) and explore how these can be aligned to create an environment conducive to international teams.

Chapter Eight

Creating the Right Organisational Context

This chapter explores the critical issue of creating the appropriate context for international teams to thrive and in particular discusses the role that senior managers have to play. It explores both their role as corporate leaders and as individuals leading international teams themselves. International teams are not created in a vacuum and often represent a microcosm of the wider organisation. If senior managers can create the appropriate environment for international teams to succeed, they will have gone a long way to creating a sustainable global capability within their organisation.

A special acknowledgement needs to be made at this point to Claudia Heimer, who provided us with access to her unpublished research on top teams in international organisations. We have incorporated some of her findings into this chapter and believe that the work she is doing in this field has important messages for senior management of multinational organisations.

> *'Globalisation is a journey, a process and it's on-going.'**

Globalisation is a journey, that needs to be proactive and conscious. Tough choices face any board of executives in creating the best strategy to achieve a local/global response for their particular product in their chosen markets. Once these strategic choices have been made, the role of the organisational leadership is to align this global *'strategic intent'*, with operational realities, the *'strategy in action'*.

To make this happen, somebody needs to decide what tasks need to be achieved to implement this strategic intent. They need to decide which structure will optimally deliver the required results, whether, for example, creating a team is the best way of achieving each one of these tasks, and if so, exactly what the team needs to do. Somebody also needs to decide how to integrate such a team into or across existing organisational structures, who will be involved and how to best support and train the team members. Somebody also needs to explain to the team leader and members how the purpose and goals of the team fit into the global strategic intent. Clearly this set of decisions

---

*Don Davis CEO Rockwell Avionics, quoted in *Financial Times*, Friday October 10th 1997.

should involve many different players, layers and functions within the organisation.

In our experience, many leaders and their organisations do not manage this alignment well. When challenged on the desire to operate around the globe, senior managers can clearly articulate the benefits to their organisations of being global: increased local responsiveness, enhanced organisational learning, lower cost base, economies of scale and more efficient processes being just a few of the reasons cited. Yet further discussions about what this means for them in practice, often result in more questions than answers. This chapter seeks to explore some of these questions and to begin to provide some signposts for the global journey.

Senior management in a company that intends to use international teams as a major driving force in capturing and maintaining global markets need to:

- Align strategy in action with strategic intent.
    - different strategic foci;
    - clearly link the purpose of your international teams to the corporate strategic intent.
- Create a supportive infrastructure.
    - organisational structure: is it a barrier or enabler for teams?
    - implement team friendly operational policies and practices: HR, Technology and Facilities.
- Role model best practice.
    - be actively involved with the international teams you create;
    - demonstrate that global working can be human;
    - actively seek to create diverse top teams.
- Assess organisational readiness.
    - pilot or 'big bang'?

Align Strategy in Action with Strategic Intent

Different strategic foci

Even a cursory glance at some of the big multinationals reveals that different companies are going global in different ways for different reasons. The reasons can be historical: being global is second nature to oil and mining and comparatively recent for most food and beverage companies. They can be cultural; companies have set up wholly owned subsidiaries within one culturally recognisable region but resorted increasingly to acquisition, joint ventures and franchises to lower the risks of operating in unknown cultural and economic contexts. Alternatively some organisational cultures lend themselves more readily to a centrifugal or centripetal global strategy. Several authors[1] have explored the impact of culture on organisational strategy and structure, and the interested reader is encouraged to become familiar with the ideas in these texts. Finally, different products require different global responses. Aeroplanes and software can afford to be more or less uniform the world over. The fact that Coca Cola is so ubiquitous is a tribute to brilliant marketing as most food, beverages, consumer goods and appliances need to be adapted to local markets.

Some companies are at the stage where they are looking to create greater efficiency between their dispersed research and design, production or sales units. On the other hand, some food and beverage and household goods companies have strengthened their local market presence by maintaining a strong overall brand name but customising products to local tastes. Their emphasis is on being responsive to the local market. Other companies are looking to capitalise and transfer learning across the whole company worldwide and into new markets, such as Coca Cola struggling to set up a bottling plant with the 'recalcitrant' Eritreans.

These three strategic lenses, global efficiency, local responsiveness and organisational learning were first articulated by Christopher Bartlett and Sumantra Ghoshal[2]. They provide a useful framework when looking at the impact of different strategic intents on the structure and processes of international teams designed to implement these strategies.

In the survey of 37 transnational teams (TTS)[3], organisational learning was the main strategic focus of most of the teams, followed by global efficiency. One can imagine that the strategic foci go through cycles depending on the type of product and stage of the company's global maturity. So, what are the implications of these three strategic foci for international teams?

Global efficiency

Global efficiency measures will include things like reduced duplication, cutting the number and cost of suppliers, creating products that are either aesthetically, practically or legally acceptable in many countries simultaneously and integrating regional distribution services and customer support.

The transnational team survey found that teams focusing on global efficiency were often purposefully understaffed to force the team to find synergy and act interdependently. This can put a significant workload on the team leader and team members, which needs to be acknowledged during the selection process. Where global efficiency is the goal, whole team training in project management, conflict and negotiation skills is often needed. The support systems and processes also need to be harmonised if not integrated. These can include pay and personnel, new technology investment and training, and tactful integration of previously different work processes.

When global efficiency is the goal, an organisation must pay attention to the equality issues highlighted in Chapter Three and ensure that they choose a solution that can be successfully implemented globally and not just push through the headquarters solution. Lack of sensitivity in the early stages can cost an organisation many of the potential gains in performance, as the following example illustrates.

> In the process of creating more efficient European project teams out of 'parallel' national teams, a senior French management team steamrollered in a French model of expert technical project leadership over the prevailing British system of independent project management.
>
> One rumoured comment from one of the French managers that caused a lot of anger was: 'Things will work when the British get the hang of it'. The result was that many highly experienced British project managers were disenfranchised in lieu of the newly appointed project leaders. Months of bad feeling resulted and talent was wasted by not considering the benefits and disadvantages of each system. The French senior managers assumed their way was best.

The key word for implementing global efficiency is 'thoughtful integration'.

Local responsiveness

Local responsiveness measures will cover the extent of customisation of goods, labelling or advertising for local markets and the resultant increase in sales or market share, the number of different foreign standards that were met with one cost effective product, fitting in (where possible) with local political, legal and economic frameworks and creating local distribution systems. Teams set up to increase local responsiveness often need to employ people that would have otherwise been marginalised in the company and who may have less international experience. For some corporate die-hards, this can feel like giving up power to those they have spent years telling what to do, as the following story illustrates.

> A large consumer goods multinational was considering its entry into the Chinese laundry market. It was assembling an international project team with members from R&D, marketing and consumer science. The Chinese market was considered to be of critical strategic importance to the organisation and the international team leader found no difficulty in getting team members allocated. Indeed a number of senior managers were interested in being on the team themselves.
>
> At one of the first meetings, the consumer science team member mentioned that there was a newly appointed Chinese laboratory technician in one of the R&D departments. They suggested that they should invite her to join the team to get a better understanding of the washing habits of the local Chinese consumers. The suggestion was quickly rebuffed by the senior marketing managers present – they had done their research, there was no need to involve 'inexperienced junior members of staff in such critical decisions'.
>
> Fortunately for the organisation, other team members thought the suggestion was valid and encouraged their colleague to informally interview the laboratory technician. The resulting information highlighted some critical gaps in the market research conducted by the American based marketing team and prevented the team investing in a product with inappropriate sized packaging, that would not have sold in the Chinese market.

Habit, language skills, different cultural communication styles and prejudices will be working against making full use of local talent as highlighted in Chapter Three. If drawn from different regions, team members are likely to have very different levels and types of expertise, different standards of remuneration, different access to basic resources such as information, technology, electricity and good phone lines. All these will impact the speed at which they can reach an effective working process.

Teams focused on local responsiveness have to listen to less powerful and minority voices.

Organisational learning

Organisational learning was rated as the strategic goal with the highest priority in the transnational team survey. Organisational learning involves improvements such as spreading innovations throughout the company, transferring technology, bringing together knowledge from different parts of the company and integrating a variety of interests. While a few companies, such as Shell, have had international project teams for at least 50 years, for most, creating international teams within their core businesses is a relatively new phenomenon and usually takes place in one or two key parts of the business first. These teams are often not only working on an innovative and more complex task than previous teams, but are also learning the processes that will enable them to work on these more complex issues across national, geographic and temporal distances.

If set up to enhance organisational learning, international teams should create a core team who bring in loosely associated temporary members to generate fresh perspectives and ideas. The boundaries of the team should be permeable to enable ideas to flow into the team and out into the wider organisation. Training and development has to be focused on creating new forms and processes of collaboration and cross-learning. Lateral thinking skills, integrating and constructive conflict resolution skills, project management and interpersonal skills become important in generating and leveraging new ideas. These are the skills that can make the most of the different perspectives created by cultural differences.

The key is not to focus on process, consensus and compromise at the expense of uncovering innovative ways of looking at and solving old problems. Interpersonal, influencing and negotiating skills become important when presenting the new ideas to the rest of the organisation.

Teams focusing on organisational learning often have a pioneering spirit, are highly motivated and need support to navigate the organisational barriers successfully.

Linking the purpose of your international teams to the corporate strategic intent

As described briefly above, the transnational teams survey (TTS) demonstrated that the jobs, staffing, training and rewards within teams will, and need to, differ depending on their main strategic purpose. Team research and experience has also clearly demonstrated that 'clarity of purpose and mission' is probably the major factor in the success of any team, and especially in more complex teams such as international teams. Yet a clear link between corporate global strategy and team purpose and contribution is often completely absent.

In the study (TTS) of 37 teams, only 3.5 per cent of the respondents were in complete agreement about the extent or not of their particular strategic contribution. The four teams with the greatest clarity were:

- one special task force who was in complete agreement that their aim was to cut costs and create global production efficiencies;
- a top team who were sure that they formulated strategy;
- a quality assurance team who were sure their contribution was to improve quality; and

- a special task force in a chemical company who agreed that they were implementing strategies for certain chemicals.

One could have hoped that the strategic contributions of the other 33 teams would be clear, but this clearly was not the case.

One might think that international teams just beginning might be more confused about where their contribution fitted than mature teams, or that many different nationalities might lead to different perspectives. However, the wide ranges in the answers of the transnational teams' survey did not depend on the type of teams, the stage of team development or the number of nationalities working in the team.

Further examples of poor understanding of purpose are illustrated below:

> The top teams of two fairly autonomous international subsidiaries of a large Italian company disagreed as to whether they were responsible for formulating and implementing strategy. Unresolved, this lack of clarity could have significant consequences for the long-term future of the organisation.

> One evolving UK/Italian joint venture feasibility study team comprised solely of engineers, were in almost total disagreement on all possible options. As the international HR manager confided 'We are having problems agreeing what we are doing together'. Not a good omen for ongoing partnership.

> In a managing global network workshop in a global pharmaceutical company, when international team leaders were asked for the advantages of working in an international team, only 3 per cent of responses concerned the contribution to corporate strategy. Over 50 per cent of the responses concerned more efficient drug development, improving networking and organisational and personal learning. While these advantages were valuable and probably what the board desired, the connection to overall corporate strategy had been left implicit.

Motivation and commitment suffer first when this connection to the rest of the organisation is left fuzzy. Team sponsors together with those formulating strategy have to break that pattern of thinking that says 'once we have had the idea, it is up to everyone else to figure out how to do it'. They have to follow the logic of why the team is being created and what it is expected to do all the way through to the team members themselves.

Teams are not necessarily created with one strategic purpose in mind. Some international teams have sometimes been intentionally created to create a flow from one goal to another. For example, a product development team might be asked to firstly establish the centralised controls and economies of scale that will achieve global efficiency in the design and planning phase. It may then pass on and delegate to local teams to create local responsiveness in the implementation phase as illustrated in the following Kodak example.

> **Accomplishing multiple strategic goals over the life cycle of a team – Kodak photo CD launch**
>
> Five regional multicultural teams were created to develop the overall strategy and plan the launch. The European launch team was originally comprised of representatives from 14 countries. The team members were purposefully chosen so that all the functions, which would be involved throughout the product life cycle, were represented within the team. In the launch plan phase each team member had to wear two hats, to represent a pan-European assignment as well as representing their country. This main team was then dissolved to a small core as the task of the implementation was sold and passed onto the country managers within Kodak who in turn appointed people with full-time responsibility for photo-CD in their country.

However, before organisations and teams can integrate a range of strategic goals into their work, they must get the basics right.

Team champions, sponsors and leaders *must* identify the key purpose of the team in relation to these three strategic lenses and *communicate it to team members*.

If the teams themselves do not understand how their work fits into the overall scheme of things, they can become unnecessarily de-motivated as they feel side-lined or irrelevant. Their effectiveness will be influenced by their power base, which in turn depends on their legitimacy within the organisation. If no-one has communicated the link between the purpose of the team and the corporate strategic intent to the wider organisation, the team will struggle to get organisational support and resources for their activities.

The more explicit senior management can be about where a team fits into the internationalisation effort, the more legitimacy these teams will have.

International teams can play an additional role in implementing strategic choices in an organisation. Current research emphasises that strategy is a dynamic process. This requires organisations to be alert to the environment they are operating in, constantly scanning for relevant cues. They must assimilate these cues from multiple perspectives to ensure they fully comprehend the possibilities open to them and they must be responsive to emergent issues that offer new potential. At the individual level, research has shown that culture influences how individuals scan and interpret information and make strategic choices[4]. Organisations must appreciate that they need different perspectives on different markets.

For international organisations to succeed in the long term, they must embed this strategic capability throughout the organisation. Senior management cannot achieve this alone, and international teams can be an essential vehicle for creating this strategic capability. However, many organisations have some way to go before this becomes a reality.

Summary Learning Points

- *It is useful for international teams to think through where their main focus fits across three established dimensions: global efficiency, local responsiveness and organisational learning.*
- *Senior managers and team sponsors need to link the purpose of each international team to the overall corporate strategic intent and communicate it clearly to the team.*
- *Senior managers must recognise the value of international teams as vehicles for formulating and implementing successful global strategies and be prepared to legitimise their role in the organisation.*

Creating a Supportive Infrastructure

Having clearly articulated the organisation's strategic intent to the international team members and highlighted how their activities contribute to that strategy, the next place to focus attention is the organisational infrastructure. Is it set up so it facilitates effective teamworking or are your international teams expending valuable energy and brain power trying to win the organisational obstacle race? Research has illustrated that there are two key aspects of the infrastructure that organisations need to be concerned about:

- organisational structure;
- operational policies and practices.

Organisational structure: barrier or enabler?

'The teams are still hampered by the 'twin peak' syndrome – you'd think the US was on another planet sometimes, not just a plane journey away – it's early days – those attitudes are not going to shift overnight.'

Creating international teams can have some very positive effects on breaking down national barriers and freeing up the internal workforce, as the following quote from an international team leader illustrates.

'I see one of the best things to come out of all this is that you are much more likely to get the right person for the job, irrespective of where they are located – it has cut right across some of the US/UK turf battles, which can only be good for the company.'

However, as companies operating globally try and reflect the complex new relationships between business streams, products and geography, they often create organisations that have their own inherent dilemmas.

'I have got too many bosses – and they can't agree.'

Some form of organisational matrix is the typical structural arrangement of many international organisations. The authority and power in these structures can be very diffuse and the dominant powerbase (eg line managers, functional heads, country managers, team leaders) often reflects the organisational culture. This institutionalisation of interdependencies affects international teams in many ways.

> You are part of the marketing function in the German subsidiary of a multinational computer company. You are working in an international team on the development of the European internet strategy with colleagues from France, the UK and Scandinavia. Who do you ultimately report to, the team leader? your local manager? or the European head of the marketing function? When judging how to spend your time, who are you likely to listen to more?

There is no one single right way to design an organisation so that international teams can thrive as the appropriate organisational design is closely aligned to the specific corporate strategy and culture. Even in a single organisation, staff will have different views about how effective the existing arrangements are for them, as these quotes from two team members show:

'It should be a strong line to the international team leader and dotted to the management line – not the way it is now – we can't get things done.'
'I am so pleased I still have our line manager, the team leader doesn't have a clue about the type of expertise you need to do our job.'

Despite there being no single 'right' answer, you should avoid creating ambiguous reporting lines and divided loyalties if you want your international teams to work effectively.

Ambiguous reporting lines

If a matrix organisation structure is implemented, it needs to be clearly articulated where the decision making authority resides: with the team leader or the line manager? The following example illustrates how damaging it can be if this is not clear.

> The international team leader said no to funding a low priority aspect of a team member's work. The team member disagreed with this decision and got clearance from his departmental head for the expenditure, who was unaware that the project leader had already refused. The team member travelled before the project leader found out. Paradoxically, the organisation had recently been restructured to give the departmental heads more power in order to reduce confusion. There was little the project leader could do, except feel undermined. Ironically, it was the project leader who had to justify the team's expenditure to senior management.

The type of decisions that can get muddled if there are ambiguous reporting lines often depend on whether the team has full- or part-time membership. If the team member is full time for a fixed term, the conflict is usually about who is responsible for the team member's development, training and discipline. If the team member is part time, the conflict usually focuses on availability, quality of work and priorities. Either set of issues can detract from the team's performance and ultimately its ability to deliver its objectives.

Divided loyalties

Even if an international team is clear where it fits in the organisation and who it reports to, it can still suffer from conflicting demands and divided loyalties. This is particularly a problem if the overall strategic direction is not clear to everyone or when different parts of the organisation have not worked closely together and do not understand each other's needs. Sometimes a line manager is under pressure to deliver a set of objectives that contradict the needs of an international team as the following example shows.

> An American vice-president with staff on an international team insisted that the American staff lost no local 'man-hours' by being involved in the team. Being part of the team was voluntary overtime. The UK team members had the full support of their director and their local work loads had been adjusted to take account of their roles on the international team. Needless to say the team soon ran into difficulties in agreeing timelines and milestones and the American team members were seen by other team members to be holding up progress.

Difficulties can arise if a team is critical of parts of the organisation that it perceives are not supporting their work. A team member may feel obliged to 'defend' their part of the business, which then makes it difficult for them to support the team fully. Similar difficulties can arise if the decisions taken by a team impact the livelihoods of some of the local colleagues of team members. This was the case in a European team in a brewing company when an Italian finance manager was purposefully chosen to be a team member so that he could break the bad news that the main factory closures would be happening in Italy.

Another problem that is becoming increasingly common, particularly for part-time team members in overly downsized organisations, is participation on multiple international teams. Loyalties can be spread so thin that the individual does not feel 'at home' anywhere in the organisation. This leads to increased turnover of staff on the international teams and a higher incidence of staff not requesting to join these teams. Some companies and international institutes have tried to overcome this by issuing guidelines on the number of significant projects one person can sensibly be involved in. In our experience it is usually two or three.

Implement team friendly operational policies and practices

International teams operate as microcosms of the wider organisation, so any inconsistencies in policies or procedures in different parts of the organisation will be thrown into sharp relief as soon as the teams start to operate. These inconsistencies or disparities can be inconsequential or have a significant impact on the performance of your international teams. One product development team we worked within a large multinational had to overcome the difficulties of working with their budget being controlled by three separate organisations, only half the team being paid bonuses for completion of critical milestones and different performance management systems being used to evaluate team members.

So, having made the decision to create international teams you need to review your practices in the following areas to ensure they are not going to negatively impact the teams' performance.

Human resources

Alignment of the HR strategy and practices is one of the critical factors for organisations who have successfully created and sustained international teams. The next chapter outlines in detail the role of the HR function in creating the right environment for international teams. However, the human resources staff will need support as they attempt to become international teams themselves and at the same time devise successful strategies to support the working of other teams. The level of detail required can be awesome, even down to the language that is used.

The senior management of the organisation should be partnering with HR to ensure it understands the strategic priorities and ensuring it has the leverage and resources to give the international teams the support they require as outlined in Chapter Nine.

Technology

Whilst the advances in computing technology have been one of the driving forces behind the creation of international teams, many organisations still fail to provide their teams with the basic compatible technologies to complete their work efficiently. Stories of incompatible versions of word processing software, databases that won't talk to each other, presentations that won't open on the screens of half the team members still abound in even the most sophisticated multinational. Even simple issues like log on passwords for computers on different locations and computer screens that are mutually comprehensible often get overlooked until the first international team is created and tries to start to work together.

Provision of appropriate technology is not confined to computing. Adequate provision of phones that have conference facilities is another simple but often overlooked requirement for international team members. Similarly, availability of appropriate video conferencing facilities – either individual or group – can significantly enhance the effectiveness of international teams. If the team has members across several time zones then phones and faxes installed at team members' homes at the company expense can make working unusual hours more bearable. There is nothing worse than sitting in an empty office, after the cleaning staff have gone home, waiting for the phone conference call that you have to participate in.

Although the initial expense of establishing these facilities may be a deterrent in the short term, in the medium and long term, the savings on travel costs and the increase in effectiveness of the organisation's international teams makes it a sound investment for organisations who are serious about globalisation. Chapter Six covered in more detail the technology issues that international teams should pay attention to, but again the role of senior management is to recognise the importance of the technological infrastructure on the effectiveness of their international teams. You cannot expect your teams to be up and running if you do not provide them with the basic tools to do their job.

Facilities

The final aspect of operational practices to mention may seem trivial, but our experience is that it is the little irritations that make a difficult role unbearable. For example, someone needs to assist peripatetic managers with security passes for all the locations where they have team members and somewhere to work when they arrive in distant offices. Arriving at a team member's site and being told that your local security badge is not valid and you will need to be escorted at all times whilst on the premises, does not engender a feeling of belonging to one organisation. Yet it is a common experience for many international team members.

Simple things like sufficient travel budgets for team members can be a major stumbling block. This is particularly the case when international travel in the past has been confined to an elite senior group of managers. This may require a fundamental culture shift that recognises that international travel is a business necessity and not a management perk. An organisation needs to understand when members of a team need to get together face to face and to provide them with the resources to do so. This is rarely a function of hierarchy and often junior members of staff who are going to be working on an international team will need to spend time together in the same place. Travel budgets should be assigned on the basis of need not status, if your international teams are to have any chance of functioning effectively.

Again you need to explore any inconsistencies that exist across functions or locations in terms of these practices. Members of one team arrived at an international airport to fly to a team meeting in the Far East to find some of them had economy tickets, whilst others were travelling business class. This did not get the team off to a good start and led some team members to feel they were being treated like second class citizens, just because they were based in a particular location.

Senior management needs to:

- *Clarify roles and responsibilities with the matrix between line and national managers and international team leaders.*
- *Involve human resources and technology experts from the start.*
- *Invest in the necessary infrastructure.*
- *Allocate travel budgets according to need not hierarchy.*

Role Model Best Practice

Having explored some of the activities that senior managers need to focus on, we now turn our attention to the senior managers themselves. What should they be doing personally to create the right environment for international teams to thrive? Our experience within organisations attempting to 'go global' indicates that the advantages and benefits of globalisation are often organisational and strategic in nature. For instance they include the ability to respond to local differences in product specifications in a cost effective manner or the ability to transfer leading edge technology to production problems irrespective of location of factory. On the other hand, the disadvantages are usually felt by the individuals and teams who are expected to deliver these strategic benefits to the organisation. Such disadvantages include long hours spent at airports or on planes, less time spent with family and friends, phone and fax calls in the middle of the night trying to resolve conflict with a team member who is several time zones away.

Too often the managers at the top of the organisation have themselves never been members of an international team and they have no personal experience to draw on. The danger of this is they can fail to appreciate the demands involved in participating in an international team. Given this situation, senior managers need to seek out, learn about, introduce and role model best practice across the organisation.

Role modelling requires

- actively seeking to create diverse top teams;
- actively being involved with the international teams you create;
- demonstrating that global working can be human.

Actively seek to create diverse top teams

> 'Japan is the major market for my drug, but I cannot get anyone from there on my team — some of the line managers seem to assume that if it works for the UK and US that is enough — I think that is a mistake.'

Your organisation is expanding globally and is considering establishing a number of international teams. If you have little personal experience of working in international teams, what do you do? You may choose to actively seek out colleagues who are different from you. You may ask yourself, 'who can I work with who can challenge the way I see the world?' This might require you to look outside your current networks for the answer or the support may be closer to home.

Look around the boardroom of your company, what do you see?

- Friends and colleagues you have known in and around the industry for years, all about the same age and from broadly the same social class?
- Mainly colleagues like yourself with functional responsibility for key parts of the business, with a couple of non-execs from prestigious institutions in countries you are trying to develop as potential markets?
- A truly diverse group of individuals reflecting the spectrum of cultures you now do business in or aspire to do business in?

Whatever your response, does it provide you with the support and challenge you need to be a successful international leader? More importantly, does it matter?

In recent years, international management theorists have debated the issue of 'requisite variety'[5], the notion that the internal composition of an organisation should reflect the complexity of its marketplace and that international organisations should have considerable cultural diversity in their management cadre. Yet experience with senior teams of successful multinationals demonstrates a rather more mixed picture.

As one CEO reflected after digging his company out of a deep crisis, 'I could not be philosophical and appoint other nationalities and women (onto the executive team), I needed people whom I could trust to say 'yes' [ie people like me]. He did not believe that a diverse management team was important to the success of the company. Similarly, many teams we work with are monocultural, often also exclusively male and have been educated through the American or European education system. Why is this?

Tradition, history and maybe a lack of courage continue to be the main forces that have created many national and international top teams[6].

Selected case studies* have also found that lack of trust in people of other cultures and the absence of strong personal networks for the CEO to produce suitable high calibre international candidates were among the main reasons. Research also suggests that monocultural top teams create less of the cross-border networking of ideas, people and resources, typical of genuinely international organisations[7]. Companies with one nationality top teams also struggled with the phenomenon of the 'glass-ceiling' and with murmurs of national mafias. Successful and ambitious managers do not stay when they feel that they have no chance of reaching the top of the company on the grounds of their nationality.

Even in organisations that have been highlighted in the press as being very effective global players this issue of diversity at the top of the organisation can be a problem. One ex-manager of ABB illustrates how his perception of this issue affected his career choices. Of American-origin, he reached a high level within ABB until he realised that the higher he moved, the more he perceived the decisions were made by Swedish people:

> 'They would allow us to debate the issues at local level, and get the value from the local and the global perspective to get the best of both, but then the decision would get taken without us, somewhere in the Swedish corridors.'

Thus, despite some international mixing at the top of ABB and the strong public commitment of the company to globalisation, for this American the message that 'we value your input' was not enough. He left the company

---

*Conducted for Ashridge International Centre for Management and Organisational Development.

because he wanted to get to the top of the company he works for and make decisions.

Multicultural and dispersed top teams do seem to display a greater curiosity for the way different cultures approach problems. Such teams tend to create international teams and networks below them to exchange best practice, to co-ordinate production on an international scale and to provide effective global customer service. Some organisations have therefore tried to break the mould and successfully create diversity at the top of the company, as the following example cited in Chapter Six demonstrates.

> MacGregor has created an international geographically dispersed top team, and rotates the venue of the monthly board meeting. The key factor with MacGregor is that four of the now six members of the executive team have known and trusted each other for many years. The newer (and younger) finance director was placed on the same site as the CEO in a tiny Finnish fishing village to enable him to experience the culture at first hand. The CEO was passionate about flying only the company flag rather than national flags. Everyone hired has to speak English, and he has fired anyone who wanted to favour one particular turf. After dispersing, the top team spent two rigorous years building up the trust, discipline, team spirit and rhythmical communication patterns to work from different northern European cities. They have flown, phoned and e-mailed the talk so to speak.

While an international mindset is arguably much more important than a mixing of passports, it is often only through getting managers from different cultural backgrounds working together, that the international mindset is created. It must be acknowledged that daily international interaction at senior levels is not always easy to create. People are not as ready to move locations as their counterparts were in the early stages of globalisation.

It is hard to motivate people to live in certain regions of the world that are perceived as unattractive. What constitutes 'attractive' is not always obvious either, for example CEOs of Swedish and Finnish companies often report their difficulties to motivate people to live in Helsinki or Stockholm, due to the high cost of living. Many have moved their headquarters to mainland Europe, especially Belgium and Switzerland to overcome this. As a result, Sweden probably produces one of the highest ratios of able international managers (to national managers) in the world.

Whatever the strengths and weaknesses of the organisation he has created, one message that Percy Barnevik drummed consistently was that if you want successful international teams, then the organisation has to make them happen by consistently challenging managers to select people outside their immediate linguistic and cultural comfort zones. If the CEO or the top team is not continuously beating and role modelling the multicultural drum, it is harder for it to happen throughout the company. Clusters will form, turfs will be protected and inequalities will persist and international teams will find they are expending much of their energies managing these inequalities rather than focusing on the task they need to achieve. As with so many organisational changes, a clear message needs to come from the top.

Summary Learning Points

- *While being internationally minded is probably more important than mixing passports, monocultural top teams tend to create a set of values and networks that make it hard for other nationalities to reach the top.*
- *Dispersed top teams can be a creative solution to creating a diverse top team that also models accommodating the different needs of the individuals on the top team.*
- *Role modelling effective international team working is a primary mechanism for embedding and reinforcing the attitudes within the organisation.*
- *Visibly acting as mentors and coaches to all international teams provides legitimacy to their task.*
- *Collecting the most air miles will not make a company globally successful.*

Be Actively Involved with the International Teams You Create

Senior managers have a critical role to play as sponsors and mentors of international teams within an organisation. Our experience of organisations where senior managers take these responsibilities seriously, indicates that the international teams they establish are more likely to operate effectively and be able to deliver on time and within budget.

Senior managers need to pro-actively put themselves forward as sponsors of new teams as they are established. They should not wait until things go wrong, but should be there from the beginning to ensure things go right. They can assist these teams in navigating through the organisational quagmire of budgetary controls and sign-offs. They can facilitate decision making by helping the team to accurately identify and influence key stakeholders and provide the team with an effective overview of the competing priorities for resource across the organisation, thereby assisting in conflict resolution. As mentors, they can coach newly appointed international leaders and team members. They can create forums to exchange common difficulties and share solutions and identify team development needs and help staff plan the appropriate activities. They can also provide an objective sounding board to talk through proposals before they are submitted to a wider audience.

Visibility is critical. Senior managers need to be seen supporting the international teams they have created. As mentioned previously, they need to give the teams legitimacy in the wider organisation, especially in the early phases of a team's life cycle. This does not mean that they have to be lenient on international teams in terms of their performance, it is about support and challenge. Some of the best international teams we have worked with have been set seemingly impossible targets by their organisations. The difference between those that succeeded and those that failed to achieve their 'stretch' goals was the ongoing active support of their senior sponsors. Even if they were absent for most of the time, they responded positively to requests for guidance and gave clear responses, even if the answer was no.

Demonstrate that Global Working Can be Human

Role modelling by senior managers is critical in setting the style of global working within an organisation. Staff often see senior managers permanently on planes, getting off the 'red eye', coming straight to the office and working through a full day, as well as using the weekends to travel to ensure that they are in an overseas office for a full working week.

It is not surprising that these organisations quickly have an escalating travel bill and an increasingly exhausted workforce. The following quote from one team member typifies the usual pattern in organisations:

> 'Unfortunately our team leader was too busy travelling to have much impact on our performance.'

As in all walks of life, we have encountered some anti-social international companies and global institutions in which senior managers seem to have lost touch with humanitarian rationale. Their power isolates them. Corporate nicknames like 'the Prince of darkness' are not uncommon. These organisations may never change, but yours does not need to join the list. If you want international teams to become your capability to work globally, you will need to think about whether the demands made by the senior managers in your organisation are sustainable in the long term.

Part of the difficulty we see in many international organisations is due to the difference in lifestyle between many senior managers and a typical international team member. Firstly, the majority of senior managers we encounter are over 45, male and have followed their chosen career for a number of years. Their model of international work is often the colonial expatriate cadre who have chosen to spend their career moving every two to three years to far flung parts of the world. The senior managers, we encounter, who are younger than this or are female, have often made a conscious decision to put their career before their family and many are single, divorced or have partners in equally responsible roles and a good live in nanny. International team members, on the other hand, can be all ages and have very diverse family and personal circumstances. They have probably not chosen to dedicate their career to one organisation and may not be prepared to sacrifice their personal life for work to such an extent.

There is increasing evidence that a macho style of globalisation (where executives compete to see who can notch up the most frequent flyer miles) is marginalising whole sections of the global workforce.

The most obvious group who are impacted are parents for whom long stretches away from home means missing large chunks of their children's growing up. As one international team leader commented, 'it's a great job if you don't want a life'. This expectation of being able to jump on a plane at a moment's notice tends to discriminate against female managers who typically still have most responsibility for child care.

However, parents are not the only ones that suffer. This style of global management is a barrier to creating a culturally diverse management cadre and may create a 'glass ceiling' within the organisation. Whilst many American managers and increasingly European managers, seem to resignedly accept this

Figure 8.1: The many hats of an international team leader – 'the hat that got lost ...'

style of global working, many cultures around the world place far more emphasis on community and family values. It would not only be personally unacceptable but also socially unacceptable to be seen to 'neglect' your community and family responsibilities in this way.

Yet even for American managers who seem to have found ways to successfully balance an international role and family life, the impact of this 'macho' style can be even more subtle as the following vignette illustrates:

> A senior manager was appointed to a newly created international role which required him to spend half his time overseas. Fortunately his children were grown up and his wife was about to take early retirement. He came to an agreement with his organisation that instead of flying business class, he would fly economy and his wife would accompany him. This cost the company no extra money and it met the needs of the couple. In addition, there were intangible benefits for the company of the wife accompanying the executive, as they were often doing business in countries where family values are held in high esteem and the wife was able to act as an ambassador for the company with clients. This arrangement worked very successfully for all concerned for two years.
>
> However, when the manager's company was subject to a take-over and the manager had to apply for a new role – again an international one – he was unsuccessful. One of the reasons given was that if he needed to take his wife with him, he probably was not up to the job!
>
> Two years later the senior management team who took this decision were willing to admit privately that they had made a mistake, but only after the 'successful' candidate had lost them significant business due to his cultural insensitivity.

Our experience of this style of global leadership is that it is simply not sustainable in the long run, neither from a financial, nor a human cost perspective. Senior managers need to demonstrate a more 'humane' way of being an effective global leader. They need to recognise that because someone is not prepared to make the same sacrifices as they have, this does not mean that they will not make an effective international team player.

They can follow the advice in Chapter Six and learn to use technology to support a rhythm of global working by, for example, conducting effective meetings using phone or video-conferences, rather than clocking up their air miles. They can also explore ways of conducting international business that meets both the needs of the company and the individuals, as the following example illustrates.

> One organisation introduced guidelines that all international team meetings had to be scheduled on Tuesday, Wednesday and/or Thursday, to enable all participants to travel during the 'core' business week. Scheduling international meetings during public holidays of any of the team members was also discouraged. This had the added bonus of encouraging team members to learn more about their team members' customs so they knew what public holidays to avoid.
>
> In practice, many managers chose to do additional personal local business when they were at a location for a team meeting and maximise their travelling time. However, this was their decision and if they needed to be back home for the weekend, international team business did not prevent that.

Senior managers also need to trust and empower their colleagues and staff to work effectively without direct leadership. This can be one of the hardest changes to make, particularly as in some organisations there will be active resistance from staff, who like the status and security of having their boss located at their site. We have experienced this in a number of American organisations, where country or regional managers were replaced with managers with global responsibility. Staff complain that they feel 'leaderless' and without someone 'looking out for them'. Helping staff to see that maximising performance at one site, or with one product or service, may not be in the best interests of the wider company is critical. Involving them in international teams can be a valuable part of their education in this regard.

Having encouraged staff to widen their horizons and participate in international teams, senior managers need to consider how they are going to expand their personal experience of working internationally.

Assessing Organisational Readiness

Probably the most critical role for senior managers in creating the appropriate organisational context for international teams to thrive is to assess the extent to which the organisation is ready to create and sustain these teams in the first place. This chapter has provided some signposts to some of the critical factors that senior managers need to pay attention to and the following chapter provides yet more detail on the vital contribution of Human Resources.

Senior management teams need to take a critical look at their organisations and ask themselves honestly, are we ready for this? They need to get beyond the long-term vision and consider the detail of how they are going to use international teams to deliver this aspiration. This does not mean they need to do the implementation themselves, but they do need to consider realistically the barriers to implementation. Otherwise the international teams that get created will struggle to survive let alone thrive. Senior management's assessment of the organisation's readiness will often determine the way in which international teams are introduced into an organisation, as discussed below.

Pilot or 'big bang'?

There is much to be said for wooing the organisation with innovative pilots. This is where an organisation selects a particular strategic or operational issue and decides to create an international team to tackle it. The international teams are initially the exception rather than the rule and much of the rest of the organisation continues to be organised locally. Companies who have adopted this approach include Electrolux.

> Electrolux started a process of rationalising and streamlining the throughput processes from production to sales across its diverse organisation. The different 'hot', 'cold', 'wet' products had different needs and annual cycles. Fewer people buy refrigerators in winter and washing machines require customising to different country preferences. A pilot team was set up in Stockholm, where the team members acted as catalysts for different parts of the processes in different sites. As managers began to see the payoffs, more sites and more processes became involved. The pilot team grew and faced its own issues of coherence and inclusion.
>
> The team leader conducted a mid-term health check as well as a survey of the processes in place to see how the managers themselves could take the process further and different sites could learn from each other to start building the critical mass to get the whole company on board. The pilot team provided the impetus to analyse the difficulties and to brainstorm.

Most pilot-led innovations seem to relate to organisational processes, rather than to structures and the technology to support those processes. The advantage here is that the international team designed to pilot the change processes and those they interact with see themselves as champions of change, often well supported in resources by top management and so motivation is often very high. They also know that the best people for the job have been called in from all over the company.

An alternative approach is the 'big bang'. This is where the senior management of an organisation decides that international teams are going to become the foundation of how they are going to conduct business globally. They typically create international teams at all levels of the organisation and these often replace existing organisation designs and local teams. The decision to implement international teams in such a comprehensive way may be the result of internal strategic choices and an assessment of organisational readiness or it might be made in response to a radical shift in the business environment in which the organisation is competing.

An example of an organisation who chose the 'big bang' route, both in response to internal strategic decisions and as a result of significant shifts in the global pharmaceutical industry was Wellcome.

> The R&D function of Wellcome had been organised regionally, Europe and America were the two primary markets. The appointment of a single international R&D Director was the catalyst for a fundamental review of the way R&D was run. It was decided that international R&D International Project Teams (IPTs) and International Medical Development Teams (IMDTs) would replace the existing parallel UK/ American teams. The decision was taken and implementation followed very rapidly within a few weeks.
>
> The organisation had not operated in this way before. Some people lost their jobs, others felt solutions were imposed and everyone, the team members, leaders, managers, sponsors and facilitators were learning at once and some of it was messy. There was a lot of learning 'on the job' and experimenting. It took about a year to really feel that it was working effectively across the organisation. Reaching agreement on some of the basic team structures, roles, and working processes was an evolving process that took several months.
>
> Yet, despite these potentially demotivating factors, there was a strong undercurrent of excitement of the possibilities of achieving so much more than before. The sense of being at the leading edge and experimenting with a new way of working was immensely challenging and rewarding for many involved. It also enabled the organisation to achieve some strategic breakthroughs in product development that simply would not have been possible under the previous regional fiefdoms. Thankfully a thoughtful HR director realised that the teams would need significant support and as described in Chapter Nine, mobilised the Human Resource department.

Clearly there are advantages and disadvantages to both approaches as Table 8.1 illustrates.

This chapter has sought to highlight the key issues that senior managers need to consider before they decide to create international teams in their organisations. The most important message is that senior management have to remember that:

Globalisation cannot be treated as the latest management fad.

Table 8.1: Advantages and Disadvantages of pilots and big bangs

	Advantages	**Disadvantages**
Pilots	One small team does much of the learning and experimenting, avoiding large scale costly mistakes.	Can take time to build up enough critical mass to make a large financial difference.
	People are motivated by volunteering to change.	Not everyone may volunteer and then it needs to be mandated.
Big Bangs	Large structural changes can be effected simultaneously.	Large scale and messy learning and experimenting to sort out all the downstream problems.
	If adequately supported can lead to large incremental financial benefits in a short time.	Needs huge amount of support and facilitation.
		Change seems to have been imposed and is therefore often resisted.

The cost to the organisation both in financial and human terms is too high. If an organisation is going to have a global strategy and operate international teams effectively, then they have to be in it for the long run – this is a marathon not a sprint. Too many organisations are currently operating globally in a manner that is not sustainable, and there is strong evidence that staff are increasingly unwilling to tolerate this way of working. There is another way, senior managers just need the vision and the courage to look to the long term.

Summary of Key Learning Points

- *Involve key players from the start.*
- *Support the organisation's strategic intent with the actions and means to carry it out.*
- *Understand the impact of different strategies on the structure and processes of international teams designed to implement these strategies.*
- *Communicate to each international team how its purpose fits into the company's overall strategy.*
- *Undo out-dated or unintentional structural hurdles.*
- *Choose a workable speed and approach to creating and developing international teams.*
- *Expect to invest significantly initially.* *(cont.)*

- *Learn by role-modelling as a top team and demonstrate how to go global and stay sane.*
- *Act as sponsors and mentors to teams and team leaders.*
- *Allocate sufficient travel budget to appropriate staff, not according to the hierarchy.*
- *Provide adequate communication technology: phones, faxes, mobiles, video conferences.*
- *Realise you are in for a marathon with steep learning curves, not a sprint.*

Chapter Nine

The Role of Human Resources (HR)

This chapter will focus on the role of human resources (HR) in global organisations and how it can facilitate the creation of an appropriate organisational context for international teams to thrive. It builds on the previous chapter which explored the role of senior management and discusses how senior managers and HR professionals need to work together if international teams are going to succeed in their organisation. Evidence of working with organisations who are at the forefront of creating and managing international teams has shown that the traditional model of international HR has not risen to the challenge. The chapter therefore proposes a more future oriented and stretching role for HR in creating and sustaining a climate where international teams can thrive. Our experience has shown us that there are three key aspects to the role of HR in organisations where international teams succeed:

- Aligning HR with the corporate strategic intent.
- HR acting as role models for international teams.
- Facilitating change to a team based organisation.

Aligning HR with the Corporate Strategic Intent

Chapter Eight explored how senior management need to ensure that the organisation's policies and practices are aligned with the corporate strategic intent and highlighted that the human resources practices, in particular, had a significant impact on the performance of international teams. This first part of Chapter Nine will discuss this in more detail and explore how HR can ensure that its activities are aligned with the overall business direction.

HR as a strategic partner

Our experience has shown us that in many organisations, senior management believe that once they have defined the global strategy for the organisation, it is often seen as an HR responsibility to provide support to international leaders and their teams.

> For example, even in Wellcome where the decision to introduce international teams followed the 'big bang' approach (see Chapter Eight), it was left to a resourceful local HR director to identify and allocate the staff to support the newly appointed international managers. This relied heavily on his personal networks across the global HR organisation. Although this support proved to be critical over the next few months, it was not given priority by senior management during the decision making process.

This is possibly because virtually any type of international problem, in the final analysis, is either created by or must be solved by people, and far too many senior executives equate 'people issues' with HR. This is not to say that HR should not play a key role in their organisation's quest to be global, as research has indicated that one of the most critical determinants of an organisation's success in the global business arena is the effective management of its human resources.

However, our experience has shown us that the effective implementation of a global strategy cannot be divorced from the formulation of the strategy. The most successful practice that we encountered was when HR defines the strategy and develops implementation plans *together* with senior management as an integral part of the strategic development of the organisation.

> In one global pharmaceutical company, HR is an integral part of the senior management teams from the board downwards. The HR representative participates equally in the discussions relating to the formulation of the business strategy and the other functional managers develop the HR strategy simultaneously. The HR representative of the management team works in close collaboration with the internal OD consultants to ensure that the processes used in the strategy process are the most appropriate for the business. In this way HR is involved in the Why? What? and How? of the business strategy process.

In organisations that are operating best practice, HR is seen in the organisation as an equal partner in the success of the business. It is seen to have a right to be at the table and is expected to add value by contributing to the bottom line. In other words, the organisation sees HR as a skilled and respected function within the company that partners with line managers to solve key strategic business issues.

HR needs to be seen as, and behave as, an equal strategic partner in the business.

Developing an HR strategy for supporting international teams

Accepting that HR is operating as a strategic partner in the business, how can HR most effectively align its activities to match the corporate strategic intent? One of the first considerations for a senior HR team when confronted with the globalisation of the organisation and the introduction of international teams, is whether they are going to respond with a holistic, strategic review of their activities or whether they are going to remain essentially regional and introduce some targeted global initiatives, eg cross-cultural management workshops?

If we assume that the organisation has moved to a truly global (transnational) organisation and is introducing international teams as core elements, then our experience indicates that the only way that HR can provide the level of support required, is if it undertakes a fundamental review of its HR strategy. Best practice demonstrates that organisations will take international HR seriously if they observe it demonstrating best practice. How can HR hope to convince line managers to work in flexible cross border and cross structural teams, if they see their local HR teams building empires and protecting their patch? The following examples illustrate different approaches and the impact on the client.

> A UK insurance organisation had recently acquired a number of businesses outside its home market, notably in America. The corporate board agreed that there was much to be gained by merging a number of aspects of the newly acquired firms into the existing business. They also realised that they would need managers to operate outside their home market far more frequently. They therefore decided to offer a global leadership programme, which would include M&A sessions, to a cadre of senior managers and HR were asked to develop a suitable offering against a number of clear objectives articulated by the board. HR was decentralised and organised locally and the UK and American HR Directors were given the task of co-ordinating the project.
>
> Six months later no programme was available and the board were getting impatient. It later transpired that there was a power struggle between the American and UK HR directors and neither would accept proposals from the other. The American HR Director would not work with a European business school and vice versa.
>
> In frustration, one of the directors contacted an international business school directly, briefed them and asked them to design a Programme. Within a fortnight the board had a proposal they were happy with. They subsequently implemented this Programme. The behaviour of the HR directors had seriously undermined not just their personal credibility, but the credibility of their function to be considered an equal business partner. A subsequently appointed international HR director found it took several months for her to overcome the negative message this had sent the organisation about the responsiveness of HR.

> In a global IT company the story was somewhat different. HR was also locally organised and decentralised, although a small corporate OD team did exist. One of the international product managers contacted her local HR co-ordinator with a number of queries about transferring a member of her staff to China on an 18-month secondment. The HR co-ordinator had never worked outside his home country and certainly had no first-hand knowledge about employment law in China. However, he assured the product manager that he would have a response to her request within the week.
>
> Using his personal networks within the organisation and externally, and using chat rooms on the Internet, the HR co-ordinator was able to get 80 per cent of the information he required. Colleagues from four other locations were able to give him examples of similar cases they had handled. However, he also recognised that the organisation did not have the necessary expertise in-house to provide all the information and they would need to pay for some external advice. He immediately contacted the product manager, explained the situation and asked how she would like to progress. She was so pleased with the prompt and comprehensive response that she readily agreed to pick up the additional costs of the HR co-ordinator using outside expertise. The client was delighted with the service from HR and the HR co-ordinator had developed his expertise about operating internationally.

There are often barriers to a fundamental review of strategy, not least ownership of budgets and resources at local and regional levels. The dominant model for HR in many global organisations is strong local functions with a small strategy group at the corporate centre. Local HR managers are often not keen to 'give up' some of their local resource to support global initiatives unless they have some element of control over that initiative. An advantage of this global HR role existing somewhere in the organisation, is that someone then has the authority to call all the relevant parties together to develop a revised strategy. This does not mean that the resulting discussions will necessarily be any easier, as you will still be working with a diverse group of individuals with a range of opinions all shaped by their cultural perspective.

In strongly regionalised or decentralised organisations initiating such a fundamental review of strategy on a global basis can be difficult, as you have additional organisational barriers to overcome. However, this is not insurmountable, as long as the key players can be brought together to create a global team at the beginning and co-create the revised strategy.

This leads us to an obvious but often overlooked success factor, which is to ensure that *all* parts of the global organisation are involved in the formulation of the revised HR strategy. Too often we have seen 'global' HR task forces created which only have members from the dominant markets or cultures as the following example illustrates.

> A working party designing a 'global' performance management system had British, Dutch and American membership, despite the fact that the resulting process was expected to be adopted by more than 40 nations world-wide. In many of the countries where it was to be introduced the cultural norms relating to performance varied enormously from the dominant norms of the working party. The resulting draft proposal never got beyond the in basket of the local HR managers.

If you are serious about creating a strategy that is going to be effective and culturally acceptable to all parts of the globe, then it is critical to include the diversity of views at the beginning. Although this may mean that the formulation of the strategy could initially take more time, this will be more than recouped when you begin to implement the strategic plans and you have real buy in around the globe. The 'start slow, end fast model' discussed in Section One applies to HR teams as much as any other international team.

Effective HR strategies are co-created by all the global players.

As mentioned earlier in the chapter, another critical issue is to ensure that the global HR strategy is integrated with the global corporate strategy. In an ideal world this should be developed together with the senior management of the organisation to ensure that they have buy in to the resulting action plans. However, if it is not possible to co-create the HR strategy then there should be a review stage built into the process that allows all the affected stakeholders to contribute. An additional advantage of involving key global managers at this point is that it gives them an opportunity to experience working in an international team and will develop their global mind set, which in turn make them more effective as sponsors and mentors to other international teams. It is important to think carefully about who the stakeholders may be now, and in the future, and get their buy in. The number of global HR strategies that have been rolled out successfully in the headquarters country and main markets, only to fail dismally when rolled out to developing markets are too numerous, as the following example demonstrates.

> An Anglo-German manufacturing organisation had introduced performance related pay and team based performance reviews into its UK, German and US plants. As it expanded into Asia and Latin America, it wanted to roll out 'best practice' to ensure that the newly acquired plants were treated equitably. This included HR 'best practice'. Unfortunately the practices that had been very successful in the 'home' markets were wholly inappropriate for the new markets, which had fundamentally different cultural expectations about performance and reward. Only after threatened strikes in four locations about the introduction of the 'best practices' did the company take some local advice on the appropriateness of the 'best practice'.

Another differentiator of an effective HR strategy for international teams, is that it is seen as a dynamic process and not an annual ritual. Effective HR functions are constantly trying out new approaches, reviewing what has been successful and how to improve areas that are not making the required impact for the business. This is all the more important, because there are, as yet, no proven answers that can be applied to all situations and our experience shows us that practitioners are sometimes ahead of the academics and consultants in this area.

Taking an Organisational Effectiveness Perspective

The current context for international HR is posing a challenge quite unlike any other it has faced. The hallmark of an organisation where international teams thrive is its ability to respond flexibly to the challenges it encounters. It is able to balance the tension between being centrally integrated and co-ordinated, yet locally responsive. If HR is to facilitate the creation of such an organisation, it needs to be looking at the company from a perspective of organisational effectiveness rather than an individual employee perspective, as illustrated in Figure 9.1.

Taking a strategic perspective requires HR practitioners to work holistically with the whole organisational system, intervening more at the organisation and team level rather than the individual level. This is turn requires certain working practices and a specific set of skills including organisation development,

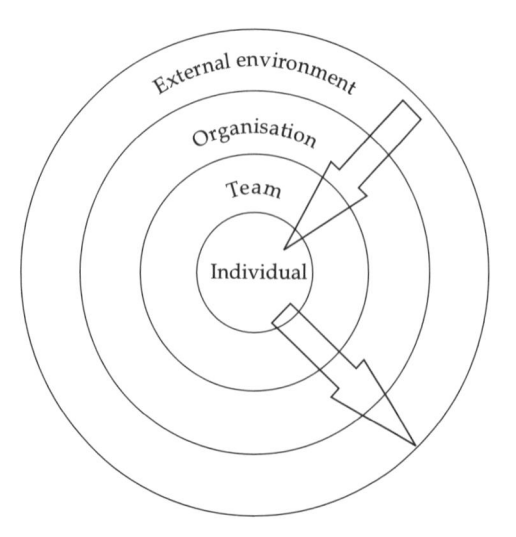

Figure 9.1: Perspectives that guide HR practices

coaching and facilitation skills. It is no longer sufficient for HR practitioners in global organisations to have effective technical skills, they must also have highly developed consulting skills and be able to effect organisational change in line with the strategic needs of business. One organisation we worked with employed the very successful strategy of pairing experienced OD professionals with senior operational HR professionals to enable them to coach and cross skill each other in their respective areas of expertise.

Effective HR practitioners will be tackling the business issues from all angles: skills training; reward practices; leadership coaching; career development. Where they do not have the skills in-house, the best international HR teams seek out experts to partner with. They do this with the intent of learning and bringing the skills in house, thereby increasing the global capability of the organisation. For example.

> Once the senior managers had selected the strategic priorities for the year, the OD team at GlaxoWellcome completed a skills audit to identify what resources they would require to support and facilitate these priorities. They then matched the skills they possessed internally to the skills required. Having identified the gaps they then sought external resources who had the necessary skills and established the appropriate relationship with them. The external resources were always partnered with an internal team member to develop the internal capability.

The current context poses dilemmas for international HR: while the global nature of the business may call for increased consistency, the variety of cultural environments may be calling for differentiation. The role of international HR is to facilitate the realisation that the parent company does not necessarily have the 'right' or 'only' way of conducting business and to manage the tension created by these dilemmas in a constructive way.

Ensure that the HR philosophy and policies are being driven by the needs of the business, rather than the business trying to accommodate inappropriate HR practices.

Increasingly, international HR has to influence the attitude of senior management in relation to international operations, in addition to introducing appropriate supporting policies and practices. The most influential way for HR to achieve this goal is to consider themselves as role models for the wider organisation – it is not do as I say, but do as I do, which has proven to be the most successful approach.

Summary Learning Points

A successful global HR strategy:

- *Is co-created with line managers.*
- *Is aligned with corporate strategy.*
- *Provides a role model for the rest of the organisation.*
- *Is seen as a dynamic process which evolves through action learning.*
- *Takes a holistic view of the organisation.*

HR Acting as Role Model for International Teams

Bringing the key HR stakeholders together at the appropriate time to work on a global HR strategy has proven to be extremely valuable in a number of organisations we have worked with. The shared experience of the organisation and the strong professional backgrounds provide a strong sense of common ground that enables a robust and coherent strategy to be developed. It also sends a powerful message to the wider organisation about how to conduct a strategic review on a global basis. HR is being seen as a positive role model from the outset of the process.

In our experience, however, by far the greatest challenge is focusing the resources in the HR function to deliver this agreed strategy in a way that role models effective international teamwork. This requires sensitive organisational design and an ability to facilitate the change to an alternative organisational structure that more accurately reflects the needs of the organisation and its international teams.

Creating an effective HR structure

One of the more visible symbols of the way HR operates is the way it is designed and structured and any changes to this structure are going to be noticeable to the clients within the wider organisation. This is another reason why it is important that key stakeholders across the global business are committed to a revised global HR strategy and support the changes that need to be made to enable HR to deliver that strategy. It is difficult, if not impossible, for HR to provide effective ongoing support to the business, while simultaneously redesigning itself, if line managers are not supportive.

> A recent merger was completed to very tight deadlines across the globe. To ensure that there was adequate HR support to manage all the integration aspects of the merger, it was agreed that the HR functions in both organisations would remain untouched until the bulk of the work was completed. A single strategic HR team was created to agree coherent practices for the newly created organisation but the implementation was handled by local HR staff.
>
> Once the majority of the integration work was completed in the wider organisation (including organisation design, selection and new team start ups), the integration of the two HR organisations began. This was led by a Board member and supported by the remainder of the Board in recognition of the pivotal role HR had played in the integration of the rest of the business. No new HR activities were initiated by the Board while the integration of HR was completed. The senior managers were acknowledging that it was just as painful and challenging for HR to be integrated and realigned as it had been for the rest of the business and someone had to be their support as they had been for everyone else.

As an organisation's global strategy develops and it operates more extensively around the world, the appropriate HR structure might need to change. One approach that is intuitively appealing, is the contingency approach, where the HR function mirrors the stage of development of the wider organisation. This is illustrated in Table 9.1.

Yet there is much evidence that HR functions are not adopting this model. Research into the structures of HR functions within global companies revealed that less than 10 per cent matched the strategy and structure of the wider organisation. This could account for some of the criticism from senior managers that HR is not delivering what the business needs, but appears to be driving its own agenda. Accessibility and responsiveness are two critical success factors for international HR. If a line manager cannot find an easy response to her issue, she will not look upon HR as a credible partner.

There is no single 'right' way of structuring the HR function. However, best practice undoubtedly means 'practising what you preach'.

The simplest observation that we can make from our experience of successful organisations is that the HR function needs to align itself to the needs of the business it is supporting *and* position itself one step ahead of the organisation, thereby acting as a catalyst and role model. It should illustrate through its actions how to operate at the next level of complexity. By acting as positive role models, HR can help to 'pull' the organisation to a more effective way of

Table 9.1: Contingency approach to international HR

- If the organisation is operating internationally using an *export* strategy, the role of international HR will be minimal. The export manager(s) are likely to be based at headquarters and come under headquarters terms and conditions and any overseas staff will be independent local agents or distributors.

- Similarly if the market grows and an overseas *sales subsidiary* gets established, if an HR function is set up at all, it is likely to be established locally and focus on the HR requirements of domestic staff.

- If the organisation continues to expand and sets up a separate *international function*, the HR staff are either located in headquarters to manage the HR needs of the expatriates or are local staff who again are focusing on domestic HR needs. It may become necessary to begin to develop expertise in areas like international taxation and relocation, although many companies contract these activities to specialist firms.

- Many *multinationals* structure themselves along global products or areas with strong local country managers. HR is often the remit of the individual countries to ensure compliance with local employment practices and legislation. However, the development of managers able to operate in international environments becomes a new imperative. Developing domestic talent to ensure responsiveness to local needs is also critical. Training and development capabilities become increasingly important at the parent company.

- In *global* organisations there is a tendency to attempt to centralise strategic areas and decentralise operational issues. If HR mirrors the organisation, it creates a small international HR function at headquarters which influences the global HR strategy, which is then communicated to domestic HR functions to implement.

- In *transnational* companies, an interdependence of resources and responsibilities exists. The aim is to create the ability to manage across national boundaries retaining local flexibility while achieving global integration. There is a need to embed matrix like behaviour, which require high levels of trust. There is a need to work strategically in the formal and informal systems, which creates a shift in the nature of the role of HR function. HR should operate as an international network of expert consultants to the organisation.

operating globally and thereby create a climate that can support successful international teams. By adopting a strong leadership role, staff in the HR function become adequately skilled for the issues the company will be facing in the future.

Be a High Performing International Team

Where HR is expected to provide support to international teams in the organisation, they should operate as global teams themselves, experiencing all the highs and lows and constantly challenging themselves to learn more about how to be effective as a global team. They should act as a role model for other teams in the organisation and demonstrate learning by doing.

The willingness to engage in action learning and experimenting with models, tools and techniques on themselves, critically differentiates HR functions who are providing leading edge support to international teams. The organisational world is changing at such a pace and effective HR functions need to be structured to respond flexibly to the changing demands. As noted in Section One of the book, different functions within an organisation globalise at a different pace. This requires HR to be able to work with a range of skills, structures and issues simultaneously.

The following stories illustrate how HR can create valuable learning for the rest of the organisation.

Noah's Ark Syndrome

The organisation had two predominant national markets: America and UK. The HR function decided to set up a number of working parties to explore international HR policy issues. Due to the size of the UK and American HR teams, the working parties were to be headed by an American or British team member. To model teamwork, it was agreed to appoint joint chairpersons, ie each working party would be headed by both an American and a UK member of staff. However, after six months of operating with co-chairs, a review of the working parties found that this arrangement was not working. It had led to increased conflict, duplication of resources and blurred accountability.

When the organisation proposed establishing global key account teams about a year later with joint leaders from marketing and sales, the experience of the HR global working parties was shared with the relevant senior managers to help them think through the implications of this decision. This helped them recognise that the proposal for joint leaders was a symptom of an underlying lack of trust between the two functions. This enabled the HR staff to work with sales and marketing on this issue as the global teams were established, thereby preventing difficulties as the teams started to work together.

> ### Creating a rhythm
>
> A global HR project team was established to design and implement a portfolio of workshops and courses to develop the business awareness of middle managers in the organisation. The team had sponsorship from key stakeholders within HR and the wider organisation. Their budget allowed them to meet face to face quarterly. Their first meeting was used to get clarity about their purpose and together they crafted an action plan with timescales and accountability for specific tasks. The meeting review of that first meeting showed that they felt energised and excited about the project and that the meeting had been a positive experience.
>
> When they came together for the second meeting, progress had not been made on substantial sections of the project – despite the commitments made at the first meeting. By the end of the first morning the meeting had degenerated into excuses and guilt blaming. All the energy was focused on identifying who was going to inform the global HR director of the lack of progress. A very different experience from the first meeting!!
>
> Fortunately one of the HR team members had previous experience of working internationally and proposed that they set up a series of weekly one-hour phone conferences and monthly video-conferences to review their progress between the face-to-face meetings. This would allow them to give each other encouragement and support while they were apart, they would identify quickly if the priorities had changed for any team member that required a reallocation of responsibility and would enable them to keep their sponsors informed.
>
> Although not all team members participated in all the phone conferences or were able to attend all the video-conferences, the meeting reviews of subsequent face-to-face meetings showed the value of the team setting up a pattern of regular communication. The team finished its task ahead of schedule. As part of its final meeting review, the team passed its learning to some HR colleagues who were working with global manufacturing teams. They were immediately able to incorporate this into the working practices of these teams with noticeable results.

Few organisations have created truly global HR teams that operate as a microcosm of the wider organisation, yet this provides the opportunity for the staff within HR to experience working globally.

Create a global HR team that develops through action learning – by constantly experimenting personally, HR staff will learn to truly understand how to support international teams in the business.

In attempting to develop the global skills of HR staff, many organisations have identified a portfolio of training courses that their staff should attend. However, this is expensive and time consuming and will not necessarily equip HR staff with the skills they require in a timely fashion. Taking a systemic learning approach has proven to be more effective and durable. Staff may still attend some 'off the job' training but the majority of their skill development should occur 'on the job' through shadowing and coaching.

Summary Learning Points

The following actions can begin to create an environment where global skill development for HR professionals occurs systemically:

- *Identify individuals within HR who already possess the right attributes for working successfully internationally, put them in key roles and use them as role models and coaches for their colleagues. Don't be afraid to bust assumptions about existing hierarchies – go for the skills.*
- *Identify individuals who are responsible for capturing and communicating the learning about global working across the HR organisation.*
- *Provide international leaders with coaches and facilitators from HR to work with.*
- *Hold workshops where HR staff can work 'in the moment' with real issues brought to the session by international leaders and their teams.*
- *Create electronic 'learning laboratories' where dispersed HR colleagues can discuss issues they are working on.*
- *Establish regular best practice reviews to embed the organisational learning.*

Facilitating Change to a Team Based Organisation

The final part of this chapter focuses on how a HR function can facilitate the transition to a more effective international team working across the organisation. It uses a case study which illustrates how one organisation created an international HR team utilising an action learning approach to respond to the globalisation of their organisation. The learning of the HR team occurred in advance of the rest of the organisation who were then able to benefit from this experiment.

226   Leading International Teams

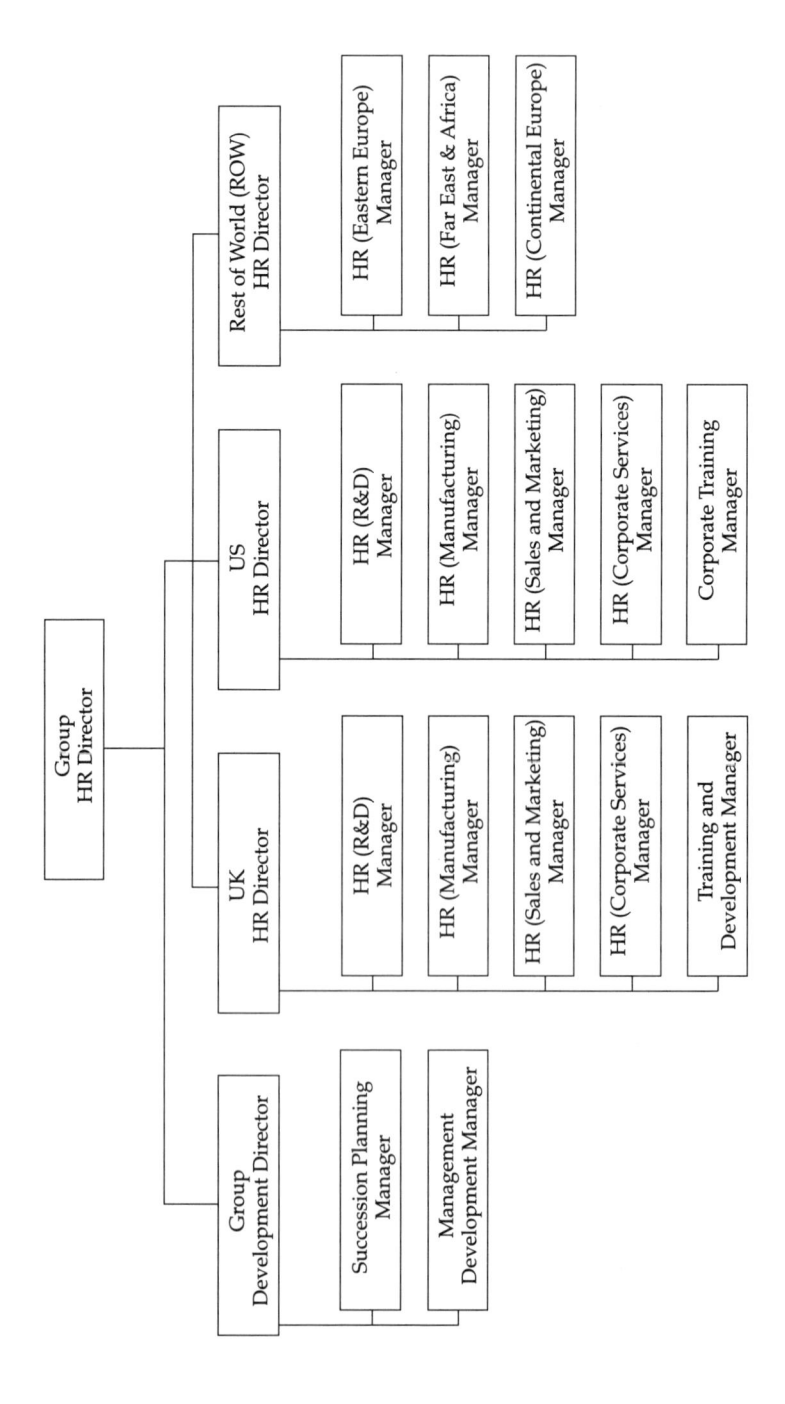

Figure 9.2: Regional HR structure

Case Study: Creating a Team Based International HR Function

The organisation had operated outside its domestic market for over a century, but had remained organised on a regional basis. The globalisation drivers in the industry included the need to have a highly efficient product development process and the need to have the ability to adapt products to accommodate local preferences in a cost effective manner. These drivers were impacting the R&D function most significantly and it was therefore decided to create a single international R&D organisation, where both the line and the matrix leadership positions were international – forcing a single point of decision making.

HR like the rest of the organisation was previously organised on a regional basis as illustrated in Figure 9.2.

As the organisation chart illustrates, each local HR function provided support to all aspects of the organisation: R&D, manufacturing, sales & marketing and corporate services (IT, finance etc) on a strictly national basis. The only part of the HR organisation which had a global remit was a small team who reported to the group HR director and had responsibility for management and career development of a cadre of senior managers globally. Thus the organisation operated a conventional HR structure for a global organisation.

As it was only one part of the organisation (R&D), that decided to organise itself globally, it was not thought to be appropriate for the HR organisation to be completely redesigned. However, it became clear very quickly that the existing structure was not sufficiently flexible to meet the changing needs of the business. The newly appointed senior director of R&D was also not interested in partnering with HR to develop a HR strategy for the new organisation. It was therefore left to newly appointed international line managers and local HR staff to identify the best way forward. An action learning style was adopted and the HR function experimented with several options over a twelve- to eighteen-month period illustrated below:

Option One: Retain the status quo and re-skill staff

This option allowed local HR staff who had previously supported the R&D organisation prior to globalisation to continue to work with their clients who were newly appointed as international managers.

This option was the initial response of the organisation as it represented the least amount of change and was low risk. No-one was clear what the impact of the organisational changes would be and it seemed premature to be making radical changes initially. However, within a matter of weeks, there was feedback from the new international managers that this approach was not providing them with the support they required. A different response was developed.

Table 9.2: Advantages and disadvantages of option one

Advantages	Disadvantages
Provided line managers with continuity of support at a time when they are facing many other challenges	Existing staff did not have appropriate skills to operate effectively in a global context
Provided opportunity for personal development for key HR staff	Local HR staff providing seemingly conflicting advice to International Managers on policies and practices
Staff knew how to navigate the informal systems to access resources	No dedicated budgets or resources to introduce any 'international' initiatives
Low risk – did not need to confront existing organisational power bases	No authority to resolve 'international' policy queries
Simplicity – did not require additional resource or reallocation of resource	The 'Noah's Ark' Syndrome – each international manager having to deal with two or more HR staff for any issue that affected their staff internationally

Option Two: Create international HR teams as pilots

The next experiment was to set up temporary international HR project teams and transfer individuals with the appropriate skills to lead these teams on a part-time basis:

The greatest success of this stage of the experiment was the ability to focus HR resources on the areas of greatest need. It was relatively easy to solve the 'quick wins'. For example, line managers with new international responsibilities simply did not understand the basic terms and conditions and employment law practices in some of the countries where they now had staff. One of the

Table 9.3: Advantages and disadvantages of option two

Advantages	Disadvantages
Focused resources in areas of greatest need	A few individuals had very high workloads and were travelling extensively to the detriment of their health and home life
Allowed HR to respond flexibly to changing requirements	Difficult for the project teams to make things happen as budgets and decision making at the senior level was still regionally organised
Low risk – allowed the regional HR structures to remain untouched	Little opportunity to transfer the learning from these teams to the wider organisation
Provided individuals with appropriate skills with career development opportunities	Temporary nature of the project teams meant that they were not given priority
	Part-time leadership roles led to role ambiguity and role overload

international HR teams developed a handbook and a series of short lunch time briefings over a very short time scale to overcome these difficulties in a consistent manner.

The greatest downfall of this option was that it left the decision making and budgetary authority residing at regional and local levels. This meant that any of the significant global changes that needed to happen were dependent on the international HR teams' ability to influence a range of stakeholders. This was taking too much time and the line managers were demanding that HR provide some more comprehensive solutions to the problems they were experiencing. They were keen to make the new international organisation successful and were supportive of HR being given the resources to make things happen. It was also clear that the impact of the globalisation of R&D was far reaching and was going to have long-term implications for the wider business. Indeed if this worked in R&D, manufacturing were keen to follow within the next eighteen months.

Option Three: Embed permanent international teams into the HR structure

The next step was to create a small core team with global roles and appoint staff with appropriate skills into the roles on a full-time basis.

The dedicated international teams were given a clear mandate by the organisation and provided with sufficient financial backing to accomplish the goals they were set. They were able to bring in expertise from outside the organisation, to enable them to 'fast track' some of the learning. A number of key projects were initiated and completed, encompassing the selection, development and rewarding of the international teams. Over twelve months, the organisation's capacity to operate effectively across the globe was making good progress.

As the organisation became more sophisticated in the way it worked internationally, the demand for support from HR grew exponentially, particularly when it came to providing facilitators and coaches for the newly created international teams. It became clear that the skills developed by the core HR

Table 9.4: Advantages and disadvantages of option three

Advantages	Disadvantages
Provided global organisation with dedicated resource	Created an 'elite' which left some staff feeling excluded from a key strategic initiative
Enabled newly appointed staff to focus on developing interventions specifically for global leaders and their teams	Concentrated the organisational learning in a few people, who quickly became the 'global gurus'.
Created new career path for HR staff	Did not provide sufficient flexibility to respond to changes in client demand.

team members needed to be transferred to a wider population. This wider population needed to extend beyond the HR function if the organisation was going to develop a sustainable capability to operate international teams effectively.

Option Four: Create a part-time international network to support the core teams

The final stage of the experiment was to create a network of coaches and facilitators to work alongside the full-time core team on a part-time basis as the needs of the organisation changed. Two members of the core team were given responsibility for co-ordinating and developing this network in addition to the other projects they were working on. The initial members of the network came from HR and from technical training teams in the business, but soon grew to include international team members from the business who were keen to pass on their learning to others in the organisation.

Having experimented with the options discussed, the solution which proved to work most effectively for this organisation was to have a full-time core global team who had the budgetary responsibility for delivering solutions to the global organisation irrespective of location. This team was staffed with individuals with the most appropriate skills irrespective of previous positions in the hierarchies of the regional structures. This team had accountability for working with senior managers to formulate the HR strategy and identify what resources would be required to deliver the agreed strategic priorities. To implement the agreed strategy, this team worked in conjunction with a network of local staff (HR and line) who worked with the international teams as coaches and facilitators on an as needs basis. This provided maximum flexibility at low additional cost, whilst increasing the organisational learning.

Table 9.5: Advantages and disadvantages of option four

Advantages	Disadvantages
Involved line managers, external experts as well as HR staff	'Messy' – needed some level of co-ordination if organisational benefits were to be realised
Developed a broader base of 'global' capability across the organisation	Some people were not comfortable with the level of role ambiguity
Provided the flexibility to meet the changing needs of the business without the need to increase overall headcount	These roles often cut across existing power bases and individuals therefore required effective conflict resolution skills to make things happen

Summary of Key Learning Points

In a review of the globalisation of this HR function, the following observations were recorded:

- *Influence the newly appointed global management team to work with you to create a global HR strategy – do not try to go it alone.*
- *Do not underestimate the amount of energy and resource required to formulate and implement a global HR strategy effectively – it is not a part-time undertaking.*
- *Identify new global roles, responsibilities and skills as soon as practical.*
- *Appoint staff based on skills required not previous responsibilities or position in local HR hierarchy – be bold.*
- *Ensure a balance of nationalities on the core team – without suffering Noah's Ark Syndrome.*
- *Provide international HR team with its own facilitator and coach – even if that person needs to be resourced externally.*
- *Ensure the whole network reviews its learning regularly with the wider organisation.*

These key learning points are valid for any HR function trying to create the right context to support its organisation's strategy to be global. For many HR staff, they will seem like significant stretches from where they are operating today. However, as Chapter One illustrated, operating globally is not going to be confined to a few large conglomerates in the future. Technology makes global working possible to even the smallest organisation and it is never too early to start learning about how to operate effectively outside your normal cultural boundaries.

Chapter Ten

Organisational Best Practices for International Teams

'The ultimate challenge of global organisations might well lie in discovering how to reproduce inside their management processes some of the vitality that cross cultural dialogue produces outside the organisation. To experiment with such internal diversity will take a new kind of leader with a more global vision, more tolerance for individual and cultural differences, more process skills in managing the inevitably more complex dialogue and the ability to creatively distil out what may initially be chaos as a more viable and competitively more adaptive posture for the organisation. The organisation that can invent, create and tolerate such leaders may well have the competitive edge in tomorrow's turbulent world.'

Edgar Schein, 1986

The previous chapters explored the roles of senior managers and HR professionals in establishing the right context for international teams to thrive. This final chapter of Section Two explores in more detail the organisational practices that need to be put in place if international teams are going to be created and perform successfully in the long term. These practices include:

- Identification of the characteristics of effective international team leaders and members
- Selection
- Development
- Evaluation
- Reward.

Our experience shows us that organisations that pay attention to these five basic organisational processes and relate them to the needs of international teams will make significant progress in establishing the appropriate context for their international teams to succeed. Senior managers, HR professionals and international team leaders and team players need to work together to identify what is appropriate for their particular organisation and teams, as there isn't one size that fits all. As illustrated in the previous chapters, the organisation has to be willing to experiment, to listen to the feedback from the team members themselves and not to seek over engineered solutions – be pragmatic.

Identification of the Characteristics of Effective International Team Leaders and Members

Some form of job analysis or role description often underpins the organisational practices we will discuss in this chapter. If an organisation does not understand and cannot articulate the content of a particular role, it will have difficulty selecting for that position if it becomes vacant, or it will not know how to develop the individuals in the role to improve their performance or how to evaluate or reward the existing performance. Our starting point, therefore, in this chapter, is a discussion of how some organisations have managed the process of identifying and classifying what to them represents an effective international team player.

Chapter Seven explored in some detail the role of the international team leader and the high expectations that are often inappropriately attributed to the role. It is not intended to replicate that discussion here, but instead to focus on examples of current operational practice.

During the late 1980s and early nineties, many multinational companies began to identify a set of competencies that they wanted to use to identify, select and appraise managers across the whole of their business. Two broad approaches have been taken. Some organisations have identified generic core organisational competencies that apply to staff irrespective of their role in the organisation, whilst other companies have focused their energies on identifying competencies for specific roles. Examples of the first approach include British Petroleum's O.P.E.N. behaviours (open mindedness, personal impact, empowerment and networking) and Matsushita's S.M.I.L.E. (speciality, management ability, international, language facility and endeavour). In both companies the competencies acted more like a tool for initiating cultural change than a comprehensive list of skills that could be used to design specific processes and, in Matsushita, in particular, the competencies sent out a strong signal about the company's intention to take globalisation seriously: being effective in the home domestic market is no longer acceptable if you want to be a senior manager. Despite not being targeted at specific roles, generic competencies of this type can still be valuable for international teams, as they send a clear message from the organisation that they wish to encourage the type of culture where international teams would thrive.

Some organisations have gone one step further and this can be a valuable building block when identifying roles for international teams. For example, Citibank intends to go through every job world-wide and describe the three main behavioural outcomes that would constitute excellence in that job. The advantage of focusing on such specific standards as opposed to competencies for managers in general, is that it enables more transparent comparison of similar roles across the whole organisation, be it for selection, development or performance review purposes.

Table 10.1: Wellcome's Effectiveness Criteria for International Project Leaders

Complex thinking	Delivering results	Influencing and motivating
Strategic focus	Action bias	Facilitative leadership
Organisational awareness	Managing ambiguity and change	Building relationships
Problem solving	Performance orientation	Interpersonal adaptability
		Influencing others

Wellcome had been using competencies (due to a dislike of the term 'competency', it called its frameworks 'effectiveness criteria') to underpin a range of its HR processes for a number of years when it globalised its R&D function. It had an existing set of global corporate core competencies which had underpinned a world-wide performance development initiative and a number of key roles had their own specific competencies identified. However, it recognised that this existing infrastructure was not going to be sufficient for providing the framework to support the newly created international teams and work was undertaken to define the effectiveness criteria specifically for international team leaders.

Given that international team leader roles had not existed in the organisation prior to the reorganisation, it was not possible to model the effectiveness criteria on existing high performers. Wellcome therefore undertook a process that included interviewing and holding focus groups with senior managers who were going to be sponsors of these teams, with managers who had led the previously national project teams and with prospective team members. They also identified organisations outside the pharmaceutical industry who already had international team leader roles and used them as benchmarks to compare the internal data. This process although lengthy, enabled a wide population to come to consensus about the characteristics that defined an international team leader in their organisation. The specific criteria are outlined in Table 10.1.

Each of the ten criteria was described in full with a comprehensive list of positive and negative behavioural indicators. For example:

Problem solving

Positive indicators
- Anticipates problems before they occur.
- Analyses the consequences of different alternatives.

Negative indicators
- Concentrates on one issue and does not consider all the options.
- Gets too involved in the details.

These effectiveness criteria were then used as the basis for selecting potential international team leaders and for identifying the development needs of existing international team leaders. They enabled a common language to emerge across the organisation and provided a level of transparency about these new key roles. This enabled individuals from all parts of the organisation to be clear about the criteria that would be used to assess them if they chose to apply for one of the roles and this opened access to the roles to staff in more parts of the organisation.

Whilst identification of criteria, either at the organisational or role level, has been valuable for a number of organisations when establishing international teams, there are a number of potential pitfalls that must be avoided. Some researchers would argue that criteria can often be criticised on three counts[1]:

1 When criteria are based on past success rather than future challenges, they keep an organisation focused on the past and do not prepare them for the challenges ahead.
2 When criteria describe the end-state attributes of current leaders rather than identifying future leaders who may not as yet have developed these attributes. It does not enable organisations to develop their long-term capability.
3 They create a single set of criteria that, by inference, is appropriate in all circumstances.

This last point is particularly critical when it comes to criteria that are to be used globally.

> When a global chemical company devised its criteria, they used two American and one British consulting companies. The result was a set of criteria that worked well for American and European managers, but was less effective in defining high performance in other cultural contexts, eg China or Japan. One author spent three hours with a senior international personnel manager of the organisation going through the very different cultural interpretations of concepts like individual performance, analytical thinking, team working and so on. This helped the personnel manager see the difficulties, but did not help gain commitment to the criteria in the wider organisation.

A final consideration before moving on to explore the practical use of these criteria. Before using an agreed set of criteria for selection and development purposes, a company has to be clear which are personality traits that need to be selected for, and which can be developed or taught. For example, to what extent can a company train someone to act with integrity, to be insightful, or to be courageous as opposed to solve problems, have a strategic focus and to adopt a facilitative leadership style? They also need to ensure that the criteria have been defined so that no cultural group is unfairly disadvantaged by their application.

Whatever the cultural biases and limitations, criteria like those illustrated have created major benefits for most companies who have introduced them. They created an international standard against which managers anywhere in the world could be identified, selected and promoted. This meant that the companies could increasingly act as large pools of interchangeable talent at senior levels. It also meant that internal vacancies focused on competencies and potential, rather than a description of the person who just left, eg 'Five years' experience with toothbrush sales'.

Summary Learning Points

- *The process of identifying characteristics is as important as the resulting output.*
- *Any characteristics identified need to be reviewed for cultural bias and understanding.*
- *A shared view of the criteria required to be an effective international team leader or member enables a more transparent selection and development process for future talent.*

Selecting International Team Leaders and Members

Having identified the criteria that an organisation wishes to use to define the roles on their international teams, the first step is usually to select individuals from the existing workforce to take on the roles of international team leaders and members. What happens when you need thirty international team leaders? You want to appoint them internally, but until that moment you have been a purely national company. This scenario is more common than you might imagine as few organisations have talent pools of potential international team players with proven experience and even fewer have the luxury of the time or money to select externally for such key roles. The selection process for these roles is therefore critical if costly mistakes are to be avoided. One organisation for whom this scenario became familiar was Global Gas, the global branch of British Gas. Their solution was as follows.

> It was essential for the criteria to be clarified in a generic way as there was no relevant international experience in the applicants on which to base any selection assessment. All managers were invited to apply so no-one was ruled out by pre-selection by other managers. Two particular activities were built into the selection process. Firstly, a realistic written case study was created that managers worked on in their own time. Their responses were rated by an expert in international working. Part of the selection interview was then given over to probing and discussing the way they thought about the different issues and how they arrived at their conclusions. The case study could then also be used to probe hypothetical situations to see how the managers thought they would react. A variety of criteria were being probed in this exercise, the depth of understanding of how to manage a different situation, the ability to analyse, be insightful, attend to the detail by looking for the clues, complex strategic thinking in an ambiguous situation, decisions about people, the ability to handle feedback and so on. It was presumed that some of the other necessary skills such as their ability to manage diverse people could be assessed from their performance in the UK.
>
> In another part of the exercise, managers were asked to come to a preliminary briefing and assessment day and to bring their spouses. There is a lot of evidence that the success of managers in international roles is strongly influenced by the support network of family and friends and it was felt that this should be acknowledged and explored from the outset. While the managers were being interviewed, the spouses were sharing their expectations, fears and experiences of being married to an international manager or having to move to another country. There was a long debate as to whether to then interview each couple together or whether that put unfair pressure on the spouse or employee. It was decided that the common briefing about the stresses it can cause, with the advice that couples did need to discuss it in depth, was enough to provide the couples with the relevant information to make an informed decision.

The need for international team leaders to respond to changes in the global energy markets forced Global Gas to work on common criteria and a creative selection solution that enabled them to build on their existing strengths and prepare staff appropriately for the rigours of these new roles. Seagram took a quite different approach when they were looking to staff teams in a global re-engineering project. When they set about creating these re-engineering teams, it was decided right from the start that all teams should be cross-functional and cross-geographical and would co-locate for eight months. Therefore, typically the choice was for an individual with high exposure who was used to working across an entire business or an entire (geographic) division. The process chosen was as follows.

> Criteria were drawn up for the team member roles by Boston Consulting Group and the Human Resources Department. These criteria were sent by the re-engineering steering group (about 4–5 senior people) to all businesses asking for nominations of individuals according to those criteria. The same criteria were used for the team leaders, although those were typically chosen among the most senior executives. Once the businesses had submitted individuals for the teams, the re-engineering leadership made the final selection and allocated people to the teams. The businesses were then obliged to release their people who had been selected. No assessment tools or processes were used and cross-cultural skills did not feature explicitly in the selection process. Finally the office of the president approved the final short list.

The advantages of this selection process were that there was commitment to the criteria and the selection decisions at the highest levels in the organisation, which was critical given that the recommendations made by these teams could have fundamental consequences on the shape of the future business. The process also allowed local business senior managers some discretion in who they nominated, again critical in getting political commitment to staffing the teams. However, feedback about the process showed that one of the disadvantages was that although it had been explained, most team members and leaders had only a rough 'generic' idea why they had been selected ... 'the best and brightest to reshape the company', 'language skills', 'people from different geography, senior and available'. Consequently the teams potentially got off to a slower start, whilst team members clarified their roles and contributions. One comment 'that receiving notice of selection in a written memo from the CEO did not create an ideal environment to think through or seek clarification' illustrated again the importance of the way the process is managed, as well as the final outcome. This is particularly critical if organisations are operating in cultures that place significant value on personal relationships to do business.

Our experience indicates that unless a well thought through and interactive selection process is applied, the leadership role will tend to go to the person perceived to have the most power and influence in the existing organisation (as illustrated in Chapter Three) and this can seriously limit an organisation's ability to respond to global challenges. For example, in the Lever Europe marketing team, it went to the German manager because Germany had the largest sales volume. In Wellcome's quality assurance team, it went to the head of quality assurance because she held the highest position in the existing hierarchy.

Often, the person selected is the headquarters' person in charge of that issue, which again diminishes the contribution of significant numbers of potential international team leaders in other parts of the organisation. For example, IBM's international Airline Support Centre based in London started with an American leader, was followed by another American leader (because the IBM airlines account teams wanted to have an American to keep in touch with the US) who fortunately changed this pattern by stating that the next director should not be American. Given that the team consisted of Americans, French, British, Germans, (East) Indians, Argentineans, Brazilians, Egyptians, Colombians, Finnish and Romanians, mostly all on international rotation, it is not surprising that attributes other than an American passport might be valuable in this role.

We are not suggesting that the people who held the roles were not the best choices from the perceived possible candidates. The first team leader was a woman. 'Very smart, can take many ideas and synthesise them into a coherent vision, everyone respects her' was typical feedback about her style. The second was the only Afro-American in senior management. The problem is that if you are not clear about what the role requires, you use selection processes based on the way national line management has been selected and you limit your pool to the hierarchical status quo, so you may be narrowing your potential field of talent.

By challenging the existing selection norms, organisations often uncover hidden talent as the following examples illustrate.

A board of executives of a financial services institution was convinced that it needed to hire in its next cadre of senior managers from external organisations. They perceived that the internal candidates were not of the right calibre to fill the international roles that were opening up. They contacted an external consultant to manage the recruitment who persuaded them to advertise all the roles internally and offer anyone who was interested the opportunity to participate in a two-day development centre. No guarantees were made other than an objective discussion about their development needs.

The Board members were trained as observers and participated in the process. To their surprise they had a high level of interest from individuals they had not considered and as a result of the process they were able to fill 95 per cent of the roles internally and identify potential longer-term successors who could be ready for all the roles within three years. They realised that their blind spot was to judge people on what they were currently doing, without considering what else they might be capable of.

> In Wellcome, the effectiveness criteria were used to select potential international team leaders and members using 360 feedback from peers. A subsequent evaluation of the process, found that 46 per cent of the international project leaders and 53 per cent of team members were female as opposed to less than 10 per cent of women in line management roles. It seems that this detailed behavioural selection approach opened up the pool of talent available and created a more transparent process than the existing line management selection process.

Summary Learning Points

- *Challenge existing selection practices – are they appropriate?*
- *Be open minded about who can apply for international team roles – personal motivation is very important.*
- *Be creative and design the selection process to meet the needs of the teams and the business.*
- *Be proactive – lack of a specific selection process will reinforce current political power bases rather than get the right person for the role.*

Developing International Team Leaders and Members

Having been selected and appointed into their new role, unfortunately too many international team leaders suffer the same experience as the following individual:

'I have had no training – I'm making it up as I go along and hoping nobody catches on – and it is a very steep learning curve – it is probably a good job I did not know how tough it was going to be or I would never have taken the job.'

The other attitude we've experienced towards development of international capability is illustrated by the following:

'IBM funds cross-cultural training if you are an expatriate, but they do not do as much if you are a national working with other countries.'

The same used to be true of many companies. However, as previous chapters illustrated there has been a marked shift away from expatriates to 'international' workers at all levels and locations of an organisation. Given the complexities and challenges of international roles, organisations are setting up their international teams to fail if they don't provide appropriate and timely development opportunities.

As the range of staff working internationally has grown, so have the development offerings. The 1990s have seen the birth of many in-house and external international management training sessions: these range from nine-month classic business school programmes, through five-week adventures for thirty consorted companies at the University of Michigan, to one-week in-house sessions in different parts of the world, and sometimes to tacking one or two days' cultural differences training onto the end of a standard course. Organisations may be also overlooking development opportunities that they already run as relevant to the needs of international teams. For example, some companies already offer career development opportunities throughout their global organisation and they may find they have a more developed pool of potential international team players than they realise. Research has shown that expatriate experience altered how managers adapted to cultural differences, learnt from mistakes, sought opportunities to learn and acted with integrity. Given this growth of development opportunities on offer, what should organisations be providing as development for their international teams if they want them to be effective?

Cross-cultural training is usually top of the list and has been suggested for many years[2]. The discussions and examples in the first section of this book provide ample illustration of why it is critical to raise the cross-cultural awareness of international teams. Without the skills to know each other and manage their inherent inequalities, international teams won't fulfil their potential. Not surprisingly, ethnocentrism (seeing everything from one cultural perspective) has been found to be an impediment to both culture specific and culture general understanding[3]. Yet many international teams are created by organisations with very strong dominant national and organisational cultures. Cross-cultural training does not need to focus only on national cultures. As highlighted in Chapter Three, organisational and functional cultures can be stronger barriers to effective international teams.

A question that is often asked is, can cross-cultural training be effective for all individuals? As one experienced manager suggested, some people seem to have a high level of curiosity and purposefully seek out people unlike themselves and others seem to be much more comfortable with their own kind. Can cross-cultural training change this?

Our experience of running this type of development intervention over a decade in many different organisations, has demonstrated that good intercultural training can aim to achieve three things:

1 A realisation that other people think, feel and behave differently and that is okay.
2 An initial understanding of one's own value structure and a realisation that knowing more is a never ending journey.
3 An uncertainty that one's own (usually taken for granted) view of the world is always appropriate and the realisation that it may fail to grasp certain situations completely.

So what are the best ways to achieve these aims? A one- or two-day interactive cross-cultural workshop can achieve the first aim of raising awareness that people are different. There are some effective consultants that offer this type of development and many teams have benefited from the insights about each other that these workshops have revealed.

Peter Aylett, who devised the week-long Shell intercultural communication workshop, believed that the best approach to learning anything about one's view of the world and one's values is by creating experiences and situations where people test their own versions of reality against those of others, either by meeting different people or in exercises and role plays. So to achieve the second two aims, you need time and experiences as close to real life as possible. This can be achieved using different types of simulation. For instance, one simulation that enables you to do this is a CIDA* exercise called 'building a culture', which provides you with the opportunity to build your own society and its norms and values as if from a blank canvas. During a week, a safe environment can be created in which participants are very quietly but continuously asked to question their own responses and actions. Feedback from participants who have experienced this development intervention indicates that the process challenges each of your core values very deeply and makes you realise that you have only one way of seeing the world and that it is not the only way.

Another approach that goes beyond a simulation is to create ad hoc project teams for a period of time (eg in Hong Kong Shanghai Bank, four days; in Nokia, four months) that work on some aspect of improving the company's strategy. Teams are facilitated by either internal or external consultants who in varying degrees train and review their interactions as a team as they work. Although this is more effective than short programmes or workshops, the teams know that they are ad hoc and that they do not need to deal with some of the underlying issues in a way a real team would have to.

A training programme would also provide a comprehensive overview of the other knowledge and skills that it is beneficial for international team leaders and members to develop including:

- conflict resolution skills;
- team problem solving technique;
- decision making techniques;
- project management skills;
- meeting design and facilitation.

Specific development tools and techniques that help teams develop their performance throughout their life cycle are outlined in Chapter Five. The formats for delivering the training that we have experience or knowledge of include:

* Canadian International Development Agency.

- being talked at by 'experts';
- doing exercises or case studies;
- role plays on video;
- being hijacked and dumped in the 'desert' or 'jungle';
- building towers;
- elaborate simulations; or
- writing guidelines for potential investors for whole developing economies.

The 'right' intervention for a particular international team will be one that meets their particular development needs, taking their cultural preferences and learning style into account. It will also depend on the sophistication of the training and development resource in the organisation and the availability of resources.

For example, Wellcome had significant managerial support to provide development for the newly appointed international teams and had access to some leading edge research and resources to design and deliver an intervention. It devised a three-day workshop for its current and potential international team leaders – Managing Global Networks.

Managing Global Networks, while it had the limitations of not dealing with actual teams it enabled team leaders to:

- work on clarifying the strategic fit of the teams;
- clarify the roles of team leaders, project managers, team facilitators, team members and the overall team structure;
- highlight the myths about each part of the organisation and the culturally different ways of doing things;
- demonstrate the use of cultural value checklists for setting ground rules;
- learn different problem solving, conflict resolution and decision making skills;
- explore the best use of different technologies in the rhythm of working together and apart;
- role play resolving some of their worst interpersonal conflicts;
- create feedback to senior management;
- brainstorm the ways forward in which the project leaders could share best practices across the business and support and learn from each other.

This intervention provided a valuable 'kick start' for all the new leaders.

Many of the development interventions discussed so far take place away from the actual work of a real international team and are to an extent 'off the job'. These can be of enormous value and are certainly better than letting them, 'figure it out for themselves'. However, it is our experience that the best way to train international team leaders and members is 'on the job' by working with intact teams with their actual issues and providing development 'just in time'.

> **'Just in time' development**
>
> For example, you are working with a team who have to prioritise a range of issues they need to take action on, as they work through each set of issues you introduce different problem solving and prioritisation techniques for them to use. The advantage is not only do they learn new skills, they also immediately know how and when to apply them.
>
> Alternatively a team may have an issue that needs resolving and there are a range of diverse and conflicting views held by team members. You can introduce conflict resolution tools and coach the team to use them on the issue they need to resolve.

The final aspect of development to comment on at this point is the issue of succession planning. Organisations should focus their energies, not just on the current international team leaders but on developing the next generation. International team working is going to become more prevalent and no organisation we have experienced has a sufficient cadre of potential leaders waiting in the wings. The development will not be wasted as the skills they acquire will enable them to be even more effective team members, even if it is a while before they have the opportunity to lead an international team themselves. Some of the approaches to developing actual and potential leaders are outlined in Table 10.2.

Table 10.2: Developing potential and actual international team leaders

Potential international team leaders	New and actual team leaders
Some overseas experience or international environment	On-going 360 degree feedback
Being a team member	Sharing best practices; social, formal, paper, electronic
Interviewing and shadowing actual team leaders	Create an experienced leaders network. They can act as mentors to new appointees
Being aware of the skills required and looking for opportunities to develop them in their current role	Specific skills training as and when needed
Being the facilitator of the team	Other company visits
	Online training, books, videos, journals, conferences etc.

Summary Learning Points

- *Do not assume staff have the skills to work effectively in international teams – even if they already have leadership roles locally.*
- *Think laterally about who needs development – it may not be those doing the travelling Don't overlook existing development opportunities for developing international skills.*
- *Developing cross-cultural awareness is critical – national, organisational and functional cultures – for effective international teams.*
- *Use a broad range of development approaches and techniques according to the cultural needs of the team members.*
- *Develop 'just in time' whenever possible.*
- *Focus development on potential as well as existing team leaders and members.*

Evaluating International Teams

As highlighted in Chapters One and Eight, international teams are often created to deliver particular strategic benefits to the organisation. It is therefore somewhat puzzling that very few organisations have effective processes or measures for evaluating the teams they establish. Where performance measures do exist, they often focus on only part of the picture, usually the output of the team or draw conclusions about performance prematurely. This can lead an organisation to come to erroneous conclusions about the performance and effectiveness of the international teams they create.

Most organisations have performance criteria at some level in the organisation, even if it is only individual work objectives that get reviewed annually. The purpose of the discussion here is not to propose an elaborate evaluation process. Instead it will focus on the key issues relating to the evaluation of international teams to enable organisations to make any modifications to their existing approach. When establishing the evaluation criteria for an international team the critical issues that organisations need to pay attention to are as follows.

Differentiate between measures of team performance and measures of outcome effectiveness

The first issue that needs to be considered here is what aspects of an international team's performance does the organisation wish to evaluate and what is the purpose of the evaluation? The second issue is how to differentiate the team's performance from its effectiveness. In this context, 'performance' is defined as the dynamics and interactions of the team, eg

- how well does the team create and sustain high levels of motivation?
- how well is the knowledge and skills of the team members used? or
- how well does the team manage its relationship to its sponsors and clients?

'Effectiveness', on the other hand, relates more to the tangible outputs expected by the organisation, eg

- the quantity of units produced to a satisfactory quality standard;
- the number and diffusion of innovations;
- milestones completed within time scales and budgets.

A team may perform successfully, yet through factors outside their control, eg a sudden decline in the market; a change in exchange rates or an unforeseen quality problem with a product, remain ineffective. The important message about differentiating between performance and effectiveness is that for far too long, international teams have only been evaluated on the effectiveness of task outcomes. This misses the richness that international teams can bring to organisations, in particular their role in enhancing the organisation's capability to operate globally over an extended time frame. As a result, companies lose not only individual motivation and morale, but also all the learning about how to work effectively as an international team in that particular corporate environment. A team needs to be evaluated on how it was performing, how well it can share that learning, as well as on the impact of the outcome.

A classic example that demonstrates the need to separate performance and effectiveness is when a pharmaceutical product development team discovers that the compound it is developing has serious toxic side effects that require the project to be cancelled. One could argue that the outcome effectiveness of the team is zero, they have not got a medicine onto the market, but this misses the point. If the team has discovered how to work well together while being spread around the world and can pass on that learning to other product development teams in the organisation, it can make a significant contribution to the global capability of the company and its ability to develop compounds and medicines faster in the future. To enable both issues to be evaluated and recognised international teams need to set clear performance as well as effectiveness measures.

> Examples of performance measures set by international teams include:
>
> - The team has set and adhered to clear goals, targets and time lines.
> - The team managed conflict constructively and maintained inclusive and open communication.
> - The team managed to effectively select and involve new members and tactfully let go of inappropriate personnel.
> - The knowledge and skills in the team have been used effectively.
> - The team effectively handled unexpected crises and deviations from the initial plan.
> - The team informed and invited feedback and actively listened to clients, sponsors and stakeholders.
> - The team scanned previous work in its area, clarified the external factors that will affect its performance and created mechanisms for staying abreast of changes in those factors.

These are general examples of performance measures. Each international team should use measures that are created for their own specific circumstances and can be used at both the team and individual level as desired. Measuring these performance criteria will be subjective. They will be gathered by interviewing or surveying team sponsors, leaders and members. In our experience, the responses are more useful and more discerning when they are clearly related to specific group events, concrete examples, decisions and objectives. Hence the need to keep a record of the group process from the start-up phase of the team life cycle. The resultant measures are then more credible to outsiders and more useful to other teams as learning experiences.

A much wider pool of people, including members of other teams, company personnel and perhaps even external clients can be included in the assessment of some of these performance measures. Again, if the team has kept a learning log of its activities in this area, it will be far easier to back up and support both internal and external perceptions of how it managed its relationship to the external environment. Clearly if a team creates innovative strategies for performing well on these issues, but has also recorded that performance so that others can learn from it, it is providing a huge wealth of knowledge about the performance of future teams, whether or not the product it was working on becomes a best seller or is shelved due to some quirk of fate.

The main item to be measured in effectiveness is the extent to which a team produces a product or outcome that adds value to the company. Which exact measurements of sales, cost, quantity, quality, number of errors, capacity, impact on processes, timing etc are most relevant will be specific to each team and product. Some will be easier to measure than others, some more effected by purely external changes than others. Production and sales teams may have a much easier task quantifying their effectiveness in financial terms than a training or facilitation team. But as mentioned earlier, the sales team's results may rely much more on market fluctuations than their performance. The facilitation team's success may depend much more on their performance but they will have a harder time coming up with financial figures.

It is important to get commitment to evaluating both the team's performance and effectiveness from line managers, because the team's performance as a team, many task focused managers will often say, is only an issue if they mess up on the outcome. Given that every company with international teams is either on a steep learning curve, paying high costs for complacency, or heading for disaster, not supporting good team performance, ignoring the learning from previous teams and then complaining when international teams crash and burn is like driving a car down the fast lane of the motorway without taking any driving lessons. Not something that organisations who are serious about globalisation are going to do.

Link evaluation of performance and outcomes specifically to the purpose of each international team.

Involve the team members

A joint process of establishing evaluation criteria brings a sense of fair play and involvement that will greatly increase the team member's motivation and hence performance. The impact of such procedural and interactional justice[4] is increasingly recognised as crucial in creating successful working environments for international teams. By involving team members in establishing the evaluation criteria, each team can assess the different level of control they have over different aspects of their work and environment and therefore what they can justly be accountable for and what they can't.

This is particularly critical for international teams as people from different cultures have different perceptions of the extent to which they can control the events around them. As described in Chapter Two, these differences spring from very different perceptions of self, deeply felt religious and social differences, different types of education, levels of wealth and even climatic differences. It is hard to feel much in control of life when rains are infrequent, unpredictable and mean the difference between living and dying. To have autonomy over resources implies that there are sufficient in the first place. Looking again at the list of performance and evaluation criteria above, each one will be subject to different cultural assumptions about and preferences for what is important. That does not invalidate the criteria themselves. It only means that they need to be arrived at after full discussions. This discussion is critical because without perceived autonomy, the link between team performance and outcome effectiveness will be increasingly beyond team members' control.*

In our experience, if the process of establishing and measuring evaluation criteria is well done it contributes more to performance, than any resulting reward structure. This does not need to be a complicated process, following these three simple steps is often all that is required:

1 First, the team sponsor, leaders and members need to clearly decide the purpose, goals and expected outcome of the teamwork.
2 Second, they need to agree how those goal and outcomes are going to be measured.
3 Third, they need to agree the timing and process by which the people involved will give and receive feedback on their work.

Such a process brings about a crucial interaction between team sponsors, leader and members. It forces team sponsors and senior management to clarify the purpose of the team and to translate that purpose into clear business objectives with measurable outcomes. This in turn enables the team leader and members to work out which aspects of the work and which behaviours will best meet these objectives and therefore the criteria on which their success will be evaluated. It also informs them which aspects of the work are already deemed important and which aspects they may have to fight for. For instance, if the sponsors have given a primary cost cutting goal and the team discovers that it will create unforeseen problems with quality; they know where they are going to need to focus their persuasive powers.

A collaborative evaluation process highlights critical barriers to success as early as possible.

Take cultural sensitivities into account

Evaluation is probably the most culturally sensitive process within international organisations. The measures chosen by the company will themselves be based on a wide range of culturally different assumptions and people will have strong preferences about how the process is conducted. Having decided the criteria for evaluation involving the teams, the next task is to decide the process. There are recognisable differences in the way that people of different backgrounds and nationalities respond to interview questions and surveys. We find Americans tend to be loathe to commit negative criticism to paper, while Finns prefer to write what they will not say directly in person. Some people will be much more explicit over e-mail, and others will treat the written word very formally.

---

*Much of what follows has been recently clarified by Brodbeck F C in *Handbook of Work Group Psychology*, ed. M A West.

Surveys give you numbers and better means of comparison, but are fraught with doubts about how each item was interpreted. Increasingly sophisticated on-line 360 degree assessment tools, that invite boss, peer and employee feedback, are being established that can be used by both co-located and dispersed teams. These tools can generate the essential intermediate team health checks for learning purposes that are all important for performance. However, care must be taken in interpreting the results.

Surveys have come back from Scandinavian countries where individuals have systematically marked each question three on a five-point Likert scale. When the respondents were questioned about this, they usually say that the answer depended on how you looked at it, and so three was the best way of stating that awareness of two possible answers. Many other Europeans seem to feel much easier about marking something a five or a one.

Similarly, in one organisation that introduced an anonymous and confidential 360 degree feedback tool for development purposes, none of the American team leaders scored below a three (six was excellent) despite verbal feedback from team members to facilitators that at least three of them should be removed for under performance. The team members were not prepared to commit this to paper even though the survey was anonymous. This has led some researchers to suggest that a ten-point scale leads to more consistent cross cultural answers[5].

Sometimes it can be the corporate culture, rather than national preferences that lead to skewed responses to surveys. For example, in some organisations, such as the UN, an unspoken corporate agreement not to rock the boat on paper has meant that giving a ratings of less than three (if five is excellent) is just not the thing to do. Evaluation becomes a yearly bureaucratic irritation instead of an innovative individual and corporate learning tool that supports people's curiosity and appetite to do better.

As a response to these difficulties with written surveys, some organisations have introduced verbal team evaluation processes. The advantage of interviews and group discussions is that the different interpretations and perceptions of the questions can be picked up, misunderstandings can be clarified and wording changed accordingly. Even then, as Chapter Two illustrated, some people can find both public and private face-to-face praise or criticism unacceptable. It may be that a combination of written surveys followed by verbal explorations of the responses may be the most culturally valid means of evaluating the performance of international teams.

Effectiveness measures, being somewhat more objective, may be easier to capture in a valid and reliable process across the world. In establishing an evaluation process for their international teams, in our experience, organisations should focus on establishing comparable effectiveness measures that are seen as acceptable globally. If organisations need to compare their international teams they should use these effectiveness measures.

Organisations then need to recognise that establishing standardised absolute evaluation measures for performance that can be normed globally is fraught with difficulty and probably not worth the effort. They should focus energy on facilitating teams to establish their own performance measures that the team can use for learning and development. Teams should therefore not only have to work through the evaluation criteria themselves, but also generate an evaluation process that works for everyone in the team.

If evaluation is going to work for the whole team, there may need to be different individual processes for arriving at a team response.

Ensure timescales for evaluation are not premature

It is critical that managers recognise that culturally diverse teams have significantly more perspectives to work through and integrate at the initial stages of their work. The 'start slow, to end fast' maxim explored in Section One of the book is absolutely critical to understand when considering the evaluation of international teams. Too many organisations have got impatient with international teams, mistakenly only focusing on outcomes and cancelling initiatives too soon. This results in low motivation among team members, who often feel they are just beginning to see the fruits of all their hard work, and significantly handicaps the organisation's ability to develop any sustainable global capability. The organisation learns nothing about how to set up and sustain successful international working in the future.

'Start slow, to end fast' is critical for evaluating international teams.

Summary Learning Points

- *To develop a sustainable global capacity, it is critical to link evaluation to the performance and outcomes of the international teams.*
- *Create measures specifically for each team that are linked to their purpose and the corporate strategic intent.*
- *Involve all the stakeholders in the evaluation process, if you are serious about getting results.*
- *Ensure evaluation measures are culturally appropriate.*
- *Don't evaluate prematurely.*

Throughout this discussion on evaluation, we have not made any explicit link between evaluation and reward, although pay for performance is currently in vogue in many multinationals. Evaluation is valuable in its own right, without a link to pay, as a tool for learning and development. However, reward is an important organisational process and one that has received much attention recently. The last part of this chapter will therefore focus on the role of rewards in creating an organisational context where international teams can thrive.

Creating Rewards Practices that Encourage Effective International Teams

Rewards need to be related to evaluation. So far we have said that in order to evaluate international teams well, senior management, human resources and team leaders need to:

- Understand that international teams are usually aiming for targets that will have much broader impact than those that can be achieved by national teams.
- Understand that as a result, premature evaluation may miss the point.
- Understand that working through to create the criteria for evaluation with team member and sponsors will probably have a far larger impact on commitment to the team and the team's goal than any reasonably equitable reward system.
- Differentiate between performance criteria and effectiveness criteria.
- Focus the time for evaluation throughout the team life cycle.

These actions will go a long way in creating a sense of focus and fairness in what the team is working towards and what they are being measured on. In fact if organisations put in effective evaluation processes, they may not need to spend much extra effort in aligning their rewards practices.

It should be stated up front that much of the energy and effort that organisations invest in creating sophisticated, equitable global rewards practices is, in our experience, rarely worth it. In our view, organisations and international teams are complex systems that can rarely be reduced to the level of simplicity required for an effective rewards process and organisations may be better focusing on the other organisational processes mentioned in this chapter.

So what reward practices are organisations experimenting with? Most of the radical team based reward experiments in America and Europe are going on in self managed teams.* They are mostly at middle and lower levels of the organisation, mostly nationally (although possibly not ethnically) homogenous and mostly co-located. It is likely the impact of these practices is as much that team members are involved in deciding how they are evaluated and how they share out their profits as whether everyone thinks that the end result is totally equitable.

*We have very little first-hand knowledge of Japanese or Asian based companies and so we confine this discussion to American and European companies.

Many Western companies seem to have gone through a cycle. The idea of performance related pay took hold in America and Western Europe and different portions of individual's pay became linked to their output and more recently to their skills development. This had some positive and disastrous effects. For many functions (eg sales, manufacturing) productivity appeared to increase for a time, in others, like R&D departments, people stopped sharing ideas before their managers acknowledged and attributed them to the individual. To overcome these effects of individuals behaviour sub optimising the organisational goals, there has been a move towards team based rewards. This approach has also had its advantages and disadvantages. One consequence was a shift from individual competition to increased inter-team competition. This then encouraged organisations to return to a total company based performance bonus or profit share, which is where many of them started before they started down the route of performance related pay.

Different practices for different teams

Our experience has been that there is no single preferred effective process for rewarding international teams, and organisations have experimented with different practices to suit the needs of their specific teams as the following three examples illustrate.

> In ABB's decentralised approach, people are rewarded on local performance, based on the outcome at the end of the year. As they increasingly need to service clients across national and regional boundaries they have been contemplating stock options or regional bonuses. Where an organisation's global strategy has been more centralised, there is often a split between international staff whose pay and rewards are relatively harmonised and local staff (usually lower in the management hierarchy) who are paid at local country rates. If international teams are a mixture of local and international staff the inequities of this system* are very apparent.

> Creative evaluation and reward can go a long way to lessen the conflicts inherent in an international matrix. MacGregor (a Finnish company in ship cargo-handling, and a subsidiary of a Swedish parent) uses an effective reward system to encourage and support co-operation across its matrix of product divisions and country units. With rewards for product sales tied to country performance and vice versa, the organisation has made co-operation a high priority for key people in the nodes of its matrix organisation. A flexible network of global customer service is the result.

*As described in Chapter Three.

> In Seagram, where the teams only lasted six to eight months, all members and team leaders stayed on their home country scheme (normal scheme) and didn't get any salary adjustment or grade upgrade. It was thought to be unnecessary luxury for the duration of the team. They got housing support (they were co-located for the duration) and could bring their spouse on company expense. The only monetary reward was through the incentive scheme. For re-engineering team members that was changed to 50 per cent on the performance of the team (metrics were part of the overall workplan of the team), 50 per cent on the performance of Seagram overall with the guarantee that they would get at least as much as what they would have got in their business unit (this just in case a business unit was doing extremely well). Given the very demanding nature of the work in the team many team members were better off in getting that kind of bonus than when they had stayed in their business unit.

As shown in Table 10.3 the transnational team survey did show that for the organisations that took part in the study the most common pattern overall was most team members on different pay schemes, paid by their home country organisations, evaluated by the team leader and using individual goals and appraisal systems. However, even in this study, the patterns did depend to some extent on the type of team.

Even in virtual teams (those that rarely or never meet), Jessica Lipnack also reports[6] that in her experience, different companies have similar mixed approaches to reward. 'Some, for example, reward one third on personal goals, one third on goals of the organisation that you report to, and one third on goals of the virtual team. Others just use input from the virtual team (eg peer reviews). Still others have decided not to reward individual teams at

Table 10.3: Reward practices by team type

Type of team	Different pay schemes	Individual rewards	Group rewards	Paid by home country	Evaluated by team leader
International joint venture	4.11	2.89	1.86	4.36	3.35
Corporate headquarters	2.89	3.76	2.9	3.28	4.31
National subsidiary	2.5	2.6	1.2	3.0	3.3
Functional teams	3.47	3.19	2.76	3.25	3.8
Regional headquarters	3.7	3.37	2.37	4.0	4.41
Business development/product launch	4.1	2.37	1.6	3.79	3.0
International task force, co-ordination team	4.0	3.44	1.72	3.37	2.6
Overall average	3.67	2.93	2.03	3.76	3.65

all – whether co-located or virtual – instead deciding to reward the whole organisation (eg Eastman Chemical, which has abandoned all team rewards).'

There is no single, easy solution to international team reward and organisations need to consider their strategic aims and organisational cultures to consider what might be appropriate in their circumstances.

The barriers to integrating rewards globally

Organisational sponsors, human resources and team leaders are up against a number of large obstacles in harmonising cross-national pay schemes. These include:

- Different home country pay schemes and levels of pay depending on the economic context.
- Different taxation and legal requirements especially in bonuses and company perks such as cars, housing, education, medical insurance etc.
- Different cultural perceptions of what is equitable.
- Part-time membership of multiple teams.
- Changing working practices.

Different home country pay schemes and levels of pay depending on the economic context

It is critical to differentiate between absolute and relative pay levels. When absolute pay levels between different countries are so different, it is hardly surprising that no company to our knowledge has equalised pay at the same level across the globe. In most cases if a 'local' person moves into a job previously held by an 'international' staff member, they remain on local pay and bonuses, even if that means vastly different absolute pay levels for the same role. The following example illustrates the difficulties of trying to alter base pay levels significantly for globally mobile managers.

> Imagine an executive from Vietnam on a good Vietnamese salary of $30,000 a year being asked to join a two-year project that is being led from the States, where his colleagues in similar roles are paid $70,000. What is likely to happen if his salary was increased to match that of his fellow team members and then he was asked to return to his 'usual' job in Vietnam after two years on $30,000 again.

It is not hard to see that maintaining a 'local' approach to base pay and adding in variable rewards like allowances and bonuses is the easiest way to begin.

Different taxation and legal requirements especially in bonuses and company perks such as cars, housing, education, medical insurance etc

One of the teams, in the video research discussed in Chapter Three, was set the task of harmonising European pay schemes to enhance the mobility of managers within Europe. There were three categories of issues. A for those that could easily be harmonised, B for those that could be resolved and harmonised with much hard work, such as the different cultural perceptions of what is a worthwhile perk and C for those that were legally impossible. Even in Europe, C was not a short list and related mostly to taxation and legal issues on company benefits.

Different cultural perceptions of what is equitable

Studies[7] suggest that many Americans still feel that it is unfair for a large part of their pay to rely on other team members. Something, we understand, many Japanese have less problem with. From the American point of view, inevitably one or two people may well end up doing a lot more work than others and that should be reflected in individually based pay. The issue of the extent to which different cultures perceive they have control over their environment, as discussed under evaluation, will also have a significant impact on how staff from these cultures will view performance related reward practices.

Part-time membership of multiple teams

Increasingly individuals are finding themselves members of several international teams over the course of a year. In many cases, part-time participation of cross-regional and other teams is more or less voluntary, 'part of the job'. The increase in use of information technology that allows people to remain spread out and contribute in many different ways and the difficulty, at the moment, in quantifying the impact of a lot of different types of knowledge work, mean that evaluating and rewarding contribution equitably becomes almost impossible, as the following example illustrates.

> A line manager in a European chemical multinational was preparing to conduct performance reviews which would determine the percentage of performance related pay his staff would receive. After reviewing the projects and work over the year of just two of his direct reports, he had calculated that he needed to get feedback from 27 international team sponsors and leaders, just to get an accurate perception of the individuals' performance over the year. This line manager had a further eight direct reports, where the picture was not much different. No wonder he felt despairing. And the amount of performance related pay available? Between 3 per cent and 6 per cent of base salary.

Changing working practices

The other challenge for organisations considering their global rewards practices is that the way people work will change so much that trying to harmonise international pay may well become a redundant exercise. It may be increasingly likely that people will have some kind of base-line contract and earn different kinds of bonuses on different teams. They will act more and more like internal consultants, 'hired for a job', rather than permanent staff and so will negotiate their rates based on their contribution to each team.

So, if base pay isn't the answer, what should organisations focus on? One aspect that has not been discussed yet is intrinsic rewards. Participation in international teams and high performance on these teams is often related to intrinsic motivations as illustrated by the following:

> *'People here are skilled, experienced and self starting. With this kind of group, professionals working together – the motivating factor is love of the job and the industry. The job changes so much that the challenges are self renewing. This keeps them involved and motivated.'*
>
> Head of IBM IASC Team in London, 1993

> *'It was more intrinsic rewards such as : access to lots of senior execs across the company (helps in a highly silo-driven organisation), exposure to CEO and senior officers, being on a mission to change the corporation, above all tremendous learning opportunity, and in most cases very good for your next career steps.'*
>
> Seagram HR Manager, April 1998

This issue of career advancement is often cited as one of the strongest motivations for participating in international teams, possibly due to increased exposure to senior management. Organisations therefore need to consider whether their evaluation and reward practices reinforce this motivation. Respondents in the (TTS) survey felt strongly that it was teams which used individual goals, appraisals, rewards and incentives, in which members were given frequent feedback, and where membership increased their knowledge of international business that most helped their careers. It was also important for careers that the members were rewarded for new ideas, good performers received more interesting work, and team members were evaluated by the team leader. Too much emphasis on home country evaluation and reward was considered unhelpful toward helping their careers.

Relevant rewards practices for international teams

So given that there is no single answer to international team rewards and there are legitimate barriers to integrating rewards practices globally, what should an organisation focus on when considering its rewards policies? The following issues if handled correctly can help organisations create relevant rewards practices for their international teams.

Decide how truly interdependent the task is

If each team member is deeply reliant on other team members to perform their part of the task, then group rewards become increasingly relevant. The management must be clear about what improvements they expect from creating a team rather than leaving a group of individuals working independently under one function.

Get rid of obvious inequities

> *'Oh – there is one thing that really causes hassle in our group – some of the Americans got bonuses when we got to our last key milestone and we did not get a bean – how is that for teamwork!'*

It can be worth attempting a harmonisation exercise and deciding what can be easily integrated, what could be integrated with some difficulty and what is legally impossible. This brings greater understanding of the different contexts for reward in the team. In some cases, common pots from a centralised budget can be used to iron out obvious differences, or to give an equitable team based reward over and above different individual pay systems.

Develop simple and transparent variable team rewards

An example would be to give everyone 10 per cent bonus on jointly agreed team goals. Alternatively split a percentage of profits after tax equitably across all the teams. Some companies see giving annual prizes for different kinds of results as the simplest way to encourage teams. The approach needs to be seen as equitable as the following example illustrates.

> One company doing incredibly well decided to reward all its employees before Christmas. However, it decided that the bonus would not be awarded to those staff who had been in the company for less than six months. The managers decided they would simply put envelopes on all the relevant people's desks. The move backfired as for quite a while no-one understood why some people got the bonus and others did not and when they found out, many disagreed with the principle.

Create a sense of fairness and openness

This means involving team members in deciding performance and reward criteria and the method of distribution. Resistance to teamwork in America has been shown to spring from team members' not being involved in deciding the rules for distributing the rewards and the lack of perceived fairness[8]. The act of working it through and voicing suggestions and concerns can placate most team members' sense of fairness even if the outcome is fairly rough and ready. This can be particularly important where international teams are forging into new areas, where nobody has clear answers. These four commonsense suggestions are sufficient to ensure that at the very least, evaluation and reward do not interfere with good teamwork.

Of all the factors in the (TTS) survey, the one that most affected the team's own perception of their overall performance* was the extent to which the team members cared about each other as people. Evaluation and rewards cannot create that care, but done badly, they can damage it. Being collectively involved in setting up the criteria and processes for evaluation and feedback can at least support this care if it is there in the company.

Summary Learning Points

- *Match the rewards practices to the needs of the organisation and the team – there is no single 'right' answer.*
- *Recognise that there are legitimate barriers to global integration of rewards practices and do not attempt to impose a 'one size fits all' from HQ.*
- *Don't get carried away by the latest reward 'fad' or fashion – at the end of the day reward will not make that much difference to the effectiveness of international teams.*
- *Decide how truly interdependent the team's task is.*
- *Get rid of obvious inequities.*
- *Develop simple and transparent variable team rewards.*
- *Create a sense of fairness and openness.*

This chapter has taken an extensive look at five core organisational processes that can significantly impact the effectiveness of international teams within organisations. Too often the design and delivery of these key processes is delegated to the HR professionals within an organisation. We believe this to be a fundamental mistake – not because we believe that the HR function is not competent to undertake such a task, far from it, rather we believe that these are processes which are foundations for an organisation's global capability. If they are aligned with the corporate strategic intent, they can free international teams to focus on the performance and effectiveness targets that will deliver business

---

*There were no external measures.

success, if they are ignored or worse conceived and implemented badly, much organisational energy will be diverted and wasted. Senior management, HR and international team leaders and members must work together to design and implement the processes and practices that facilitate the ability of the teams to deliver.

Summary of Key Learning Points

- *Align key organisational processes to the purpose of the international teams and the corporate strategic intent.*
- *Involve all the key stakeholders in the procedure of developing the processes so that they fully understand the barriers to global integration.*
- *Ensure alignment between the core processes – for example, don't try and reward outcomes that are not being evaluated.*
- *Engage team leaders and members in the design and development of these processes to increase their commitment to the output.*
- *Create forum to share best practice across the organisation.*

Chapter Eleven

International Teams in the Future Scheme of Things

This chapter first summarises the key messages in this book. However, if managers are then hoping for a bulleted summary of the future, we have left that task to others. We choose to first look at three views of the future, one based on technology, one on the quality of the natural environment and one on the quality of human interaction. We show how including all of them in a view of the future, challenges many of the stereotypes that create the problems outlined in Chapter Three. We then briefly consider how technology will change the way people will work and interact. However, we then abandon practicalities and end by imagining how some of the ancient and emerging scientific disciplines and analogies can allow us to look at these teams from different angles. These may well deepen our understanding of how to harness and celebrate the richness inherent in our differences.

The Key Messages in the Book

This book is about creating the organisational capacity to manage globally by using international teams effectively. It has fallen into two parts. The first section is aimed directly at existing or potential international team members and leaders. It describes in some detail the knowledge and skills that he or she will need to be effective. The second section recognises that the effectiveness of an international team will depend on the organisational context. If teams are to be successful, then key people within that organisation have to actively ensure that the cultural norms, unwritten rules, organisational systems and structures and the human resources functions are supporting and facilitating each team.

This leads to what we have termed the systemic approach. This is one where the organisation creates a cascade of learning and experimentation that supports and enables these teams to work together. It demands a huge commitment to change any part of the old organisational processes that hinder these teams being successful. In Wellcome, for instance this meant a complete rethink of the role of a project leader, of human resources and the development of an international facilitation network.

The key messages for international team leaders and members

International teams are more complex than national teams in four key ways:

1. The different nationalities within the team are likely to create greater communication difficulties and different expectations.
2. The organisational contexts and balance of power may exacerbate those difficulties.
3. An international team is likely to be working on a complex broad target that has significant impact on the future profitability of the company.
4. It will also probably do much of its work on communication technology while being spread across large distances and time zones.

This means that there will be many facets to the leader's role. A leader cannot abdicate responsibility for getting the work done, however, with the help of a facilitator, the team members can soon learn to take responsibility for maintaining effective interaction that supports the task. This leaves the team leader freer to act as the conduit between the team, key stakeholders and the organisation as a whole and to promote the team within the organisation.

A team leader benefits from understanding the many different ways in which cultural differences can influence the interaction within the team. By anticipating difficulties and having the ability to look below the surface at the root causes of some problems, the team leader can assist and be assisted by a good facilitator in keeping communication effective. Not only that, but he or she will also have a key role in diffusing the inequalities that will also hinder effective interaction. A set of timely useful practices have been described in Chapter Four which support the interaction and teamwork throughout the team's life cycle.

Because the team is probably geographically dispersed, a team leader has to work out with good information technology experts what technology can best support the team's task. Much can be achieved by using relatively simple existing technologies, eg telephone, fax, e-mail effectively. However, especially in the case of building documents and designs at a distance, shared replicative databases and document exchange facilities are very helpful. The team leader has the responsibility of establishing a disciplined rhythm of working together face to face and working apart. In doing so he or she needs to work out what needs to be done in expensive face-to-face time and to establish a common agreement on how to work apart.

International teams do not exist separately from the organisations, which created them. The team leader needs support from key people and must be clear about what that could be. Senior managers should have explained very clearly how the team's purpose fits in with the overall strategy and have provided supportive resources and infrastructure. The team leader should understand the criteria upon which he or she was selected and have agreed workable expectations with senior management. If senior management is difficult, it is advisable to create a network of international leaders to lobby for adequate support and a sane lifestyle. It is a job that can be highly rewarding and stimulating as well as turn into an eighteen-hour a day nightmare.

The key messages for team sponsors, CEO's, human resources and line managers

International teams help a company most when they are working towards a meta-target that will have a dramatic impact on organisational profits and knowledge. A target that also needs high initial investment and a longer time frame for a much bigger financial impact. A drip by drip approach to supporting and investing in these teams is unlikely to be sustainable. ABB has been successful because it took a dramatic step ten years ago, and persisted. BP Exploration put aside £13 million for its virtual teamwork project and gave them five years to become internally self-sustaining. Other European business leaders have recently rated these two companies as Europe's two most admired companies. Perhaps the motto is 'only the brave survive'.

The top teams have to mirror what they want to see happen in the company as a whole. Their cultural make up will represent the company's global spread and they will be actively learning and demonstrating how to work across large distances. As they create their global visions of expansion and profitability they also need to think through the 'how?'. Human resources and organisation development experts need to be equal partners in the top-level discussions. Teams in these departments will also be culturally mixed and practising what they preach.

The structure of international teams needs to be workable. We have demonstrated that being a 'hopping' line manager three weeks here, three weeks there, does not work. However, an international project leader can lead a team spread across the globe, especially if there are strong counterparts in each location. The key is discipline and rhythm in communication and decision making and using what is available in communication technology effectively.

There needs to be enough international teams to create a critical mass*. Companies with enough critical mass will create flexible common systems, update them and have a project dedicated to exploring the potential impact of new technologies. These companies will have a huge advantage over others taking a slower road.

There needs to be a standard, but flexible model of best practices and interventions for international teams which allows for a wide range of specific interventions to be used in any cultural context at the appropriate time. Just as human resource/training teams in different locations within the same company have to forge a common but flexible approach, so do human resource/training and support teams across strategic alliances. New international teams need to be

---

*Many organisations have different standards, policies and technologies at locations around the world. This is not ideal, but has to be recognised as the starting point for many organisations.

facilitated and fully supported until the learning becomes systemic within the organisation. This may well take five to ten years.

If the number of middle managers has been cut, the organisational memory is usually transferred into a virtual network of managers turned consultants. Creating inter-connected pools of international managers and project leaders is one way of bringing that crucial global knowledge and learning back within the company. Many creative and extensive multi-media methods are being set up to spread that learning systemically through the organisation. Increasing numbers of companies have knowledge managers*.

Much pro-active work needs to be done to prevent internal rivalry, and protecting one's own turf from re-emerging. More attention needs to be paid to the balance between the task and process and profit and people. Management thinking tends to swing back and forth between the two with each swing heralded as a 'new' approach by the management gurus. Top transnational writers[1] have recently stressed the need to go from strategy, systems and staffing to purpose, processes and people and there is now a swing towards the power of the individual rather than whole teams. Whatever the swings and however many wheels are re-invented on the management merry-go-round, managing the interactive processes is now recognised as equally important to the long-term stability and excellent growth of the company as achieving highly effective products and outcomes by co-ordinating and using knowledge and expertise well. So what of the future?

'Globalisation' is Just Warming Up

We have defined globalisation simply as 'economic interdependence between nations'. Some argue that there was more international trade decades ago than now. What is visible now are the large multinationals that function in many countries simultaneously and the growing conformity around key branded products. Given the spate of mergers, strategic alliances and joint ventures, there is clearly an ongoing pressure to become yet bigger and to command adequate market share in more and more national and regional markets.

Large companies will invest heavily in technology and human resources to transform their companies into focused global operations, made up increasingly of international project teams. Small companies and innovative networks will find niche markets between the cracks of the big companies and be able to exploit them with entrepreneurial arrangements based on trust and mutual benefit. As Hermann Simon suggests, small companies can usefully aim high, establish a psychological lead, go deeply into a niche, innovate through slow

*See www.brint.com.

incremental stages and deal directly with customers anywhere in the world[2]. Other companies will remain regional, extending themselves through strategic alliances and joint ventures. In other words, whatever the extent of 'overseas' sales decades ago, true economic interdependence between nations and the spread to mega 'global' companies and alliances has just been warming up these last ten to twenty years.

With regard to management science, so far, much of it has originated in America. It is spreading and other parts of the world digest it at great speed and in huge quantities, especially the Japanese and South East Asians. The fact is that with the shrinking of the global market, Western management will continue to watch and learn from the East just as much as the East will continue to watch and learn from the West. Ford will continue to learn the benefits of a certain amount of centralisation, just as Honda will continue to learn the benefits of being responsive to certain local preferences. Suitable hybrids such as Acer in Taiwan and Toyota in America will continue to emerge. China, India, Russia, Africa and Latin America have so far not had much say in the international management field and that, rightly or wrongly, is unlikely to change much in the immediate future. They will be expected to integrate as best they can, into the current international global business world where a certain set of products and business practices will continue to spread. The split between those that are affected by American, Japanese and hybrid forms of management will, we believe, increasingly be *within* countries, not so much between countries.

Although companies pay consultants like Tom Peters a lot of money to make them aware that they live in turbulent, chaotic times and going a little crazy would be profitable, organisations seem naturally conservative and we therefore doubt we will see any really fundamental change in the purpose or leadership of global companies. By fundamental change, we mean that we have not heard, for instance, of any management guru suggesting that a company scrap the position of CEO or create a top self-managed team with rotating functional leadership from different levels of the company. In fact, current debate is how to have smooth succession into this often controversially highly paid top job. At the moment, the most admired companies tend to have the most visible individual leaders.

Aside from a few admirable attempts at something different like Ben and Jerry's, distinct vertical differentiation of power and wealth within a company are remaining the norm, even if there are fewer, broader layers in the middle. This vertical differentiation also seems to be the most accepted pattern for distributing wealth in an increasingly global capitalist society. This will continue to have some difficult social repercussions in many parts of the world where the gap between rich and poor is getting wider.

Looked at pragmatically, trouble will brew in countries where there are significantly more poor than rich, or lots of people keen to get rich quick. Already the managers of large businesses in these areas, be it in Africa, Latin

America, Indonesia or parts of America, live behind high walls, managed gates and electric fences, with dogs and radio alarm back up and nowhere to safely go for an ordinary thing like a walk. The more dangerous and unstable these areas become, the more difficult it is to do good business.

Alongside this reality come calls for 'equal power' in international teams and leaders becoming coaches, stewards and mentors. We believe that many consultants will keep banging the meritocratic, 'involve different people equally' drum. As some people from developed and 'developing' countries gain the 'right' education and values, they will be accepted into the elite profiting from globalisation. Perhaps two of the most salutary research findings described in this book are that 'the greater the number of nationalities in a team, the less people wanted to work together again', and that the more team members 'cared about each other as people' the more that increased their ratings of their overall performance. We tend to prefer working with and to care more about 'people like us'. 'Like me' will increasingly be 'having the same material wealth, education and access to global information as me' with nationality becoming less important.

Once inside this elite with international access, all the best of what is now being suggested may well be happening; communities based on trust, highly diverse yet all being respected. People will be rewarded for the financial and human value they add to the company and be treated 'equally' with lots of say in what they do each day. Outside these companies, the reality may well look very different. Many companies will feel mostly helpless or uninterested to change the different social, political and economic environments in which they work. For those serious about moving into new markets, they will increasingly look beyond current lack of experience and opportunity and replace the use of expatriate managers with well-trained local people working in dispersed international teams. In order to prevent the kind of negative stereotypes described in Chapter Three arising, companies need to stop rating the world through the lenses of economic strength and technical wizardry and see that each area has its own issues to solve.

Ways of Looking at the Future

As Figure 11.1 points out, it is probably far harder to bring the butterflies back to New York than for a manager in Kenya to get connected onto a desktop video system. Even so the world is almost always measured according to technological development. From that viewpoint, some countries such as America are 'developed' and others, such as Kenya are 'underdeveloped' or 'developing'. From this perspective, at this point in the book we would need to wow the reader with exotic visions of cyberspace, one ahead of the technology that is already pouring out of the likes of Silicon valley. We would then need to extrapolate how it will affect the way people will work in future. This, in our

Figure 11.1: Progress?

humble opinion, would be a limited view, even if it is the one that excites many managers.

Aside from technology and natural environment there is another important futuristic view that says that improving the quality and skill of human interaction is the basis for a secure and happy future. Human interaction and social systems need improving everywhere. America persists in thinking that bombing Iraq is a viable option, the Irish and Israeli peace talks rumble on, the Hutus need to learn to live peacefully with Tutsis and vice versa, the heads of Turkish and Greek Cyprus went to school together but now find it politically more expedient to spend millions of dollars pointing missiles at each other, and a massive bomb just ripped through Nairobi, killing over two hundred innocent people and injuring over four thousand.

The annals of history and endless science fiction movies tell us over and over again that many of us still believe that the only way to deal with the bad guys is to kill or zap them. All that has changed over the years is more advanced technology to do it. Despite centuries of opportunity, our ability to settle our differences through negotiation and other social mechanisms has not improved much. Now suppose that by implementing best practices international teams would not be influenced or adversely affected by inequalities or preconceived stereotypes. We believe that this would be a small but profound revolution in people's sense of self worth and the freedom and opportunity to be who they want to be and to appreciate others. Perhaps an even more profound revolution than being able to interact from any place at any time through a fully equipped virtual meeting facility.

If countries are looked at through at least these three lenses; the quality of human interaction, the quality of the natural environment and the level of technology, then the loaded perceptions that some are much further advanced than others are less clear. It becomes easier to acknowledge that each area has different sets of problems that they need to tackle in order to make life rewarding, safe and full of personal choice for as many people as possible. Some fundamental shifts are in order.

The Future for International Teams

International teams are here to stay. In fact they are only warming up and will be coming in many shapes and sizes. Companies can be assured of a critical mass of research and expertise emerging in the next ten years. This will hopefully do much to clarify which factors are most relevant to team performance. So far, we are convinced that in most cases, what happens in these teams is more sensitive to organisational context and different types of inequalities than to cultural differences per se.

International teams will continue to need to work pro-actively until the 'international team basics', outlined in Chapter Four, become automatic reflexes within and between organisations. New and useful models will emerge. Interventions, cross-cultural translation, international facilitation and interactive individual and team learning spaces will go on-line and be readily available. Hopefully, international teams will not become homogenised and complacent, but will dig ever deeper into the creative depths of their differences.

What technology will offer

Given the amount of ingenuity, money and energy being invested, the technological and subsequent information revolution will continue unabated at a faster and faster pace. Technology will allow certain countries to miss out whole steps that other countries had to go through.

One presumes that from the human interaction perspective, technology is being designed to fulfil the overriding desire to participate from anywhere anytime without being tied to being in a certain place at a certain time. The increasing and rapid development in these wireless 'anytime, anyplace' technologies will make commuting and heading into crowded offices increasingly redundant.

It will do this by:

- Shifting the power increasingly to the user by allowing selective pulling down of information from vast knowledge databases, as and when needed.

There will be much less need to push information from one person to another.
- Increasing the ease and hopefully, emotional fullness of complete interaction at a distance, either one on one or in large or small team meetings.
- Taking over routine processes such as certain standard information flows, arranging meetings, scheduling etc.
- Helping teams to plan, update and keep track of their progress on the task, passing on information from one team member to another as needed, reminding the relevant team member of deadlines, searching out relevant solutions etc.
- Creating on-line interactive exercises and discussions to establish the purpose, goals, roles, ground rules, sources of unity and difference with the team. Interactive team reviews will be available, as will imaginative team process templates to guide the team through fast start up processes.
- Providing interactive on-line cross-cultural facilitation, translation, coaching and problem solving on technical, infrastructure, hardware, software and team process issues.
- Providing new ways to track, evaluate and 'price' knowledge outcomes based on individual contribution.

The result will be that teams will increasingly work solely in the 'team information space' that team members set up in cyberspace and access through their videos, voice respondent gadgets and flexible computers. The biggest threats to competent work will be power cuts, computer viruses and network overloads. Technology will be developed to respond to these threats.

For the individual team members, these facilities will allow greater autonomy about what work they do and when. One may be able to work smart by writing in a number of responses to the outcome of a decision being made elsewhere in the team. When the decision arrives at your workstation, the computer reads it and the appropriate prescribed answer for that outcome is sent off while you are climbing Mount Fuji. So hopefully, based on increasing demand, technology will assist people in not having to be on line 24 hours day and night, while still being able to participate from any place any time.

With regard to interpreting messages, as Chapter Six points out, although the information revolution allows for greater spread and ease of communication, current information technology also allows for greater miscommunication. An important role of good expatriates was to act as on-site cultural buffers and mediators. Now many companies bring locals to the headquarters and send them back to mediate, sometimes with just as disastrous results as with some parent company expatriates, such as when Hong Kong Chinese are expected to know about mainland Chinese practices. Nevertheless, excellent 'dispersed' communication practices will be needed to replace face-to-face on-site mediation.

The revolution in information technology is also becoming a revolution between generations. Young people will grow up 'chatting' with people from different countries and cultures in their own bedrooms, no doubt sharing their commonalities more than their differences. For many large organisations, teams that never meet will be created from lower levels that are already quite at home on-line. There will be increasing pressure from the bottom up for each level to teach the next level up how to do what they want to do without travelling. Members of the top team are still likely to travel independently, meeting face to face with large groups of workers. They will broadcast and emphasise the overall purpose, philosophy and guiding principles of the company. There will be increasing pressure to also spend much of their time responding to e-mails and joining in on-line discussions.

The managers underneath this may well still travel to meet each other one on one, or in complex decision making task forces that make major strategic changes. Given the freedom and support, they will be the sources of growing company knowledge, the movers, experimenters and shakers. They will in turn be organised (or organise the experts; technicians, engineers, accountants etc) into increasingly locally based, but simultaneously virtually connected international teams that can work at a distance. Some may have to meet if the task is groundbreaking, novel and totally new outcomes are being sought. Others will be able to design, gather, collate and work data, integrate systems and create new ones successfully at a distance without ever meeting. They will all be technologically adept.

Technology may come that allows us to see and transmit subtle and tangible emotional messages, to put all our jostling values, opinions and experiences into the information space which then creates a decision that accounts for them all. Who knows? So far each technology has added to and only gradually completely replaced the ones that went before.

As more people get 'connected', there will be many different configurations of teams. Teams with defined membership and definite boundaries and a set task will probably become the exception rather than the rule. All sorts of linkages, co-operative patterns of work will emerge. New and useful typologies[3] will be adopted and new forms identified. Although the model in Chapter Four may well soon speak to the exception, the underlying principles and interventions will still be useful as cultural differences and inequalities will still be potentially difficult to benefit from.

Team members will be recruited and rewarded according to their skill base. Many companies as such, will dissolve into networks of short-term contracts. Team members will increasingly be as good as their last performance, and probably invest in technology that will search relevant websites for on-going team work opportunities. There will be a huge scope for learning and re-inventing your skills in a highly competitive market. People in Silicon Valley will say, but this is not the future, it is the present. For farmers in Rwanda, it is as far away as the Milky Way. Technology will only seriously change the way the world works as a whole as it spreads and supports the desire for improved human interaction . . . the much needed social revolution.

The Social Revolution

So what of the social revolution in international teams? As mentioned in Chapter Three, there are three main kinds of inequality that can have a negative impact on the performance of an international team. Structural inequality where there are more people from one nationality than from any other. Linguistic inequality, where some people speak the working language as a mother tongue and perceptual inequality, were some people have more power and influence because of their perceived social standing, not necessarily because of their skills and contribution to the team.

While automatic translation may do something for linguistic inequality, technology per se will not change the others. That takes good team processes and a change in attitude and mindset. As mentioned above, both could be part of what would then be seen as a social revolution. One that will come about through the interaction between the realisation that certain behaviours lead to poor performance and instability, the use of best practices and collaborative technology. Certain changes are predictable.

The team basics will be embedded

Firstly, the team basics listed in Chapter One and expanded into international teams in Chapter Four, will become more and more entrenched as they are pushed and taken up by all kinds of organisations. More and more people will know and accept generically what a team needs to do when they start, do the work and finish. This will lead to 'instantaneous teams' with very short start up times with people who have never met before, forming, doing the work and breaking up with greater ease. Increasingly people will become comfortable with going through the same processes at a distance using increasingly sophisticated technology.

Templates for handling differences

In this book we have illustrated the cultural value checklist that we have found very useful. Fons Trompenaars has produced an interactive version of his cultural dimensions that managers can analyse where they stand against many country norms. Another group, Transnational Management Associates, have created a simulation to take people through the live implications of making decisions based on Fons' cultural framework. While we cannot say how, one gets the impression that just as David Sibbett is using his graphic talents to create team process templates, templates for handling cultural differences will go on line, be projected and become increasingly complex as well as good fun. The only caveat would be that in creating a sophisticated tool, managers might not be prepared, in spirit and feeling, for when they encounter the edges of the industrialised world. That said, we look forward to see what develops. A lot more will probably be usefully said about culturally different patterns of cognition and logic[4] and the need for greater emotional intelligence[5] in international teams both which may become common additional aspects of the 'basics'.

The interplay of timing, team processes and parts of the task will become increasingly crucial

Once the team processes and task phases have been understood and embedded, there will be increasing focus on timing and rhythm in teams[6], especially those processes that can happen synchronistically and lead to major leaps in productivity, paradigm shifts and helpful 'catastrophic' events. For those wishing to dig deeper into the interconnectedness, messiness, complexity and transformative learning potential of these teams, the analogies and 'new' thinking are already available. Systems thinking, chaos theory, complexity theory and alchemy offer themselves as alluring candidates.

Analysing teams using systems thinking will show the interdependence of the organisational, team and individual levels and perhaps be the most useful model to assist in connecting the work of and events in a team to the organisation as a whole. One of the features of systems thinking is to explain unforeseen blockages created by good intentions or seemingly harmless actions. This may turn out to be very helpful in getting senior managers to understand the consequences of their seemingly harmless actions and attitudes. It may also be useful in demonstrating to teams at all levels of the company that by doing it right, they too can have an impact on the whole... create a 'far from equilibrium' change.

Chaos and catastrophe theory are alluring because they help to move us away from the linear models that have dominated team thinking to perhaps give us a description of those strategic moments, where something just clicks in a team. It can help us think about fields of creativity held in reasonable coherence by special attractors, which may be the ground rules or common sources of cohesion. They may inspire some teams to let go of too rigid procedures by realising that seemingly chaotic patterns of interaction and approaches can be underscored by patterns of order at other levels. The task is to identify the underlying patterns to see if they are leading the team where it needs to go. Reflecting back on the team called Bank 2 in Chapter Three, their response to their chaotic friendly interaction was to impose rigid order, which drained all the energy in the teams. They needed to look deeper to other sources of order that would have allowed free interaction but that guided it in a more useful way.

New scientific thinking has also emphasised the importance of each team member being able to know and understand themselves in relation to others[7]. Maintaining one's core identity, while forging creative ways of co-ordinating one's activities with others is a key aspect of high performing international teams. However, the analogies of chaos theory will probably remain more as juicy analogies and descriptions of possible underlying principles. They will serve to shift the focus onto accepting/inviting non-linear processes, but are unlikely to act as predictors of what will happen in any one international team. A phone call to Mandelbrot[8] some years ago about the possibility of explaining the interaction of international teams with chaos theory, elicited the response, 'I am humble, I stick to fractals'.

Complexity theory helps us understand that coherent complex systems can emerge from a few simple central principles. We are suggesting that practising what you preach throughout the organisation, actively creating level playing fields from inherent inequality, and agreeing clear ground rules for interaction are three of the key principles essential to allow international teams to become creative and involved in highly complex processes. It is a useful perspective and further in-depth exploration will say much about the rhythms and timing that create complexity from simplicity.

For those more drawn to allegorical thinking, alchemy is alluring because the processes that lead to transformation in a sealed crucible are multidirectional and complex. It recognises that processes that are seemingly negative can be a necessary part of transformation. Preparation, descent, grounding, putrefaction, coagulation, mortification (wounding), awakening, nourishment, extension, multiplication, union, rippling, encircling, all lead up to transformation. A transformation happens out of time, where what has gone before ceases to exist. When a critical mass of best practice and understanding has been reached, something seems to happen in many teams, some kind of coalescence. Team members may not be able to fully describe what has changed, only that things work much better and old personality and emotional problems don't bother them anymore.

In future, all these four disciplines may provide creative and thought-provoking different angles on what happens in international teams and change the way some people think about them. As process templates and certain ways of starting teams become embedded, these may be helpful in shaking up things that have then become too rigid again. They will help teams to break out of set norms and to look afresh at different ways of working. Once the team basics have become second nature to most team members, these more complex and intricate processes may become the subject of exploration and study and reveal interesting and sometimes quirky insights.

We are sure that if the value and richness of cultural variety is to be harvested and enjoyed, we need to passionately love our differences and protect them from overriding norms. Structured processes and best practices are invaluable in preventing dominance or unnecessary homogenisation. We remind the reader of our initial analogy of weaving. That international teams may weave a brown cloth, but closer inspection reveals that the individual threads are bright yellow, red, blue, green, pink and so on, not a uniform brown. Such threads can be unravelled and re-woven into many different patterns, whereas uniform brown thread will only ever weave brown cloth. We need to keep our individual colours bright while working effectively with others if cultural differences are to be turned to our advantage. We look forward to watching all the ways that others will unravel our work, re-weave and develop it in order to better understand how to work collaboratively across cultural, social, economic and geographic distances and so improve the quality of human interaction and the effectiveness of international teams.

We have emphasised that in order to be successful in handling the high risk high pay off nature of these teams, team leaders, members and organisational leaders will need to go for a full quota of interventions and support activities. This is a marathon not a sprint. Given the time, money and effort involved, this means everyone involved should consider deeply what they are doing and why they are doing it before starting down the road. On that note, we end with an Indian story.

> One sunny afternoon, a fisherman was lying on a beach with a small bunch of fish beside him. An American tourist came along and asked if he could buy the fish. The fisherman explained that they were for his family and not for sale. The American pointed out that even if he sold the fish to him, there was plenty of time left to catch more and that way he would earn some money. The fisherman asked what he should do with the money. The American explained that he could hire another man and together they could catch ten times as much fish by staying out all day and sell the catch for even more money. 'And what then?' asked the fisherman. 'Well then', said the American, 'you can hire teams of men and two or three boats and after a whole week of fishing make even more money.' 'And what then?' asked the fisherman. 'Then you can build a house for you and your wife and let other people fish for you' replied the American. 'And what then? asked the fisherman. 'Well, then you can lie back and enjoy yourself', explained the American. 'This is what I am doing now', replied the fisherman.

Appendix One

Definitions of Culture

'The historically created designs for living, implicit, explicit, rational, irrational, non-rational which exist at all times as the potential guides for the behaviour of man.'

Kroeber and Kluckholn's version (1952) after discovering 164 different definitions.

'Culture rarely intrudes into conscious thought.'

Herskovits in *Cultural Anthropology* (1954) A A Knopf, New York.

'Man is an animal suspended in webs of significance he himself has spun. I take culture to be those webs, and the analysis of it to be therefore not an experimental science in search of law, but an interpretive one in search of meaning.'

Clifford Geertz in *The Interpretation of Culture* (1973) Basic Books, New York.

'A set of basic assumptions ... shared solutions to universal problems of external adaptation and internal integration ... which have evolved over time and are handed down from one generation to the next.'

Edgar Schein in *Organisational Culture and Leadership*, (1985) Jossey-Bass, San Francisco. Peter Aylett's favoured definition on the Shell Intercultural Communication workshop.

'The collective programming of the mind which distinguishes the members of one human group from another' ... 'this covers what I have been able to measure.'

Geert Hofstede in *Cultures Consequences* (1980) Sage Publications.

'The more difficult question is perhaps' can you name anything that is not encompassed by the definition of culture?'

Fons Trompenaars *Riding the Waves of Culture* (1993) Nicholas Brearley publishing.

Sets of Cultural Dimensions

Geert Hofstede

- Power distance – the degree to which power is shared unequally.
- Uncertainty avoidance – the degree to which people build structures and processes to avoid uncertainty in the future.
- Individualism/Collectivism – the degree to which a person and context focuses on the individual or the group (based on Margaret Mead (1961), Kluckholn and Strodbeck (1961) and Parsons and Shils (1951).
- Masculinity/Femininity – the degree to which the society endorses masculine qualities (material success, money, assertive, competitive) or feminine qualities (nurturing, intuitive).
- Confucian Dynamism – virtue in relationship versus absolute truths – the degree to which people take a long-term thrifty view of the future that values and accepts status and shame or a short-term view based on reciprocity, tradition, protecting your 'face' and steadiness.

Fons Trompenaars

Based on Parsons and Shils (1951)

- Individualism (self-orientation) versus collectivism (collective orientation).
- Neutral (affectivity) versus affective relationships – the extent to which people restrain their emotions or display them, needing for a response.
- Specific (specificity) versus diffuse relationships (diffuseness) – the degree to which people limit the relationship to others to specific spheres or put no prior limitations on.
- Ascription versus achievement – the degree to which you judge others by who they are or by what they do.
- Universalism versus particularism – the degree to which you apply general standards to all or take particular relationships into account.

Based on Kluckholn and Strodbeck (1961)

- Time orientation – the degree to which people define themselves by the past, present and future and whether they see time as sequential or synchronous (see E Hall, *The Dance of Time* (1983)).
- Relationship to nature – the extent to which we believe that we can control nature and our destiny versus the extent to which we think we are controlled by nature and fate.

Some Relevant Books and Articles

- G Hofstede (1980) *Culture's Consequences* abridged edition, Sage Publications, Newbury Hills.

    An in depth classic look at how Hofstede arrived at his dimensions and the results when he processed the databases of two *large* IBM organisational climate surveys conducted in 1968 and 1972.

- F Trompenaars (1993) *Riding the Waves of Culture*, Nicholas Brearley publishing.

    An easy to read introduction on how cultural differences affect business life based on a large database of 15,000 managers. Unlike Hofstede's work, the questionnaires were intentionally designed to measure cultural differences based on the seven dimensions of Parson and Kluckholn outlined above.

- S Schneider and J L Barsoux (1997) *Managing Across Cultures*, Prentice-Hall Europe.

    An intelligent and well studied book on the implications of culture, their effect on key management practices and strategic planning and human resource management and how to manage cultural differences.

- Abraham Kaplan (1996) 'Management and the Structure of Culture' in (Ed) Mel Berger, *Cross-cultural Team Building*, McGraw-Hill International, UK.

    The most elegant chapter on the deep implications of different cultural conceptions of time, space, the degree of enforcement of cultural norms and causality on working patterns. Clearly this was a fitting epitaph for a learned, wise and erudite mind.

For the latest books, CD's, cross-cultural practitioners, see the web page at McGraw-Hill ... http://www.mcgraw-hill.co.uk.

Appendix Two

Sample Form for Counting the Contributions of Team Members

Team: **Time**

Name	Short	Medium	Long	Clarifying/ questioning	Obstructing/ ignoring	Initiating	Supporting/ facilitating
SN							
NP							
TCP							
FM							
MS							
PO							
XC							

Sample International Teams Cultural Value Checklist

The following set of questions are laid out on a scale with descriptions of two opposite approaches to an issue on either end of the scale. The scale itself is not cumulative and is there only to provide reference points. Please mark on the scale with a **cross** where **you personally would like it to be** and with **a circle, how you think it is in your team.**

For example, the first scale reads:

| For effective interaction the team should first create a set of ground rules and stick to them | Effective ground rules will develop through the relationships in the team. |

1   ②   3   4   5   ✗   7

If your **personal** belief and preference is that ground rules will develop through relationships then score the X up the right-hand end of the scale. You may think that within the **team (or department/organisation) in general** there is an understanding that ground rules will be more effective, so you score the circle near the left-hand end of the scale.

1) For effective interaction the team should first create a set of ground rules and stick to them.	Effective ground rules will develop through the relationships in the team.
1 2 3 4 5 6 7	
2) The team leader should make the final decisions after consulting with the group.	The whole team must reach consensus after group discussion.
1 2 3 4 5 6 7	
3) Expressing strong emotions is inappropriate in the workplace.	Expressing all feelings openly and honestly is the only basis for a working relationship.
1 2 3 4 5 6 7	
4) It takes a long time to get to know someone before you are able to work well together.	So long as the specific area of expertise is clear, the rest of someone's individual attributes are unimportant when working together.
1 2 3 4 5 6 7	

5) Project leaders should be appointed because of their political pull and expertise in getting things done in the organisation. 　　1　　　2　　　3　　　4　　　5　　　6　　　7	Project leaders should be appointed because they are technically brilliant in the relevant area.
6) High performance is reached by finishing one thing at a time before starting the next. 　　1　　　2　　　3　　　4　　　5　　　6　　　7	High performance is reached by working on many aspects of the broad picture at the same time.
7) Each person is responsible for his/her own performance. 　　1　　　2　　　3　　　4　　　5　　　6　　　7	There are factors beyond a person's control that can affect his/her performance.
8) Effective teamwork comes from highlighting and working with differences. 　　1　　　2　　　3　　　4　　　5　　　6　　　7	Effective teamwork comes from highlighting and working with similarities.
9) One should only say things that are relevant and that are carefully thought through. 　　1　　　2　　　3　　　4　　　5　　　6　　　7	Talking about things that simply come to mind can lead to interesting ideas and greater creativity.
10) Both appreciation of and dissatisfaction with other people's behaviour should be pointed out directly to them. 　　1　　　2　　　3　　　4　　　5　　　6　　　7	Appreciation of and discomfort with other people's behaviour is best expressed in subtle indirect ways.

Sample Team Interaction Review

1) The team has established an effective common working pattern while recognising individual differences.

Strongly agree   neither agree nor disagree   strongly disagree

   1   2   3   4   5   6   7

2) The team is constantly improving the effectiveness of its interaction and is able to pass on this skill to other teams in the organisation.

Strongly agree   neither agree nor disagree   strongly disagree

   1   2   3   4   5   6   7

3) All the team members participate fully and feel equally involved, wherever they are based.

Strongly agree   neither agree nor disagree   strongly disagree

   1   2   3   4   5   6   7

4) Everyone feels as accountable for the outcomes as the team leader.

Strongly agree   neither agree nor disagree   strongly disagree

   1   2   3   4   5   6   7

5) I am comfortable with the decision making processes and leadership style of the team.

Strongly agree   neither agree nor disagree   strongly disagree

   1   2   3   4   5   6   7

6) The team handles conflict in a creative manner.

Strongly agree   neither agree nor disagree   strongly disagree

   1   2   3   4   5   6   7

7) We have made the most of being a multicultural team and have continuously used a wide variety of experience and thinking in our final decisions.

Strongly agree   neither agree nor disagree   strongly disagree

   1   2   3   4   5   6   7

8) I have been listened to, my skills have been fully utilised and my ideas have been seriously considered and discussed.

Strongly agree   neither agree nor disagree   strongly disagree

   1   2   3   4   5   6   7

9) The team has found the most effective way of using all the communication tools and modes available when working together and apart.

Strongly agree   neither agree nor disagree   strongly disagree

   1   2   3   4   5   6   7

10) The team has found the most effective way of passing on its message to the rest of the organisation.

Strongly agree   neither agree nor disagree   strongly disagree

   1   2   3   4   5   6   7

Annotated Bibliography

Chapter One: International Teams in the Current Scheme of Things

Global trends and global work:

Bartlett C and Ghoshal S (1989)
Managing Across Borders: the Transnational Solution
Hutchinson Business Books

   Management gurus have written many books that apply to global as well as national strategies since the publication of this book a decade ago (eg Hamel and Prahalad, *Competing for the Future* and De Geus *The Living Company*). However, the models and discussions that were based on ten years' research in nine companies seem to remain the most salient and relevant when talking about 'going global'. Whether or not companies have become 'transnational' and despite the lack of discussion on many practical managerial issues; global efficiency, local responsiveness and organisational learning remain powerful explanatory forces for many of the different ways in which companies are co-ordinating, structuring and organising themselves around the world.

Bartlett C and Ghoshal S (1995)
Transnational Management: Text, Cases and Readings in Cross-border Management 2nd Edition
Irwin

   A practical and informative handbook, where the authors not only summarise the most recent research on cross border management, but also illustrate their original models through a range of comprehensive case studies. Whilst not illustrating 'the answer', these cases do provide the reader with an insight into real companies struggling with the issue of becoming 'global'. Widely recommended to students in the field of international management as a good introductory text.

O'Hara Devereaux M and Johansen R (1994)
Globalwork: Bridging Distance and Culture and Time
Jossey Bass, San Francisco
Authors are based at the Institute of the Future, Menlo Park, California, Tel: +1-415-854-6322, E-mail: ohara@iftf.org

   Based at the Institute of the Future which has taken a lead in exploring cross cultural collaborative work, these two authors describe the main fault lines in the new global business landscape. They then look at the multicultural, technological, facilitation and leadership skills necessary to work effectively across cultural, geographical and temporal distances. The second half of the book describes case studies based on US relationships with the Pacific Rim, Mexico and Canada before ending with a look at the dominant norms within the multicultural American workplace and working anytime, anyplace. The book has useful models and lots of good advice, but the structure does not allow for easy access and collation of the 'what to do' learning points.

Rhinesmith S H (1996)
A Manager's Guide to Globalisation: Six Skills for Success in a Changing World
Robert D Irwin

Steve Rhinesmith is an experienced political and managerial globetrotter. The six skills of globalisation he describes cover how to develop a global competitiveness; how to manage complexity and organisational adaptability; how to manage uncertainty, multicultural teams and personal and organisational learning. Although the chapter on multicultural teams is not well thought through, the book as a whole is a good overview of the managerial as opposed to operational challenges of globalisation. There is a useful, extensive but unqualified bibliography.

The information revolution:

Cairncross F (1997)
The Death of Distance: How the Communications Revolution Will Change Our Lives
Harvard Business School Press

The book opens with the trend spotters guide to new communications; thirty developments that Cairncross feels will indicate the death of distance, eg the irrelevance of size, the loose knit corporation, increased value in niches. This is an easy to read speculative book for business people who want to thank about the possible impact of the information revolution on their lives. Cairncross is a senior editor at the *Economist* and the book achieves the same definitive readable style, based on lots of interesting facts, but not strong on alternative viewpoints or other possible realities. This is a good thought-provoking optimistic look at what technology might do.

Tapscott D (1997)
The Digital Economy and *Growing Up Digital: The Rise of the Net Generation*
McGraw-Hill

The first book, the Digital Economy explores the promises and perils of the age of networked intelligence. It is a good basic run through of doing business in the age of technology growth. Tapscott outlines most of the issues in the first third of the book while the rest is made up of examples in different functions and sectors, such as design, manufacturing sales and government, travel, education and media. The second perhaps more interesting book is based on some 300 interviews predicting how the 2 to 22-year-olds growing up with interconnected technology may reshape society. It suggests that rather than becoming isolated techy zombies, future generations will use technology to broaden rather than replace the many ways in which they interact, socialise, learn and work. Better organised and much more interesting than 'the Digital Economy', this book suffers the same problem as Cairncross', drawing simplistic conclusions and lacking of different perspectives from kids not immersed in technology. Nevertheless it makes a good thought-provoking read.

Teams:

Bennis W G and Biederman P W (1997)
Organising Genius: The Secrets of Creative Collaboration
Perseus Press

Warren Bennis and Patricia Biederman have produced an anecdotal easy read book illustrating the successes of seven different collaborative teams. Perhaps an antidote to the drier *Wisdom of Teams*. You have to be prepared to treat each team separately and to pull out your own learning points despite the practical conclusions at the end of the book. However, the storytelling style means that the same team basics get repeated in each story.

Hitchcock D E and Willard M L (1995)
Why Teams Fail and What to Do About It: Essential Tools for Anyone Implementing Self-directed Work Teams
Irwin Professional publishing

Whether or not you are thinking of implementing self-directed work teams, this easy to read well laid out book takes you through solutions to the common reasons why many teams fail; inappropriate roles, low confidence, inadequate support, focusing on the wrong thing, poor appraisal and leadership problems. Hard hitting, tough on managers and down to earth practical advice make this a very accessible book that not only warns of the pitfalls, but also draws on the authors' considerable experience in avoiding them in the first place.

Katzenbach R and Smith D K (1993)
The Wisdom of Teams: Creating the High Performance Organization
Harvard Business School Press

The chances are that if you are reading this book, you have already read this now classic best seller. The success of this book lay in two simple models. First, collating, outlining and illustrating the 'team basics'; those things that every team needs to do to be successful such as having a small number of people, with complementary skills, committed to a common purpose with mutual accountability. Second, coming up with a developmental team performance curve of how a working group can develop from being a potential team into a high-performing team. The authors then backed up these two simple models and discussions on team leadership with in-depth case studies to create a classic on teams.

Robbins H and Finley M (1995)
Why Teams Don't Work: What Went Wrong and How to Make it Right
Peterson/pacesetter Books

This book shares all the things that you experience and discuss with your colleagues about the rubbish and difficulties you are going through with some teams and team members, but usually do not read in dry 'how to get it right' books on teams. It talks to the people actually in the teams, not to highbrow managers. One of the problems is that it does it in very strong American vernacular that makes it hard to understand internationally. Good on a wide variety of real things that go wrong, eg resistance; team sadism; 'hot potato' tasks and 'turf wars' to name a few. Overall you need to structure and pull out the solutions for yourself and the authors are still in forming, storming, norming, performing mode when it comes to moving teams through stages toward success.

Chapter Two: Know Your Team

Cultural differences:

Hampden-Turner C and Trompenaars F (1994)
The Seven Cultures of Capitalism: Value Systems for Creating Wealth in the United States, Britain, Japan, Germany, France, Sweden and the Netherlands
Piatkus

An overview of capitalism in all its different shapes and guises. Based on a survey of 15,000 senior managers from around the world, this book shows how culturally instilled values and customs not only affect the way that countries conduct business but also determine economic success. The authors examine the fundamental valuing processes without which wealth creating organisations could not exist and reveal the different approaches that each country takes. A readable text that builds on the authors' work with individual managers and extrapolates their hypotheses to an organisational and national plane.

Hofstede G (1984)
Cultures Consequences: International Differences in Work-related Values abridged version
Sage Publications

This book laid the ground work for recent acceptance that cross-cultural differences will have a significant impact on international business and collaboration. It is useful to look at this original book for two reasons. Firstly to understand the scale of the survey and to see the detailed results. Secondly, to understand the constraints of the work, eg Hofstede used an existing questionnaire in one corporate culture that hired particular types of people from each culture. He then looked to see which questions could be related to already existing robust dimensions, though the links are sometimes tenuous.

Once these limitations are clear, it can be useful to read his second book, *Cultures and Organization* (1991), McGraw-Hill. This book extrapolates the original findings into organisational reality and also adds in discussion on the fifth dimension, 'Confucian dynamism', and the six dimensions of organization culture that became the basis for his analytical tool, DOCSA (diagnosing organisational culture for strategic advantage).

Redding S G (1990)
The Spirit of Chinese Capitalism
W De Gruyter

Gordon Redding was for a long time Head of the Hong Kong University Business School. He demonstrates his in-depth understanding of the region in this fascinating cultural analysis of the Overseas Chinese in East and South East Asia. It is an excellent reminder that the cultural dimensions described by Trompenaars and Hofstede's work were chosen by two Dutch men. While they talk about individualism versus collectivism, power, uncertainty and control over nature, Gordon Redding talks about the family, networks, filial piety, face, bounded trust, frugality and pragmatism. Moreover, he points out how the ideographic Chinese languages support a very practical rather than abstract way of thinking. Even if you are not going to work with overseas Chinese, this excellent book is a timely reminder that we will also see cultural differences through our own limited cultural lenses.

Schneider S and Barsoux J L (1997)
Managing Across Cultures
Prentice Hall

This is a comprehensive studious book on how cultural differences affect many aspects of organisational life. Perhaps the most unique part of the book is the middle section 'culture and management practice' that looks at 'culture and organization', 'culture and strategy' and 'culture and human resource management', three areas that Susan Schneider has studied and researched in depth and tend not to be covered well elsewhere. Each chapter ends with questions or suggestions and a useful list of relevant endnotes, yet this is not a simplistic 'how to' book, but instead covers the ground thoroughly, raising the important issues. Although not as easy to read as some, it gives the reader a solid base to work from.

Trompenaars F (1993)
Riding the Waves of Culture: Understanding Cultural Diversity on Business
Nicholas Brearley London

Fons Trompenaars chose seven existing cultural dimensions that cover human interaction as well as fundamental outlooks. Unlike Hofstede, he then developed a questionnaire specifically to elicit cultural differences. After some years of working with Shell, consulting and teaching, he not only had a large database but lots of examples of the way in which these differences affect international business. A skilled and much liked presenter who has brought the message of cultural differences to hundreds of companies around the world, this book reads like a well grounded workshop. Fons has developed interactive programmes where you can assess your own cultural standing and compare with others, and created specialist packages for many countries around the world. An excellent introduction to the way cultural dimensions play out in international business.

Cross-functional teams:

Parker G M (1994)
Cross-functional Teams: Working with Allies, Enemies and Other Strangers
Jossey-Bass Publishers

This is an easy to read anecdotal book with lots of examples. Parker starts by looking at the advantages of these teams, which have become the necessary norm in many companies over the last decade. He then lists the common barriers to success; limitations of leadership, confusion about the team's authority and so on and spells out the solution in the following chapters. After a brief chapter on management's role, the book ends with a discussion of tools, a survey and an annotated bibliography. What is missing is any in-depth analysis of how and why certain departments and professions will see the world differently and, therefore, what it takes to creatively work towards a common goal. As the only book specifically on the subject, there is room for more.

Chapter Three: The Impact of Inequalities

A classic book on inequalities is Blau P M (1977), *Inequality and Heterogeneity*, Free Press, New York. It clearly distinguishes between the two concepts and describes how they come about and the social realities that create them.

The impact of tokenism is well described in Moss Kanter R (1977), *Men and Women of the Corporation*, Basic Books, USA, and of majority and minority influences in (Ed) Moscovici S (1985), *Perspectives on Minority Influence*, Cambridge University Press.

Some thought-provoking recent chapters on dominant identity, the effects of group proportions and multiple identities can be found in (Ed) Jackson S E, Ruderman M N (1995), *Diversity in Work Teams: Research Paradigms for a Changing Workplace*, American Psychological Association, Washington DC.

Chapter Four: Implementing Best Practices

Team toolkits:

(Ed.) Berger M (1996)
Cross-cultural Team Building: Guidelines for More Effective Communication and Negotiation
McGraw-Hill UK

This books pulls together a wide variety of authors on the issue of culture and teams. As mentioned in Appendix One, the chapter by Abe Kaplan is probably one of the most erudite on 'what is culture'. Paul Kingston's chapter is an excellent case history of dealing with the issue of language in an Anglo-French merger of GEC-Alsthom. Imre Lovey amply demonstrated the problems of unequal expectations between wealthy Americans and newly 'capitalised' Hungarians working together. Dennis Clackworthy from Siemens outlines his excellent in-depth work on how differently Americans and Germans approach conflict resolution. While dealing with specific examples and nationalities, all these chapters have lessons for all.

Rayner and Associates
Virtual Teams
Rayner & Associates Inc

This practical large format handbook takes would-be virtual teams (that can also meet face to face) through the 13 disciplines needed to be effective. These disciplines include virtual team building, establishing a team charter, and working across boundary conditions. Well laid out with clear sequences of questions to ask, template questionnaires and good practical advice, this is a useful unfussy handbook that can be adapted to working across cultures.

Senge P et al (1994)
The Fifth Discipline Handbook: Strategies and Tools for Building a Learning Organisation
Currency Doubleday

While not written for international teams, or even teams, per se, this handbook provides a wealth of models, tools and techniques, which are readily adaptable for the purpose. With its excellent references, it points the reader to further texts and ideas, but also focuses on practical tips about how to use these ideas in practice. While professional facilitators will probably get the maximum benefit from this handbook, the language and ideas are accessible to international team players in general.

Chapter Five: Facilitating International Teams and Key Interventions

Butler A (1996)
Teamthink: 72 Things to Make Good Smart, Quick Decisions in any Meeting
McGraw-Hill

Easily accessible and well organised, this book is a bevvy of tools and ideas with which teams can enjoy improving their meetings. Toys and music may not be for everyone, but something else will be useful from the six techniques to brainstorm ideas, eighteen ways to gather information, eleven ways to make decisions and seven ways to implement them. A book to skim, pick from, adapt and use.

Heron J (1989)
The Facilitator's Handbook
Kogan Page

While not written specifically with international teams in mind, this book covers the basic skills and expertise required by an effective facilitator. It includes dimensions and models, group dynamics, planning, meaning, confrontation, feeling, structuring, valuing and creating a style. It focuses on the role of the facilitator in relation to the team and does not explore the wider organisational context of the role in any depth. A good introductory text.

Schwarz R (1994)
The Skilled Facilitator: Practical Wisdom for Developing Effective Groups
Jossey Bass Publishers, San Francisco

A professional book, it opens with in-depth analyses of the facilitator's role and what makes groups effective. This is followed by important chapters on how to contract with the group and identifying different behaviours. The next part of the book looks at how to intervene at different stages and deal with conflict and emotions. The format is not that accessible and is probably more useful for skilled facilitators wanting to think about what they are doing rather than beginners wanting to know what to do at each stage and how to deal with common problems. An excellent comprehensive book on the theory and practice of facilitation that would be well complemented by something more accessible.

Chapter Six: Leading in the Information Space:
Teams and Technology

Information/knowledge working:

Boisot M (1995)
Information Space: A Framework for Learning in Organisations, Institutions and Culture
Routledge

This book is a challenge for the grey cells. It looks in detail at how data becomes information and how six different stages of a 'social learning cycle' do different things to information. There is an excellent chapter on how culture economises on data/ information processing and leads to the need for variety as well as both converging and diverging forces within an organisation. Thought provoking and not for the faint-hearted ... look out for his apparently more accessible new book *Knowledge Assets*, Oxford University Press.

Fisher K, Fisher M D (1998)
The Distributed Mind: Achieving High Performance Through the Collective Intelligence of Knowledge Work Teams
Amacom

The Fishers take the basics about teams and rethink them. For example, when the teamwork is based on organising and creating knowledge. They cover in particular the different ways in which knowledge teams need to become self-managed, 'vertically' multiskilled and create multiple communication channels. Companies need to organise into learning lattices and support rather than control these teams. They discuss the issue of maintaining creativity and describe the seven competencies of boundary managers, the main role of knowledge team leaders. The chapters on virtual teams and matching technology to the team are very general. Overall, this is a well researched, well thought out useful book.

Collaborative technology:

Robert Johansen et al (1991)
Leading Business Teams: How Teams Can Use Technology and Group Process Tools to Enhance Performance
Addison Wesley, OD Series (Paperback)

This very readable classic gives an in-depth analysis of the dynamics of working together and apart. Using Drexler and Sibbett's team model, its wonderfully illustrated exploration of what was going to come with new technology and groupware facilities, and how that will fit into team dynamics, will remain true however fancy the technology becomes. It is an excellent introduction to the different modes of working together and apart, same place, same time different place, different time different place and so on. It goes on to describe the different options of information technology and groupware to improve effectiveness when working apart.

Johansen has a gift not only of portraying the future and being one of the first to appreciate the value of groupware, but also of portraying that future peopled by people and not machines.

New technology:

Creighton J L, Adams J W R (1997)
Cyber Meetings: How to Link People and Technology in Your Organization
Amacom

The book opens with a futuristic scenario exploring how people will be able to connect up and interact in the future. Its strength is that rather than immediately highlighting new technology, it stresses that managers first need to think about what they want to do and the nature of the relationships that they need and then see how technology can best support them. They first examine the collaboration systems of an organisation and then what is coming and likely to come out of Silicon Valley and elsewhere in terms of technology. The book ends with a useful chapter on deciding which technology to choose and how to introduce it. Probably a must read for all teams, the book will need a follow up on how to make best use of high tech collaborative technology across cultural, temporal and geographical distances.

Lipnack J, Stamps J (1997)
Virtual Teams: Reaching Across Space, Time and Organisations with Technology
John Wiley and Sons
website http://www.netage.com

Building on their consistent messages of best practices in *The Team Net Factor* and *Age of the Network*, Lipnack and Stamps give a first-hand account of what some companies are achieving with high technology. Building on a looser definition of a 'virtual' team (ie a virtual team works across space, time and organisational boundaries and only in extreme cases never meets face to face). Chapter One is a good introduction to 'why virtual teams' and it outlines the basic interaction between people, purpose and links. Using their effective mixture of stories, theory, practical ideas and vision, the authors then work through various forms of working apart. The book culminates in a very useful toolkit for 'working smart' pulling all the lessons of the book together and ends on a muse on virtual values.

Look under 'virtual team' in Amazon.com for imminent new books.

Chapter Eight: Creating the Right Organisational Context

Binney G and Williams C (1995)
Leaning into the Future: Changing the Way People Change Organisations
Nicholas Brearley

Explores how leaders need to be able to lead and learn simultaneously by 'learning while doing' and 'seeing clearly'. It explores conventional approaches to managing organisational change and concludes that the either/or choices of the past cannot provide solutions for today's complex global environment. The authors provide case studies and examples of leaders and organisations to illustrate their ideas, which makes the book both readable and practical.

Morgan G (1997)
Images of Organisation New Edition
Sage Publications, Inc

This book helps managers multiply their ability to see, understand and redesign organisations to fit today's extraordinary challenges. It challenges conventional wisdom about how to define and understand organisations and provides managers with alternative perspectives on issues that are very familiar to them. Given that leaders of global organisations and international teams need to be able to assimilate and incorporate multiple perspectives into their view of the world, this book provides an accessible yet challenging starting point.

Van der Heijden, K (1996)
Scenarios: The Art of Strategic Conversations
John Wiley & Sons

Challenges managers to face up to uncertainty and ambiguity in the future for their organisations and explores how to introduce processes to facilitate strategic conversations across a myriad of stakeholders. A very readable and practical account of how to use scenarios – different plausible future environments – to explore the choices facing the organisation, in a way that encompasses and acknowledges both the formal and informal systems.

Chapter Nine: The Role of Human Resources (HR)

(Ed) Kirkbride P S (1994)
Human Resource Management in Europe: Perspectives for the 1990s
Routledge

A collection of papers aimed specifically at the HR manager who wants to become conversant with the particular issues of transnational HRM. The focus is Europe, rather than the wider field, but the topics addressed are equally applicable to non-European organisations attempting to work outside their home markets and the contributions are from Europeans and Americans. The first section explores a model of European HRM and compares and contrasts it to Japanese and American models, whilst later sections pick up the emergence of the former Eastern European states. A number of case studies help to illustrate the key issues in a practical way.

Perkins S J (1997)
Internationalisation. The People Dimension: Human Resource Strategies for Global Expansion
Kogan Page

Drawing on practical experience across all continents of the world, it shows companies how to design and implement a human resource strategy within the context of an overall business strategy for internationalisation. It includes detailed cases on all the major topics including selection, international teams, performance management and developing global managers and the examples are drawn from right across the world. A good introductory text for HR professionals and managers alike.

Chapter Ten: Organisational Best Practices for International Teams

Very little on international teams, but a good read on team rewards in general.

Kohn A (1995)
Punished by Rewards: The Trouble with Gold Stars, Incentive Plans, A's, Praise and Other Bribes
Houghton Mifflin Co

Kohn challenges the widely held assumptions that incentives lead to improved quality and increased output in the workplace and in school. He suggests that they tend to punish, disrupt relationships, ignore underlying reasons for behaviour, discourage risk taking and undermine genuine interest and self-motivation. He instead proposes that collaboration, meaningfulness and autonomy act as much better motivators. Well researched, written with authority and humour, this is not your pat book on how to manage team pay.

How to Measure the Results of Work Teams
Zigon performance.
http://www.zigonperf.com/contact.htm

Chapter Eleven: International Teams in the Future Scheme of Things

The future:

There are many versions of futuristic writing. Three books that could be of interest to someone wanting to think about how the world may shape up are:

Fukuyama F (1996)
Trust: The Social Virtues and Creation of Prosperity
The Free Press

McRae H (1995)
The World in 2020: Power, Culture and Prosperity
Harvard Business School Press

Toffler A (1991)
Powershift: Knowledge, Wealth and Violence at the Edge of the 21st Century
Bantam books

Especially in the last one, the authors suggest that the quality of human interaction will play a significant part in the future prosperity and stability of different nations and global regions.

The new sciences:

Chaos

The first accessible book on chaos theory was a review of how the theory evolved, by James Gleick (1988), *Chaos: Making a New Science*, Penguin USA. While filling the pages with all the interesting characters that contributed in different ways, Gleick also managed to use descriptive prose, sketches and photographs to persuade you that you can understand the complicated terminology and maths behind the theory. Naturally those involved in the physics and maths of chaos will no doubt regard it as shallow. Even more shallow then but an excellent source of visual analogies to get oneself out of purely linear thinking is Briggs J and Peat F D (1989), *The Turbulent Mirror: An Illustrated Guide to Chaos Theory and the Science of Wholeness*, Harper and Row, London.

Complexity

Mitchell Waldrop attempted to do what Gleick did with Chaos theory in Waldrop M M (1992), *Complexity: the Emerging Science at the Edge of Order and Chaos*, Penguin UK followed soon after, by Roger Lewin in Lewin R (1993), *Complexity: Life on the Edge of Chaos, the Major New Theory that Unifies All Sciences*.

While the characters and evolution of their thinking makes fairly interesting reading, it is worth heading more for the work of the original thinkers. Even if you just get as far as the first four chapters in Kauffman S (1995), *At Home in the Universe: The Search for Laws of Self-Organization and Complexity*, Oxford University Press NY, you get a good feel for what is meant by how a few simple principles can create complex systems.

Similarly Richard Axelrod's two books: *The Evolution of Co-operation* and, more recently, (1997), *The Complexity of Co-operation: Agent Based Models of Competition and Collaboration*, Princeton University Press, make fascinating accessible reading on the computer modelling experiments and theorising that have provided a 'scientific' basis for co-operation.

System dynamics and systems thinking

The most read book that first incorporated systems thinking and other bits of 'new thinking' into organisational change and learning is Senge P (1990), *The Fifth Discipline: The Art and Practice of the Learning Organization*, Doubleday Currency.

Again it can be well worth going back to some of the original work, such as Jay Forrester's (January 1971), 'The Counter-intuitive Behaviour of Social Systems', *Technology Review* (pp 52–68), to understand how seemingly 'good' decisions can lead to very negative outcomes. There are now also good journals and consultancies working to make qualitative and quantitative sense out of this holistic way of looking at organisational processes. Try http://web.mit.edu. under research and look at the Centre for Organisational Learning and the Systems Dynamics group.

Alchemy

Aside from very accessible books like Ramsay J (1997), *Alchemy: The Art of Transformation*, Thorsons UK, good classics are Jung C G (1967), *Alchemical Studies*, translated by R F C Hull, Routledge and Kegan Paul, and the question and answer format of Von Franz M L (1980), *Alchemy: An Introduction to the Symbolism and the Psychology*, Inner City Books, Toronto, Canada.

Currently one of the most successful books linking management and the new sciences has been Wheatley M (1994), *Leadership and the New Science: Learning About Organization from an Orderly Universe*, Berrett-Koehler Publishers Inc. Written in a discursive musing style, Wheatley explores the implications of Newtonian Physics on organisations. She then takes some of the findings of quantum physics and complexity theory and some natural truisms and links these through metaphor rather than operational reality to situations and organisations that she has encountered. This graceful easy to read book can make many managers reflect on some of their basic assumptions, but will not give them the practical solutions of how to rethink their organisations. She takes this lyric approach one step further with her later book with Kellner Rogers M (1996), *A Simpler Way*, Berrett-Koehler Publishers, which will appeal to those happy to take themselves further into a self-propelled journey (and read much of the further suggested readings) and not to those seeking ready-made solutions.

Endnotes

Chapter One: International Teams in the Current Scheme of Things

[1] These figures are quoted in Fisher K and Fisher MD (1998) *The Distributed Mind: Achieving High Performance Through the Collective Intelligence of Knowledge Work Team*, Amacom, NY.
[2] Sanborn M (1992) *TeamBuilt*, Making Teamwork Work, Sanborn & Associates Inc.
[3] Canney Davison S (1995) 'Intercultural Processes in Multinational Teams', unpublished PhD thesis, London Business School.
[4] Snow C, Snell S, Canney Davison S and Hambrick D (1993) *Transnational Teams: A Resource Guide*, International Consortium for Executive Development and Research. Lexington, Massachusetts.
[5] Story in 'the Last word', *The East African*, March 30–April 5th 1998 (p 11).
[6] Jarvis J (1997) in *Cultural Diversity at Work*, Gildeane Group.
[7] Snow et al (1993) ibid.
[8] Canney Davison S (1995) ibid.

Chapter Two: Know Your Team

[1] Geertz C (1973) *The Interpretation of Cultures*, Basic Books, NY. Tiredness H et al (1972) *The Analysis of Subjective Culture*, J Wiley, NY.
[2] Hofstede G (1980) *Culture's Consequences: International Differences in Work-related Values*, Sage, Beverley Hills.
[3] Triandis H (1994) 'Cross-cultural Industrial and Organisational Psychology' in (eds) M Dunnette and L Hough, *Handbook of Industrial and Organisational Psychology*, Vol 4 (pp 103–172), Consulting Psychologists Press, Palo Alto, CA.
[4] In learning language: eg Hall B J and Gudykunst W B (1987) 'The Intergroup Theory of Second Language Ability' (research note), *Journal of Language and Social Psychology*, Vol 5 No 4 (pp 291–302). In causal attribution: eg Taylor D M and Jaggi V (1974) 'Ethnocentrism and Causal Attribution in a South Indian Context', *Journal of Cross-cultural Psychology*, Vol 5 (pp 162–171). In self perceptions: eg Moghaddam F M and Taylor D M (1987) 'The Meaning of Multiculturalism or Visible Minority Immigrant Women', *Canadian Journal of Behavioural Science*, Vol 14 No 2 (pp 121–136). In performance in school and expectations and motivation to achieve: eg Naidoo J (1980) 'New Perspectives on South Asian Women in Canada', in (ed) N A Nyiri and T

Miljan, *Unity in Diversity: Proceedings of Interdisciplinary Seminars at Wilfrid Laurier University*, Vol 11 (pp 199–266), Waterloo, WLU Press. In behaviour in groups: eg Katz I et al (1958) 'Behaviour and Productivity in Bi-racial Groups', *Journal of Abnormal and Social Psychology*, Vol 61 No 3 (pp 448–456).

[5] Devine P G (1989) 'Stereotypes and Prejudice: The Automatic and Controlled Components', *Journal of Personality and Social Psychology*, Vol 56 No 1 (pp 5–18).

[6] Ratiu I (1983) 'Thinking Internationally: A Comparison of How International Executives Learn', *International Studies of Management and Organization*, Vol XIII No 1–2 Spring–Summer (pp 139–150).

[7] Prothro E and Mellikan L (1955) 'Studies and Stereotypes: Familiarity and the Kernel of Truth Hypothesis', *Journal of Social Psychology*, Vol 41 (pp 3–10).

[8] Adler N (1986) *International Dimensions of Organisational Behaviour*, PWS Kent, Boston (p. 74).

[9] Triandis H and Vassilou (1967) 'Frequency of Contact and Stereotyping', *Journal of Personality and Social Psychology*, Vol 7 No 3 (pp 316–328).

[10] Naidoo J (1980) ibid. See endnote 4.

[11] Meyer H D (1993) 'The Cultural Gap in Long Term International Work Groups: A German-American Case Study', *European Management Journal*, Vol II No 1 (pp 93–101).

[12] Eg see Church A T (1982) 'Sojourner Adjustment', *Psychological Bulletin*, Vol 91 No 3 (pp 540–572). Weiss S (1994) 'Negotiating with Romans – Part 2', *Sloan Management Review*, Spring (pp 85–99).

[13] Tioborn I (1982) *Living Abroad: Personal Adjustment and Personnel Policy in the Overseas Setting*, Wiley, Chichester and Hofstede G (1980) ibid.

[14] Eg Kirkman B and Shapiro D (1997) 'The Impact of Cultural Values on Employee Resistance to Teams: Towards a Model of Globalised Self-managing Work Team Effectiveness', *Academy of Management Review*, Vol 22 No 3 (pp 730–757).

[15] Duncan Crundwell (1996), CEO of Solid State Logic 'An Analysis of the Implementation of a Self Managed Work Team Structure'. Unpublished dissertation.

[16] Hsu F (1985) 'The Self in Cross-cultural Perspective' in (ed) A Marsella et al, *Culture and Self: Asian and Western Perspectives*, Tavistock, NY. Markus H R and Kitayama S (1991) 'Culture and the Self: Implications for Cognition, Emotion and Motivation', *Psychological Review*, Vol 98 No 2 (pp 224–253).

[17] Kumon S (1984) 'Some Principles Governing the Thought and Behaviour of Japanists (Contextualists)', *Journal of Japanese Studies*, Vol 8 (pp 5–28).

[18] Eg England G W and Harpaz I (1983) 'Some Methodological and Analytical Considerations in Cross-national Comparative Research', *Journal of International Business Studies*, Vol 14 (pp 49–59). Triandis H (1990) 'The Self and Social Behaviour in Different Cultural Contexts', *Psychological Review*, Vol 96 (pp 506–520).

[19] Redding G S (1990) *The Spirit of Chinese Capitalism*, De Gruyter, NY.

[20] Wai Ling Young (1982) 'Inscrutability revisited' in (ed) Gumperz J J, *Language and Social Identity*, Cambridge University Press (pp 72–84).

[21] Lee H Y and Bolster F J (1992) 'Collectivism – Individualism in Perceptions of Speech Rate', *Journal of Cross-cultural Psychology*, Vol 23 No 3 (pp 377–388).

[22] *See* Schneider S and Barsoux J (1996) *Managing Across Cultures*, Prentice-Hall.

[23] Hayashi R (1988) 'Simultaneous Talk – from the Perspective of Floor Managers of English and Japanese Speakers', *World Englishes*, Vol 7 No 3 (pp 269–288).

[24] Bond M and Yang K S (1982) 'Ethnic affirmation versus cross-cultural accommodation', *Journal of Cross-Cultural Psychology*, Vol 13 No 2 (pp 169–185).

[25] Condon W S (1982) 'Cultural Microrhythms' in (ed) M Davis, *Interaction Rhythms: Periodicity in Communicative Behaviour*, Human Science Press, NY (pp 31–52).

[26] *See* Goleman Daniel (1995) *Emotional Intelligence*, Bloomsbury Publishing Plc.

[27] Triandis ibid *see* endnote 9.

[28] Lee Lynt (1993) 'Discourse Modes in Participative Decision-making in Hong Kong and Australian Banking Contexts', unpublished doctoral thesis, Macquarie University, Australia, September. Lee studied forty-four meetings in Hong Kong (working in Cantonese) and Australian banks (working in English) and analysed the participative decision styles.

[29] Meyer ibid.

[30] Clackworthy D (1996) 'Training Germans and Americans in Conflict Management' in (ed) M Berger, *Cross Cultural Team-building*, McGraw-Hill.

[31] *See* Butler A (1996) *Teamthink*, McGraw-Hill.

[32] Moss Kanter R and Corn R I (1994) 'Do Cultural Differences Make a Business Difference? Contextual Factors Affecting Cross-cultural Relationship Success', *Journal of Management Development*, Vol 13 No 2 (pp 5–23).

[33] Blau P M (1977) *Inequality and Heterogeneity*, Free Press, NY.

[34] Moss Kanter R (1977) *Men and Women of the Corporation*, Basic Books, NY.

[35] Maass A and Clark R D (1984) 'Hidden Impact of Minorities', *Psychological Bulletin*, Vol 95 (pp 428–450).

[36] Ferrari S (1972) 'Human Behaviour in International Groups', *Management International Review*, Vol XII No 6 (pp 31–35).

[37] *Sunday Times*, October 12th 1997.

[38] Moss Kanter R and Corn R I ibid.

[39] Hofstede G (1991) *Cultures and Organisations*, McGraw-Hill, UK. Boisot M (1995) *Information Space*, Routledge UK.

Chapter Three: Managing Inequalities

[1] 'Time's up for the man from head office' Tony Jackson, *Financial Times*, October 8th 1998.

[2] Canney Davison S (1995) 'Intercultural Processes in Multicultural Teams', unpublished PhD thesis, London Business School.

[3] Earley C et al (1997) 'An Empirical Assessment of Transnational Teams', paper for Academy of Management, Boston, Massachusetts.

[4] Kingston P (1996) 'Bridging the Language Gap Through International Networking' in (ed) M Berger, *Cross-cultural Team Building*, McGraw-Hill.

[5] Maruyama M (1985) 'Mindscapes: How to Understand Specific Situations in Multicultural Management', *Asia Pacific Journal of Management*, Vol 2 No 3.

Chapter Four: Implementing Best Practices

[1] Eg Snow C, Snell S, Canney Davison S and Hambrick D (1993) *Transnational Teams: A Resource Guide*, International Consortium for Executive Development and Research,

Lexington, Massachusetts. Mankin D, Cohen S G. and Bikson T K (1996) *Teams and Technology*, Harvard Business School Press, Boston.
[2] Unpublished comment by Max Boisot, *see* Boisot M (1995) *The Information Space*, Routledge, London UK.
[3] Katzenbach J R and Smith D K (1993) *The Wisdom of Teams*, Harvard Business School Press, Boston.
[4] Eg Hitchcock D and Willard M (1995) *Why Teams Fail and What to Do About it: Essential Tools for Anyone Implementing Self-directed Work Teams*, McGraw-Hill.
[5] Snow et al (1993) ibid.
[6] Eg Johansen R et al (1991) *Leading Business Teams: How Teams Use Technology and Group Process Tools to Enhance Performance*, Addison Wesley, OD Series, Reading, Massachusetts.
[7] Drexler A B, Sibbett D and Forrester R H (1988) 'The Team Performance Model' in (ed) Reddy W B and Jamison K, *Team Building for Productivity and Satisfaction*, NTL Institute for Applied Behavioural Science and University Associates Inc, San Diego (pp 45–61).
[8] For an exploration of the notion of fields structuring space or behaviour *see* Wheatley M (1992) *Leadership and the New Science*, Berrett Koehler Publishers.
[9] *See* Redding S G (1994) 'Comparative Management Theory: Jungle, Zoo or Fossil Bed?', *Organization Studies*, Vol 15 No 3 (pp 323–359).
[10] *See* Trompenaars F (1993) *Riding the Waves of Culture*, Nicholas Brearley Publishing, London.
[11] Adler N J (1991) *International Dimensions of Organisational Behaviour*, PWS-Kent Publishing Company, Boston, Massachusetts.
[12] Maznevski M (1994) 'Understanding Our Differences: Performance in Decision-making Groups with Diverse Members', *Human Relations*, Vol 47 No 5 (pp 531–552).

Chapter Five: Facilitating Teams and Key Interventions

[1] Pinto J K and Slevin D P (1989) 'Critical Success Factors in R&D Projects', *Research Technology Management*, Vol 32 (pp 31–36).

Chapter Six: Leading in the Information Space: Teams and Technology

[1] *See* Lipnack J and Stamps J (1997) *Virtual Teams: Reaching Across Space, Time and Organisations with Technology*, John Wiley and Sons Inc, New York. Creighton J L and Adams J W R (1998) '*Cyber Meeting: How to Link People and Technology in Your Organization*', Amacom, NY. Fisher K and Fisher M D (1998) *The Distributed Mind: Achieving High Performance Through the Collective Intelligence of Knowledge Work Teams*, Amacom, New York.
[2] *See* eg DPE parcel delivery service in Hasting C (1993) *The New Organisation*, McGraw-Hill, UK.
[3] Eg Johansen R *et al* (1991) *Leading Business Teams: How Teams Use Technology and Group Process Tools to Enhance Performance*, Addison Wesley, OD Series, Reading, Massachusetts. Creighton J and Adams J W R ibid. See endnote 1.

[4] Eg Gallupe R B, Dennis A R et al (1992) 'Electronic Brainstorming and Group Size', *Academy of Management Journal*, Vol 35 No 2 (pp 350–369). Aiken M, Krosp J et al 'Electronic Brainstorming in Small and Large Groups', *Information and Management*, Vol 27 (pp 141–149).

[5] Pinsonneault A and Kramer K L (1989) 'The Impact of Technological Support on Groups: An Assessment of the Empirical Research', *Decision Support Systems*, Vol 5 (pp 197–216).

[6] Nunamaker quoted in 'Here Comes the Pay Off from PC's', *Fortune*, March 23rd 1992.

[7] Eg Greenwood T (1993) 'International Cultural Differences in Software', *Digital Technical Journal*, Vol 5 No 3 Summer (pp 8–20).

[8] Aiken M, Martin J, Shirani A and Singleton T (1994) 'A Group Decision Support System for Multicultural and Multilingual Communication', *Decision Support Systems*, Vol 12 (pp 93–96).

[9] Ishii H (1990) 'Cross-cultural Communication & Computer Supported Co-operative Work', *Whole Earth Review*, Winter.

[10] Boisot M (1995) *The Information Space: A Framework for Learning in Organisations, Institutions and Culture*, Routledge, UK (p 119).

[11] Mike Beyerlein on e-mail.

[12] Nohria N and Eccles R G (1992) *Networks and Organisations: Structure, Form and Action*, Harvard Business School Press.

[13] Goleman D (1995) *Emotional Intelligence*, Bloomsbury Publishing Plc.

[14] Trompenaars F (1993) *Riding the Waves of Culture*, Nicholas Brearley, London.

[15] Armstrong D J and Cole P (1995) 'Managing Differences and Distances in Geographically Distributed Work Groups' in (eds) S Jackson and M Ruderman, *Diversity in Work Teams: Research Paradigms for a Changing Workplace*, American Psychological Association, Washington, DC. Canney Davison S (1996) 'Leading International Teams' in (ed) M Berger, *Cross-cultural Teambuilding*, McGraw-Hill, London.

[16] Kydd C T and Ferry D L (1994) 'Managerial Use of Videoconferencing' (case study), *Information and Management*, Vol 27 (pp 369–75). Gowan J A and Downs J M (1994) 'Video Conferencing Human-machine Interface: A Field Study', *Information and Management*, Vol 27 (pp 341–356).

[17] Maznevski M L and Chudoba K M (1997) 'Effective Virtual Transnational Teams: Conceptual Model and Initial Empirical Test', paper given at the Academy of Management, Boston, Massachusetts.

[18] See Cairncross F (1997) *The Death of Distance: How the Communications Revolution Will Change Our Lives*, Harvard Business School Press (p 257).

[19] Dix J (1994) 'Teaming with Technology', *Network World*, Vol 11 No 2 (pp 8–16).

[20] A point shared by Mike Beyerlein in e-mail discussion.

Chapter Seven: The Role of International Team Leaders

[1] Laurent A (1983) 'The Cultural Diversity of Western Conceptions of Management', *International Studies of Management and Organization*, Vol XIII No 1–2 (Spring–Summer), M E Sharpe Inc (pp 75–96).

[2] Snow C et al (1993) 'Transnational Teams: Strategic Contributions and Leadership Roles', unpublished paper.
[3] Maznevski M (1994) 'Understanding Our Differences: Performance in Decision-Making Groups with Diverse Members', *Human Relations*, Vol 47 No 5 (pp 531–552). Maznevski M L and Chudoba K M (1997) 'Effective Virtual Transnational Teams: Conceptual Model and Initial Empirical Test', Paper given at the Academy of Management, Boston, Massachusetts.
[4] Trompenaars F (1993) *Riding the Waves of Culture*, Nicholas Brearley, London (p 143).
[5] Canney Davison S (1994) 'Creating a High Performance International Team', *The Journal of Management Development*, Vol 13 No 2 (pp 81–90).

Chapter Eight: Creating the Right Organisational Context

[1] Hofstede, G (1980) *Culture's Consequences: International Differences in Work Related Values*, Sage. Trompenaars, F (1993) *Riding the Waves of Culture: Understanding Cultural Diversity in Business*, Nicholas Brearley Publishing.
[2] Bartlett C A and Ghoshal S (1989) *Managing Across Borders*, Hutchinson Business Books.
[3] Snow C, Snell S, Canney Davison S and Hambrick D (1993) *Transnational Teams: A Resources Guide*, International Consortium for Executive Development and Research, Lexington, Massachusetts.
[4] Schneider S and Barsoux J L (1997) *Managing Across Cultures*, Prentice Hall, Europe, Chapter Five (pp 106–127).
[5] Heimer, C. (1994) The Principles of Requisite Variety and the Composition of Executive Boards of International Companies: Implications for the Internationalisation of the Firm, MSc Dissertation, Birkbeck College, University of London.
[6] Heimer C and Barham K (forthcoming) 'International Top Teams: Putting them Together and Making them Work', Ashridge International Centre for Management and Organisational Development, Berkhamsted.
[7] Lei D and Slocum J W Jnr (1992) 'Global Strategy, Competence Building and Strategic Alliances, *California Management Review*, Fall (pp 81–97).

Chapter Ten: Organisational Best Practices for International Teams

[1] McCall M, Spreitzer G M and Mahoney J (1993) *Identifying Leadership Potential in Future International Executives: A Learning Resource Guide*. Or the International Consortium of Executive Research and Development, Lexington, Massachusetts.
[2] Eg Chemers M M, Fielder F E, Lekhyanda D and Stolurow L M (1966) 'Some Effects of Cultural Training on Leadership in Heterocultural Task Groups', *International Journal of Psychology*, Vol 1 No 4 (pp 301–314). Anderson L R (1983) 'Management of the Mixed Cultural Work Group', *Organisational Behaviour and Human Performance*, Vol 31 (pp 303–330).
[3] Wiseman R L, Hammer M R and Nishida H (1989) 'Predictors of Intercultural Communication Competence', *International Journal of Intercultural Relations*, Vol 13 No 3 (pp 349–370).

[4] See eg Kirkman B L et al (1996) Employee concerns regarding self-managing work teams: A multidimensional justice perspective. *Social Justice Research* Vol 9 (pp 27–47); and further work by Kirkman B and Shapiro D (eg endnote 7).

[5] Hui C C and Triandis H C (1989) 'Effects of Culture and Response Format on Extreme Response Style', *Journal of Cross-cultural Psychology*, Vol 20 No 3 September (pp 263–298).

[6] Jessica Lipnack on e-mail September 1997.

[7] Kirkman B and Shapiro D (1997) 'Why Team Members Won't Share: Individual and Team Level Correlates of Employee Receptivity to Team-based Rewards', Paper presented at the Academy of Management, Boston, Massachusetts.

[8] Kirkman B and Shapiro D ibid.

Chapter Eleven: International Teams in the Future Scheme of Things.

[1] *The Individualised Corporation* (1997) Bartlett and Ghoshal Heinemann.

[2] Simon H 'The Hidden Champions', paraphrased in *Financial Times*, Friday October 24 1997.

[3] Such as those outlined by Mankin D, Cohen S G and Bikson T K (1996) *Teams and Technology*, Harvard Business School Press, Boston.

[4] Eg Maruyama M (1985) 'Mindscapes: How to Understand Specific Situations in Multicultural Management', *Asia Pacific Journal of Management*, Vol 2 No 3.

[5] Daniel Goleman (1995) *Emotional Intelligence*, Bloomsbury Publishing Plc.

[6] Eg McGrath J E and O'Connor K M (1996) 'Temporal Issues in Work Groups' in (ed) M A West, *Handbook of Work Group Psychology*, John Wiley and Sons Ltd.

[7] Wheatley M (1993) *Leadership and the New Science*, Berrett-Koehler Publishers, San Francisco.

[8] A key figure in the emergence of chaos theory and author of *Fractals: Form, Chance and Dimension*.

Index

360 degree feedback, failure of in certain organisational contexts, 250
ABB (Asea Brown and Boveri) 15, 24, 25, 155, 202, 253, 263
Acer, as succesful hybrid, 265
Ad hoc project teams, use in developing international team skills, 242
Adaptation
 'good' and 'bad,' 43
 to different cultures, 43
Aylett P. 242

Ben and Jerry, wealth distribution in, 265
Big Bang approach, establishing teams through, 209–11
BP (British Petroleum) 263
 OPEN behaviours, 233
British Gas, selection process of international team leaders, 236

CIDA, (Canadian International Development Agency), cross-cultural exercise from, 242
Citibank 233
Communication technology and emotional exchange, 150–53
 and emotional 'sync', 152
 as an equaliser?, 149
 best uses of, 141–46
 creating new types of results with, 155
 future possibilities, 146
 planning the support of, 92
 the cross-cultural argument, 146–50
 the future for, 268
Conflict resolution
 in different cultures, 53–56
 in virtual teams, 162
Contributions
 balance in individual amounts of, 68
 patterns of in international teams, 68–70
Counting contributions, sample form for, 278
Cross-cultural training, for developing team leaders, 241
Cultural differences
 about equitable rewards, 256
 five factors to manage 34
 impact on teams, 33–64
 in attitudes towards self managed work teams, 40

 in conflict resolution, 53
 in contexts of unequal power, 2
 in decision making, 56–58
 in preferred evaluation methods, 249
 in the use of communication technology, 150
 no need to fuse, transcend or resolve, 1
 the need to understand early in life cycle, 97
 using a cultural value checklist to elicit, 97
Cultural norms *See* Appendix One
 statistical research on, 39–40
Cultural value checklist
 administration of, 131
 example of a, 279
 to identify cultural differences and similarities, 97
Culture
 cultural dimensions, examples of, 276
 defining, 34
 definitions of, 275
 ethnicity as a guide to, 37
 has both individual and group aspects, 35
 has both subjective and objective aspects, 35
 nationality as a guide to, 37
Cultures
 different status in organisations, 58
 the impact of 'dominant,' 80
Current technologies
 advantages and disadvantages of
  desktop video conferencing, 145
  external e-mail, 143
  facsimile, 142
  group decision support systems (GDSS), 143
  group video conferencing, 144
  groupware, 144
  internal e mail, 142
  internet, 143
  shared databases, 144
  teleconference, 142
  telephone, 142
  virtual offices, 145
Data sharing technology, impact of, 140
Decision making
 and interruption patterns, 73
 in different cultures, 56–58
Dominance, patterns of, 80

Economic strength, different perceptions of, 24
Effectiveness criteria, for international team leadership, 234

Ethnicity, as a guide to culture, 37
Evaluation
  culturally sensitive, 249
  different time scales for international teams, 251
  involving team members in, 248
  issues at different stages of life cycle, 135
  of international teams, 245–51

Facilitation, key interventions in life cycle, 124–38
Facilitator
  aware of cultural bias, 122
  conflict resolution skills of a, 116
  deciding if you need one, 93
  diagnostic and analytical skills, 116
  engaged with organisation and team, 121
  knowledge needed by, 118–20
  knowledge of adult learning, 120
  knowledge of business principles, 119
  knowledge of facilitating change, 119
  knowledge of OD, 119
  language skills of a, 117
  lived through major change, 120
  need for emotional and professional support, 123
  need for extensive toolkit, 117
  need for passion, 123
  need for physical and emotional resilience, 123
  passive versus active roles, 113
  political awareness, 122
  realtime planning and design ability, 118
  reasons you may need, 115
  reducing presence, 106
  selecting and developing a, 115–24
  skills of a, 116–18
  the purpose and role of, 111–38
  transferring skills of, 114, 138
  use of culturally responsive feedback, 118
  useful experience for, 120–22
  working with unfamiliar topics, 117
Ford Motor Company 28
Future, ways of looking at the, 266–68

GDSS (group decision support systems), findings about, 146
Geographical distance, assiting outliers, 158–60
Glass-ceilings, because of preferential nationalities, 202
Glaxo-Wellcome 15, 26, 28, 84, 87, 89, 92, 100, 106, 156, 164, 170, 173, 210, 214, 219, 234, 238, 240, 243, 261
  outcomes of project leaders training course, 243
Global Gas See British Gas
Globalisation
  definition of, 14
  just warming up, 264

Ground rules
  function of, 99
  leading to rich results, 101
  strong enough to manage heat, 101
  use of cultural value checklist to set, 98
Group behaviour
  different expectations of, 53–58
Groupware, its importance in maintaining involvement, 107

Heated debates, successful channeling of, 104
Hofstede G. 119, 130, 275, 276, 277
Honda 265
Hong Kong
  comparison of two teams, 84
  contribution patterns in teams, 69
Hong Kong Shanghai Bank, ad hoc project teams in, 242
Human interaction, the need for improvement in, 267
Human Resources
  acting as a catalyst, 221
  acting as a role model for international teams, 220–25
  aligning with corporate strategic intent, 213–20
  and strategic alignment, 198
  as a strategic partner, 213
  creating effective structure of, 220
  developing a strategy to support international teams, 215–18
  facilitating change to a team based organisation, a case study, 225–31
  strategy, the organisational effectiveness perspective, 218
  the role of, 213–31
Humour
  light–hearted incidents, 86
  need for face to face interaction, 97

IBM (International Business Machines) 147, 277
  airline support centre, 239
Ideas, the need to follow up good, 84–86
Ikea 28
Inequalities
  managing them in international teams, 65–87
  the difficulty of addressing directly, 81
  three types in international teams, 58
Information technology See Communication technology
Information, as a global commodity, 140
Integrating diversity, brief discussion about, 109
Interactional justice, importance of in evaluation, 248
Intercultural synergy, discussion of, 109
International elites 266
International team leaders and members, key messages for, 262–63

International teams advantages and
    disadvantages of, 16
  and structural inequality, 66
  contribution patterns in, 68–70
  creating effective rewards for, 252–53
  definition of, 11
  developing a supportive HR strategy,
    215–18
  developing leaders for, 240–45
  evaluating, 245–51
  focusing on specific ones first, 27
  four phase model of team life cycle, 88–110
  functional and professional cultures in, 61
  geographic spread of, 60
  greater communication difficulties in, 20–21
  HR acting as role model for, 220
  identifying leadership for, 233–36
  interruption patterns in, 72
  leadership of, 166
  managing inequalities in, 65
  most satisfied in video research, 86
  numbers of nationalities in, 22
  optimal size, 67
  pilot or big bang approach to establishing,
    209–11
  position in organisations, 25
  preconceptions, prejudices and stereotypes,
    their impact on team dynamics, 78–82
  selecting leaders of, 236–40
  structural inequality in, 66
  the added complexities
    from different nationalities, 19
    from the organisational context, 21–25
  the future for, 268–71
  the reasons for, 1
  the three trends creating more, 14
  typology of, 26
  use of communication technology in, 139–65
  usual composition of, 22
Interrelationships, building face to face, 97
Interruption patterns
  and decision making, 73
  in international teams, 72
Interventions
  communication charters, 131
  cultural value checklist, 131
  establishing working practices, 130
  evaluation issues at different life cycle stages,
    135
  feedback and process skills, 132
  mapping the team life cycle, 128
  role negotiation, 128
  stakeholder analysis, 128
  team reviews, *See* Team review

Language, choosing the working one, 70
Languages
  affect how people think, 46
  change as they spread, 45
  different meanings of silence and pauses, 46

  different uses of simultaneous talk, 46
  difficulties with similar, 71
  some precise and some imprecise, 45
Leadership
  and different types of task, 169
  and strategic focus, 168
  at different stages of life cycle, 169
  components of a training programme for,
    242
  culturally appropriate style, 175
  development for international teams, 240–45
  effectiveness criteria for in Wellcome, 234
  identifying for international teams, 233–36
  in IBM Airline Support centre team, 239
  'just in time' development, 244
  managing boundaries, 170
  negotiating resources, 172
  no fundamental change in global companies,
    265
  of international teams, 166–80
  of virtual teams, 160–63
  outcomes of training course in Wellcome,
    243
  reducing team presence, 106
  selection for international teams, 236–40
  selection process in British Gas, 236
  selection process in Seagram, 237
  sharing the role in international teams,
    178–79
  technical or process skills in international
    teams, 167–68
  the need for ethical clarity, 177
  the need for strong support, 177
  the role of cross-cultural training in
    developing, 241
Leadership style
  adapting to different cultures, 50
  Australian and Hong Kong Chinese
    comparison, 51
  the meaning of participative, 51–52
Learning points
  about adapting cultural norms, 43
  about culture, 41
  about languages in teams, 50
  about speech patterns in international teams,
    77
  culturally different team processes, 57
  for a successful HR strategy, 220
  for developing leaders, 245
  for evaluating international teams, 251
  for HR facilitating change to team based
    organisation 231
  for HR teams, 225
  for identifying team leaders, 236
  for international team leaders, 180
  for senior management creating a supportive
    environment, 200
  for senior management on creating top
    diverse teams, 204
  from the video research, 87
  on creating right organisational context, 211

on culturally different leadership styles, 53
on functional cultures, 62
on geographic spread, 61
on international teams in general, 32
on key organisational best practices, 260
on managing inequalities, 82
on recognising inequality in teams, 60
on rewarding international teams, 259
on selecting team leaders, 240
on structural inequality, 70
on use of communication technologies, 165
Learning, sharing the team's, 108
Lever Europe *See* Unilever
Likert scales, in evaluation, 250
Logic, culturally different patterns of, 75

MacGregor Navire 71, 153, 203, 253
Management science, dominance of American, 265
Matsushita, S.M.I.L.E. 233
Measures
    distinguishing between team performance and outcome effectiveness, 245–48
    examples of outcome effectivness measures 247–48
    examples of performance measures, 247
    the need to separate performance from task outcome, 246
Meeting
    planning first of team, 94
    when to meet face to face, 154–58
Meritocracy, difficulties in realising, 266
Metaplan, advantages and use in international teams, 124
Michigan, University of, teams programme, 241
Mitchell, Steve, and strategic moments, 100
Multinationals
    certain departments internationalise first, 28
    responses of different, 15

National identity, playing it down, 80
Nationalities
    different status in organisations, 58
    numbers in different types of teams, 26
    the restricted range and level of, 22
Nationality, as a guide to culture, 37
Nokia, ad hoc project teams in, 242
Non verbal communication in different cultures, 48

Organisational context
    best practices in, 232–60
    complexities added by, 21–25, 21
    creating supportive infrastructure, 195–200
    creating the right one, 187–212
    glass-ceilings for non dominant nationalities 202
    three factors to manage, 34

Organisational readiness, assessment of, 208
Organisational strategy
    ambiguous reporting lines, 197
    divided loyalties, 197

Participation
    counting as a feedback tool, 83
    creating a balance in, 82
Participation curves, optimum in different cultures, 83
Personality
    and adaptation to different cultures, 42
    in different cultures, 42
    sometimes overrides cultural differences, 66
Peters T. 265
Pilots, establishing teams through, 209–11
Preconceptions and prejudices, the impact of on team dynamics, 78–82
Preparation, 3 × 1 for international teams, 89
Purpose, of team linked to strategy, 192

Questionnaires
    use in team start-up, 126
    use of prior to teamwork, 94

Research
    Ferrari in ILO, 59
    findings on reward and motivation, 254–57
    findings on strategic foci, 189
    findings on strategic foci, 189–92
    fit with organisational strategy, 96
    introduction to video, 3
    results of video, 65–87
    statistical limitations of research on cultural norms, 39
Review, sample of a team interaction, 281
Rewards
    and part time membership of multiple teams, 256
    barriers to global integration of, 255
    different practices in, 253
    effective for international teams, 252–53
    relevant practices for international teams, 257
    the cycle of experimentation, 253

Schein E. 232
Schrage M. 1
Seagram 3, 33, 65, 96, 170, 171, 174, 254, 257
    selection of international team leaders, 237
Second language speakers
    and type of task, 77
    costs and benefits for, 47
    impact of international experience, 73
    impact on contributions, 47
Self-fulfilling expectations, no evidence of, 79
Self, understanding of in different cultures, 42

Senior management
    actively involved with teams, 204–5
    actively seeking diverse top teams, 201–4
    demonstrating humane global working, 205–8
    key messages for, 263–64
    role modelling best practice, 200–201
Shell, Royal Dutch 15, 191, 242
Simons H, on small companies, 264
Size, optimum for international teams, 67
Stereotypes
    facts about, 38
    misuse of to push a dominant norm, 79
    their impact on team dynamics, 78–82
    unhelpful, 38
Stereotypical remarks, apparent ranking in, 80
Strategic intent, aligning HR strategy with corporate, 213–20
Strategic moments, definition and management of, 100–101
Strategy
    aligning team with strategic intent, 188–92
    three strategic foci, 189–92
Systemic approach, to team development, 2

Team information space 140
Team interaction review, sample of a, 281
Team life cycle, four phase model, 88–110
Team members
    interviewing prior to teamwork, 94
    selection of, 91
Team processes
    actions taken when things went right, 86–87
    broadcasting successes along the way, 106
    clarifying vision, mission, goals and objectives, 91
    co-ordination of tasks, 110
    different cultural expectations of, 53–58
    effective generic, 18
    implementing the team basics, 95–96
    importance of four phase model in review of, 135
    managing the interaction, 82–83
    questioning the interaction, 83–84
    rotating meetings, 158
    sculpting like an art, 110
    setting action plans at first meetings, 99
    sharing the learning, 108
    start slowly, end fast, 95
    structured for rich results, 104
    the need for structure, 2
    the need for team basics, 18
    the need to structure the interaction, 84
    when to meet, 154–58
Team review
    at end of life cycle, 107
    different methods of final, 137
    different methods of, 133–34
    half time health checks, 105
    importance of four phase model in, 135
    the importance of, 74
    use of drawing in, 137
Team sponsors, the importance of identifying and involving, 89
Team start-up
    exercises used in, 127
    use of questionnaires, 126
Teams
    differentiated from workgroups, 17
    dispersed or virtual, 4
    skewed, tilted and balanced, 59
Toyota, as succesful hybrid, 265
Translation, difficulties for teams, 71
Trompenaars F. 119, 130, 271, 275, 276
Trust, building in different cultures, 97

Unilever 28
    selection of team leader, 238

Values
    and adaptation, 43
    understanding other people's, 36
    weighing up in different situations, 36
Virtual teams
    leading, 160–63
    paradoxes of virtual conflict, 162

Weaving, analogy with, 2
Wellcome *See* Glaxo-Wellcome
Work patterns, changes in due to communication technology, 140
Working apart, actions when, 157
Working together, actions when, 156

Zeneca pharmaceuticals 19